The Civilization of Crime

The Civilization of Crime

Violence in Town and Country
since the Middle Ages

Edited by

Eric A. Johnson and Eric H. Monkkonen

University of Illinois Press
Urbana and Chicago

© 1996 by the Board of Trustees of the University of Illinois
Manufactured in the United States of America
1   2   3   4   5   C   P   5   4   3   2   1

This book is printed on acid-free paper.

Library of Congress Cataloging-in-Publication Data

The civilization of crime : violence in town and country since the
Middle Ages / edited by Eric A. Johnson and Eric H. Monkkonen.
p.   cm.
ISBN 0-252-02242-4 (cloth : acid-free paper). —
ISBN 0-252-06546-8 (pbk. : acid-free paper)
1. Violent crimes—Europe—History. 2. Violent crimes—Cross-
cultural studies. I. Johnson, Eric A. (Eric Arthur), 1948–
II. Monkkonen, Eric H., 1942–
HV6937.A18   1996
364.94—dc20   95-50201
                                                        CIP

In memory of Herman Diederiks

1937–1995

Contents

Introduction

Eric A. Johnson and Eric H. Monkkonen

Are the violence-laden cities of much of present-day North America and parts of Britain and continental Europe condemned to an increasingly violent future by certain laws of historical development? Are cities inevitably more violent and crime-ridden than small towns and villages? What social, economic, and attitudinal factors account for the evolution of criminal behavior over time and across national boundaries? Was village and town life more peaceful in the distant past? These are some of the significant questions that the authors in this volume seek to address. Coming from seven different countries, the authors are all recognized criminal justice historians. Here they have combined their efforts to challenge much of what both scholars and laypeople in Western society have come to believe about the nature and causes of violence and crime in the past. Their work could help us make more informed policy choices about our future.

The focus of this book—violent crime in the city and the countryside—features one of the elemental distinctions made in the context and definition of crime and crime control. Over time there have been both large and subtle shifts in this elemental dichotomy. The classic city had walls to keep armies and criminals out. Gangs were in the countryside. Today, at least in the suburbs and rural parts of the United States, many people would like to wall cities to keep criminals and criminal gangs *in*. In the past, city safety came often as a result of increased state authority and power as well as a change in mentality on the part of the population. Today the nature of the city as well as the countryside has changed, becoming more complex and varied. We have much to learn from our rural and urban past, not least of all concerning questions of order, authority, and mentality.

Some of the essays in this collection may seem to be inattentive to customary social theory. Where are the classical social thinkers who address the centuries-long transformations of the West? Durkheim, Weber, and Marx are underplayed, as is even Michel Foucault. Instead, a shadowy figure, Norbert Elias, appears, his presence announced by the English historian James Sharpe's reference to the "civilizing process," in the first chapter. Starting from differing (if traditional) theoretical perspectives, a large number of historians of crime have become more interested in Elias because his work better describes what they have found than has that of other social thinkers. Even if all of the contributors to this volume do not explicitly see their work as grounded in the theories of Elias, almost all of them, although they study different societies and come to their work from a variety of intellectual perspectives and national backgrounds, have discovered that their empirical findings do not fit with customary social theorizing.

Three decades ago, it could have been said that historians of crime were far more optimistic about studying everything around crime than about studying crime itself. The latter pursuit was considered elusive primarily because empirical estimates concerning crime's volume and severity seemed to be unattainable, at least for crime in earlier times. Therefore, historians set about researching everything surrounding crime—legal institutions from the penal system to modes of enforcement, popular and elite attitudes, court systems and crimes coming to courts. Few historians asked what might to an outside observer seem to be initial or fundamental questions: How do crime rates and trends in the past compare with those in the present? What were crime rates and trends in the past?

In addition to exercising caution in directly confronting questions about the long run of crime, historians were similarly reticent to make international comparisons. The reasons: crimes are legally defined actions, and legal systems vary enormously among nations. In addition, national mechanisms for dealing with crime, national attitudes—indeed, all of the aspects of crime that historians felt they could study—seemed incomparable in any clear sense. So responsible scholars usually balked at international comparisons as well as at describing long-run change.

Presumably, these two areas—international comparisons and long-run change—would be the primary points of interest most people would have when it comes to old crimes, so it is no wonder that the history of crime and justice never became a scholarly growth industry. Yet, those researchers who began working seriously on crime and crime-related topics continued to pick away at the subject; their small number grew ever so slightly, but steadily.

A major organizational and intellectual turning point came when a small group of scholars in the Netherlands began meeting in 1973. Known as the "Dutch group," this loose organization contacted even smaller groups of historians in other nations (such as a group in the United States organized through the Social Science History Association [SSHA]) and arranged for several sessions on the program of the International Economic History Conference in Edinburgh, Scotland, in August 1978. Out of this critical conference the Dutch group was reborn as the International Association for the History of Crime and Criminal Justice (IAHCCJ), with a newsletter published biannually as a supplement to *MSH Informations* of the Maison des Sciences de l'Homme, Paris. The first issue appeared in February 1979. In 1991, with issue 14, its name changed formally to the *IAHCCJ Bulletin* with a special issue honoring the scholarly contributions of Yves Castan. Meanwhile, in North America, the Canadian/American serial *Criminal Justice History* began publication in 1980.

Just five months after the Edinburgh meeting, the IAHCCJ initiated a series of annual meetings, usually in Paris, with international meetings occurring every three or four years. Its members often attend the SSHA meetings in the United States, and through its newsletter an international network of scholars shares ideas, bibliography, and calls for conference papers. At the same time, the bibliography of monographs and research articles expanded to the point that a mastery of all the literature is no longer possible.

The present volume offers some of the fruit of the growing international collaboration among criminal justice history organizations based in Europe and America. Its genesis came at the third major international conference of the IAHCCJ, a meeting attended by some thirty leading criminal justice historians who came to an island in the Stockholm archipelago in early July 1990 to discuss the theme of "crime in town and country." Subsequently, panel sessions on the theme of crime and modernization over the whole of European history were organized for the 1991 and 1993 annual meetings of the SSHA, held in New Orleans and Baltimore, respectively. Many of the participants at the original Stockholm conference took part in those American meetings and refined their arguments through further contact with American scholars and each other. The present volume, therefore, took root on both the European and North American continents and represents close teamwork among European and American scholars concerned with the history of crime over the long term.

As this volume demonstrates, the slow, low-key growth in organizational connections and knowledge has finally brought about a surprising scholarly consensus. It is now assumed that crime—in particular personal violence—in the Western world has declined since the early Middle Ages until very recently. This simple statement encompasses the two aspects of crime that scholars expected never to approach: international comparison and lengthy trends. This generalization is itself still open to more precise specification, to a large amount of detailing, and to demanding empirical refinement.

At least one problem exists: in detailing long-term trends, the more crime historians are able to fix the numerator (the count of crimes), the more they must define and find the denominator (the population against which the crimes are indexed to produce a rate). It becomes an enormous challenge to achieve accuracy in the denominator, especially since it should be adjusted for age and gender and then made precise to the geopolitical unit for which the crime data are available. Historians will not be able to use the vague estimates that have previously satisfied them. Nor can they easily rely upon the work of demographers, who typically have reconstructed the birth and mortality patterns of samples, rather than the size and shape of a particular region's population.

The authors of the following chapters explore the details of this unexpected generalization about the long-term decrease of violence in Western society, but a few points about the theoretical impact of this generalization must be stressed. One of the most notable effects of the recent work on the history of crime as demonstrated in this volume has been to force historians to reassess (or assess for the first time) the work of the sociologist Norbert Elias. Without a doubt, his work has gained the greatest respect of any single theoretician. Elias's significance has come to be recognized in part because his descriptions of the "civilizing process" match so well what crime historians have been finding. That he wrote his major works touching on violence in the late 1930s with little social historical research to confirm his ideas makes his theoretical formulations all the more impressive.

Elias ties the control of individual impulse to the growth of powerful states and courts in Europe; he claims that the state's monopoly on violence (a notion from Weber, of course) "makes the use of violence more or less calculable, and forces unarmed men in the pacified social spaces to restrain their own violence through foresight or reflection."[1] He argues that this imposition of self-control began with the "transformation of the nobility from a class of knights into a class of courtiers,"[2] and that impulsive violent behavior slowly came under control in the princely courts of the sixteenth and seventeenth centuries. Elias's work has many substantive implications that historians would have found unacceptable thirty years ago: first, that control of violent behavior emanated from courts; second, that urban centers would have more "civilized" behavior; third, that areas where state systems had not yet penetrated would be more impulsively violent; and, fourth, that, over time, violence would decline.

It is these and many other implications of Elias's work that may have impeded its acceptance in the immediate postwar years, for what he said ran contrary to a different and more persuasive theoretical sequence. This argument, originally associated with classical sociological theorists such as Tönnies and Durkheim, and later elaborated on by Park and Burgess of the Chicago school of sociology, held that, with the breakdown of family and community (*Gemeinschaft*) and the rise of mass society (*Gesellschaft*), especially through urbanization, industrialization, and the class alignment of capitalist societies, crime has increased. Since crime did increase somewhat (in America at least) following World War II, and dramatically subsequent to 1968, this other line of sociological theory made much sense. Elias's discussions of the control of violent impulses in "civilized" societies seemed out of touch. So, for historians of crime, the slowly growing conviction that crime has decreased, not increased, over the centuries; that the countryside used to be dangerous, not safe; that, as Barbara Hanawalt put it, "fur-collar crime" was a major threat—all of this changed the status of Elias from curiosity to prescient thinker.

Elias's work also ran contrary to something else painfully evident in our century—violence by the state. Elias himself was the victim of such violence, spending much of his life in exile. Several observations are in order here. This book is *not* about violence by the state, but that means neither that such violence is insignificant nor that the authors of the individual chapters are unconcerned about such violence. The authors use the work of Elias to help understand social behavior in the context of the nation state. They do not use his theories to explain state behavior. An underlying critique might be to ask how we can see the expansion of the modern state as spreading more orderly and civilized behavior while it at the same time has spawned mass executions, "ethnic cleansing," and genocide. The point is, of course, that this book is not about all violence, but about a particular kind of violence, violence on the individual level. Most historians have been by tradition and training best equipped to analyze activities by states—political takeovers, revolutions, wars, and violence against citizens. Recording the history of everyday life, of private life, of families, is a relatively recent pursuit, and the study of the history of crime is very recent.

Some will speculate that the apparent increase in civility, the decrease in the acceptability of violence between persons, came about as the state increased its legitimate monopoly on violence, but that in turn, the state itself became increasingly violent. In this scenario there would be fewer crimes between individuals but more large-scale assaults by states. In the Middle Ages there should have been less state-sponsored genocide and warfare, and fewer executions; the rise of the nation state should have been accompanied by greater interpersonal safety and more fearsome state violence. This argument implies some sort of balance sheet of horror, one that we are not yet capable of providing. The careful analyses of crime in this volume do not try to measure exactly the amount and nature of crime across wide jurisdictions; the questions have more to do with what crimes show about the state and society. The idea that crime decreased from the Middle Ages until recently is interesting and important, but its exact measures are not yet the object of major research efforts.

Other impacts of the research represented here are now being evaluated. That the results demonstrate the benefits of comparative work has led to a new, multi-institutional, collaborative project on courts and violence in the Nordic countries, involving many scholars, including some of the contributors to this volume. Throughout Europe, younger scholars in law, history, and sociology faculties have begun a host of new projects following on and amplifying the work so far accomplished.

One concern common to people in most Western societies is the recent rise in crime rates. Is it possible that the long historic decline in crime has ended? Do we have any understanding of the foundations that prevent criminal violence? What is the deeper relationship between individual and state violence? These worrisome and urgent problems propel us to probe more deeply crime in the past.

◆ ◆ ◆ ◆

The essays in this book treat the nature and genesis of violent criminality in European communities and societies—from Paris during the Hundred Years' War in the fourteenth century and Arboga, Sweden, in the mid-fifteenth century to Amsterdam and Norrköping, Sweden, in the 1980s. They provide remarkably consistent evidence from several different national contexts that the distant past was far more violent than the more recent past and indeed even the present; and that the great decline in the level of interpersonal violence took place sometime between the seventeenth and eighteenth centuries—a period marked by the rise of state control over the population, but a time considerably before the great wave of urban-industrial growth and expansion during the nineteenth and twentieth centuries (see, especially, the essays by Sharpe, Österberg, and Spierenburg). The essays also demonstrate rather conclusively that the popular *de la violence au vol* (from violence to theft) "modernization" thesis does not hold up to empirical verification (see Sharpe, Österberg, Diederiks, Weinberger, Johnson). Hence the perceived decline in violence over the long term was in fact real and not merely a spurious correlate of a growing interest in prosecuting property crimes in bourgeois society. Whereas violence certainly did decrease over the centuries, there is no solid evidence that property crimes actually increased.

The essays also challenge many other historical-sociological theories and common folkwisdom and provide rich and nuanced detail about the crime problem in town and countryside in nearly all corners of Europe since the late Middle Ages. Among other things, they demonstrate that contemporary organized crime is hardly new. Criminal gangs and networks were pervasive in both urban and rural settings in centuries' long past (as set forth by Egmond). The essays show that the church had much to do with the change in popular mentality from an acceptance of violent acts in medieval and premodern society (as in fifteenth- and sixteenth-century Naples, described in Mancino's essay) to a condemnation of such activity during the seventeenth and eighteenth centuries (as in Sundin's examination of several Swedish communities). They provide strong proof that critics both in the past and in the present have no justification for blaming cities and city populations for violence, as more often rural areas were associated with violence than urban ones in most societies' pasts (Diederiks, Johnson); and that, once again, the predominantly rural societies of the distant past were far more violent than the predominantly urban societies of both the recent past and the present (Cohen, Sharpe, Österberg, Spierenburg). But, finally, as Spierenburg so intelligently points out, even if it is folly to romanticize the far from tranquil village life of the past, it is also wrongheaded to think that our distant ancestors were much less happy in their tumultuous and violent lives than most of our parents and grandparents were or we are in our far safer and apparently more "civilized" communities. Love and happiness might well have coexisted harmoniously with even fatal outbursts of passion.

The chapters in this book are grouped in two sections, the first treating long-term trends from the medieval era to the present and the second exploring various aspects of crime and justice in town and country in briefer time periods but often in more detail. The first three essays, by the English scholar James A. Sharpe, the Swedish scholar Eva Österberg, and the Dutch scholar Pieter Spierenburg, assess all of the empirical evidence in their respective countries pertaining to long-term trends in homicide and, to a lesser extent, to other forms of criminality.

Previous to these essays only the English case had received much attention. J. A. Sharpe is one of the leaders in the English debate between several leading scholars like himself and Lawrence Stone and more recently J. S. Cockburn, an exchange played out in recent years in several books and articles—most prominantly perhaps in the pages of the English journal *Past and Present.* Sharpe takes a fresh look at the English evidence in his chapter here, "Crime in England: Long-Term Trends and the Problem of Modernization." In it he argues that "the overall pattern seems clear"—namely that there can be no doubt that there was a long-term decline in English homicide rates from the fourteenth to twentieth centuries. Sharp warns, however, that "the pattern with property offenses is less unequivocal," but that "the great decline in homicide in the seventeenth century was not accompanied by a rise in property offense prosecutions, but rather by their diminution." Finally Sharp argues that Elias's arguments work much better for explaining English crime trends than "modernization arguments" based on the urbanization and industrialization of the last two centuries, as "discussing the 'modernization' of English crime is complicated by the fact that much of it looks very modern from a fairly early date."

The findings presented here by Eva Österberg in her essay, "Criminality, Social Control, and the Early Modern State: Evidence and Interpretations in Scandinavian Historiography," and by Pieter Spierenburg in his essay, "Long-Term Trends in Homicide: Theoretical Reflections and Dutch Evidence, Fifteenth to Twentieth Centuries," coincide with Sharpe's evidence. The evidence on homicide trends reported by the two scholars is compared in table I-1 (though here the homicide rate is reckoned per million inhabitants, instead of per thousand in Österberg's tables or per hundred thousand in Spierenburg's, and recalculated from their figures so as to apply to whole centuries instead of to decades, which figure in their more precise discussions).

Clearly these figures, rough as they are, demonstrate that the English case is no anomaly. The homicide rate in fifteenth- and sixteenth-century Amsterdam and Stockholm was quite similar to the rate for England and very high (about on a par with the most murderous American cities of the 1980s and early 1990s, which are, according to a 1993 article in the *New England Journal of Medicine,* by far the most violent places in the industrialized world). The big drop in the rates, although they had started to decline more gradually in both countries earlier, came in the second half of the eighteenth century. After that time both countries' rates appeared to hold steady through-

Table I-1. Estimated Yearly Homicide Rate per Million Inhabitants in · Sweden and Holland, Fifteenth to Twentieth Centuries

Century	Amsterdam[a]	The Netherlands	Stockholm	Sweden
15th	500	—	425	330
16th	200	—	280	300
17th	75	—	340	300
18th				
first half	80	—	—	165
second half	20	—	7	
19th	14	5	30	15
20th				
first half	—	5	6	—
post–WWII	60[b]	25[b]	8[b]	—

a. Amsterdam figures are for homicide victims, not including infanticide.

b. Dutch figures for post-WWII are for 1985–90 for the Netherlands, 1987–90 for Amsterdam. Stockholm's figures are for 1966–70.

out the nineteenth century and the first half of the twentieth before increasing somewhat in the last thirty years.

In her essay Eva Österberg adds an assessment of minor crimes of violence and of thefts to her careful study of homicide trends in Sweden and some neighboring Scandinavian lands since the fifteenth century. Though her evidence seems to indicate some rise in property offenses in the post–World War II period, she sides with Sharpe in rejecting the modernization argument about a shift from violence to theft in bourgeois society. She writes, "The notion of a shift 'from a violent society to a thieving society' is too simple a model for the description of changes in criminality in Scandinavia." Rather, her nuanced examination of crime trends and the rise of the power of the state in Scandinavian history leads her, if admittedly with some reservation, to support Elias's concept of a "civilizing process" in explaining the long-term change in mortal violence.

Spierenburg adds to Sharpe's and Österberg's criticisms of the "violence-to-theft" thesis and agrees with them in siding with Elias's "civilization argument" in explaining long-term trends in homicide in Amsterdam and the Netherlands since the fifteenth century. Besides his lengthy theoretical discussion, and his judicious assessment of previous Dutch studies of homicide trends, Spierenburg provides a cautious treatment of his own compilation of the Amsterdam figures from the seventeenth to nineteenth centuries. By examining coroners' inquests for the period between 1667 and 1816, Spierenburg is also able to make important statements about the role of women in homicide offenses, the motivation of murderers, and the relationship between killers and their victims. Here he adds support for Elias's theory by demonstrating that cases of premeditated homicide increased over time with fewer people being killed by strangers. Finally, he concludes that his evidence "casts serious doubts on the thesis that Dutch society traditionally has been nonviolent in comparison with other European lands"; nonetheless, he also concludes that the recent rise in Amsterdam's homicide rate is out of step with the rest of the country and probably occasioned by its status as a major center of the drug trade.

In her study "The Hundred Years' War and Crime in Paris, 1332–1488," the Israeli historian Esther Cohen leads the way for the more specialized essays in part 2 of the volume, arranged chronologically, by carefully exploring the nature of violence in late medieval Paris. Though "the sporadic nature of the sources" makes it difficult for her to calculate verifiable crime rates, her evidence points to a lusty and violent society with the majority of the cases in the available records concerning "brawls, street fights, and casual violence." Also she finds a surprisingly high level of continuity during and after the Hundred Years' War as "thirty years after the end of the war, the picture of urban crime remained unaltered. . . . The most typical cause for arrest in 1488 was the same in 1332." Richly descriptive, her essay provides flesh and blood to the picture of violent crime in late medieval society and demonstrates that the high level of violent crime in late medieval France corresponded closely with that of England, Sweden, and Holland. As she explains: "Violence was not even deplorable. It was a part of life, one of the ways one dealt with other people."

The Italian historian Michele Mancino provides yet more flesh and blood in his in-depth treatment of several cases of rape, murder, and other forms of violence in sixteenth- and seventeenth-century Naples, in an essay entitled "Ecclesiastical Justice and Counter-Reformation: Notes on the Diocesan Criminal Court of Naples." His chapter is particularly important for detailing the often crucial role of the church in its conflict with the state for the control of the hearts and minds of the people. The church, he finds, was generally tolerant of crimes of the flesh if intolerant in cases of crimes concerning the spirit. This, he shows, was in sharp contradistinction to the position of the state authorities. Hence the rise of the state's authority in premodern Europe would seem to mandate a shift in attitudes toward, and the practice of, violence in premodern society, as Elias and the other authors argue.

The Dutch historian Florike Egmond's essay, "Between Town and Countryside: Organized Crime in the Dutch Republic," demonstrates that the Dutch case does not fit stereotypes about banditry, usually associated with the countryside, and the organized underworld, usually associated with cities. As she argues, "organized crime in preindustrial Europe turns out to have been much more varied than suggested by the dual model of picaresque rural bands and urban underworlds." Comparing gangs and organized crime networks in the highly urbanized Dutch province of Holland with criminals in the more rural province of Brabant, Egmond shows that by at least the seventeenth century in Holland there was already a well-organized crime network, far more advanced than mere congeries of bandits, which operated with "interurban connections" and an "organizational pattern of overlapping networks, and a tendency toward specialization." Additionally her evidence suggests that criminal bands were also highly organized in the more rural province of Brabant but that they were much more violence prone in their method of operations than their urban counterparts, thus again lending credence to the view that violence was more commonly associated with the countryside than the city in premodern society.

The final member of the "Dutch group" in this volume was also in many ways the leader of that group. Herman Diederiks was the president of the IAHCCJ from its inception until his death in August 1995. In his essay entitled "Urban and Rural Criminal Justice and Criminality in the Netherlands since the Late Middle Ages," Diederiks reports on the findings of a huge research project, known as "SR18," conducted at the University of Leiden on Dutch criminal cases in several localities, most dating from the eighteenth and nineteenth centuries. His quantitatively based essay complements Spierenburg's and Egmond's chapters as he focuses on several other types of crime and criminal justice issues that affected the urban/rural dichotomy in criminal behavior. These include the relatively frequent presence of criminal courts and justices in rural and urban areas and the differences in penalties doled out in town and countryside. Of his many important findings, his evidence about the overarching role of males in violent acts, more so in rural than in urban areas in the eighteenth century, is of great interest to criminal justice historians as so little systematic evidence about the role of gender in premodern society exists for any country. Finally his evidence pointing out that "the rural countryside showed more male and violent criminality" than the cities of eighteenth- and early nineteenth-century Holland adds further proof to the central argument of nearly all of the authors: violence has not been a particularly urban phenomenon throughout most of the last several centuries.

In another largely quantitative study of local regions in nearly the same period, entitled "For God, State and People: Crime and Local Justice in Pre-industrial Sweden," the Swedish historian Jan Sundin also finds that women's criminality was greater in the towns than in the countryside. Focusing his study of the seventeenth through mid-nineteenth centuries, Sundin examines the "judicial revolution" that coincided with the rise of the state's dominance over local affairs and the impact these had on crime and justice in two Swedish provincial capitals and their surrounding countryside. Perhaps more than any of the other essays, Sundin's work helps to explain in detail why homicide rates dropped so precipitously in the period in Sweden and presumably in several of the other societies as well. As he discusses in detail, the decrease in violence was associated with a change in how one's honor was preserved, from fistfights in the seventeenth century to court litigation in the nineteenth century. Also he attributes the decline to a decrease in weaponry among the citizenry, to an increase in church discipline, and to the fact that "society at large became more peaceful, which was undoubtedly the case after the warlike seventeenth century."

Barbara Weinberger, an historian of modern England, in her essay "Urban and Rural Crime Rates and Their Genesis in Late Nineteenth- and Early Twentieth-Century Britain" focuses on the role of the police in the industrial heartland city of Birmingham and its surrounding region. Examining the police's role in generating the crime statistics in several types of offenses from poaching and drunkenness to common assault and simple larceny, she argues that "the higher and much more volatile offense rate in the city is evidence of a higher degree of police activity" and that "there was really no substantive difference" between Britain's rural and urban areas.

Although Eric A. Johnson, in his study of "Urban and Rural Crime in Germany, 1871–1914," employs far more quantitative data and displays far less caution in interpreting the crime statistics than does Weinberger, his findings and overall conclusions are quite similar. Furthermore, Johnson points out that the alleged connection between urban communities and serious crime has essentially been an ideological position that conservatives have frequently argued so as to condemn their political enemies—urban workers, socialists, and ethnic minorities. His evidence, based on coroners' records for murder and manslaughter and on court records for assault and battery and theft in over one thousand localities over a span of more than thirty years, shows conclusively that violent crime was not a common characteristic of German cities during the period of that country's great urban and industrial expansion. Violent crime was much more often associated with poor and discriminated-against Polish and Lithuanian minorities who usually lived along Germany's eastern borders. Thus the perceived crime rates were largely manufactured, by a conservative and discriminatory political order and criminal justice system.

Taken in sum, the chapters in this book point to the following conclusions: (1) violent crime has decreased over the last five centuries; (2) violence was a common and often tolerated, if not fully accepted, form of dispute settlement in the rural areas and villages that dominated premodern society; (3) a major drop in violent crime in most countries took place in the seventeenth and eighteenth centuries; (4) this drop was associated with a "civilizing process" whereby dispute settlement was gradually worked out in court more often than in potentially deadly brawls in taverns and on streetcorners—the growth of the state's power and monopoly over violence helped to retard interpersonal violence; (5) throughout the centuries as today, women have been far less prone to violence than men, but urban women have been more often involved in violence than have rural women, suggesting that their behavior has been quite different from that of men, whose violent acts were a more common feature of the countryside than of the town; (6) cities have not usually had exceptionally high crime rates in most societies in the past.

Finally, even though the historians in this volume have demolished any notion that there was a peaceful golden age in premodern times, they have created the image of a much more civil period during the nineteenth and early twentieth centuries, an era distinguished by expanded state control over violent behavior. As the twentieth century draws to its seemingly chaotic close, with crime rates soaring, are we not discovering only belatedly that during those years Western nations were in some sort of golden age? And is it possible that whatever the causes of the long decline in crime, they no longer obtain?

Notes

1. Norbert Elias, *The Civilising Process,* 2 vols. (Oxford, 1982), 239.
2. Ibid., 236.

PART ONE

Long-Term Assessments:
The Middle Ages to the Present

1

Crime in England: Long-Term Trends and the Problem of Modernization

James A. Sharpe

Toward the end of the reign of Queen Elizabeth I a petition reached Lord Scrope, one of Her Majesty's leading officials in the north. The petition aimed to bring to Scrope's notice the misdoings of "the Graymes and their clanne." These, the petitioners claimed, were they to be described fully, "wold contayne a volume." As it was, the brief catalog in the petition was impressive enough. The Grames had attacked a lesser royal official, John Musgrave, the land sargeant, firing "above thirtie dagges and gunnes" at him. Musgrave escaped only when local people rescued him. The Grames had sprung one of their number, John Grame, alias Jock of the Peartree, from prison during the assizes, or superior court sessions, at Carlisle. They had kidnapped an eight-year-old boy and held him hostage to use in exchange for Watt Grame, "a notable thief in prison." They ran a protection racket in their area, burning the houses and assaulting the persons of those who did not cooperate, while Richard Browne, who had killed one of their number while defending his goods, not only had his house burnt but also had to "buy his peace." They had assaulted the son of a justice who had helped convict one of their number, had impeded the hue and cry, prevented the sheriff from serving writs, and carried out numerous robberies, sometimes with the aid of Scots. They were also easing "men of good service" out of tenancies and replacing them with Scots and other "badd people," doubtlessly with the intention of consolidating their local power base. The petitioners claimed that more than three of the Grames had been outlawed for murder, burglary, and other of-

fenses. The Grames' counterpetition, professing their loyalty to their mon-
arch and their attachment to law-abiding ways, is belied by constant references to their misdeeds in the relevant documentation.[1]

However much of a menace to their neighbors and a nuisance to royal
officials the Grames may have been, they perform a useful service to the modern historian by providing an ideal-type example of late medieval crime. Such
crime, by 1600, was more likely to exist on the Anglo-Scottish border than
anywhere else in England, but perhaps it had been prevalent in other areas
in the fifteenth century. It was a criminality where a "clanne" of blood relatives and their associates could create an area where the royal writ ran, at best,
very insecurely. It was a criminality that depended on organized intimidation
and protection racketeering. And it was, above all, a criminality that depended
on violence, the violence of hard men who, from their late childhood, had
been accustomed to fighting as a normal part of life. It was a criminality, then,
that reflected a low level of penetration by the state, a low level of respect for
its laws, and a set of social mores that depended heavily on loyalty to kin and
that set great store by violence as a means of dispute settlement.

Thus we see one possible model of premodern crime. This coexists
uneasily with another view that uses our own current social preoccupations
to create a cozy mirror image of the modern situation. This view of premodern crime, like so much conventional wisdom about the preindustrial world
(one thinks of the extended family and the stable village community) has
proved pervasive. Howard Zehr, referring to "some of Western man's most
basic assumptions about both crime and modernity," gently lampooned the
resulting conventional wisdom:

> Everyone knows that crime is more frequent today than it was in the sta-
> ble rural milieu of our parents and great grandparents. In fact, many
> would agree, such a trend is inevitable. Modernity implies a decline in
> respect for conventions, a reduction in social controls, a lessening of
> appreciation for the rights and property of others. What could be more
> logical than that delinquency should accompany the modernisation pro-
> cess? Moreover, the growth of cities is usually considered a major cata-
> lyst in this development. . . . The city, in the popular view, is character-
> ised by instability, impersonal relationships, social disintegration and
> weakened social controls: it is the paradigm of modern society.[2]

Here Zehr neatly sets out the conventional wisdom about the transition from
"premodern" to "modern" society, and the main elements of how this process affected crime and delinquency.

Insofar as historians have turned their attention to the process, they have generally agreed that crime "modernized" over the period of the industrial revolution in the nineteenth century, and that this process involved changes in both the content of crime and the levels of organization behind it. Thus Michael Weisser, in an early and not altogether successful attempt to plot large-scale changes in criminality, postulated the emergence of a "new crime," a phenomenon that began in the sixteenth century as a consequence of a number of very familiar processes (demographic growth, increased geographical mobility, more marked social stratification, urbanization, and a greater gap between rich and poor) but which did not reach fruition until the nineteenth. By the eighteenth century this "new crime" was becoming evident in the more economically advanced sectors of Europe: "this period witnessed the emergence of new forms of criminality that reflected the ongoing transition to industrial life. These newer types of crime occurred most frequently in areas and among populations that were directly confronted with the effects of modernisation—places where industry and commerce developed in the earliest and most obvious sense."[3] Most scholars who have addressed the problem will have agreed that the salient feature of this new crime was the prevalence of property offenses, as opposed to crimes of violence: Howard Zehr summed it up by referring to "a modern pattern of crime, where violence is relatively low compared to property crime, and a 'premodern' pattern of high levels of violence relative to property crimes."[4]

We now know far more about the history of crime than Zehr did when he subjected the conventional wisdom about crime and modernization to scrutiny in 1976, and certainly more than we did when this conventional wisdom was formulated, around the beginning of the twentieth century. In this chapter I will review this conventional wisdom in the light of the English experience of the history of crime. There are two grounds that make this exercise an attractive one. First, in traditional historiography England has been portrayed as the pioneering industrial society. Although it is currently fashionable to be skeptical about the extent and impact of the Industrial Revolution,[5] even those scholars who have challenged the significance traditionally attributed to it cannot ignore the concrete impact of industrialization and urbanization: London, the biggest city in Europe, was expanding constantly throughout the nineteenth century. With this expansion came that of other, and new, great urban centers: Manchester—the "shock city" of the Industrial Revolution—Leeds, Liverpool, and Birmingham; lesser centers, such as Halifax, Huddersfield, and Preston; and, if we extend our view to the other parts of the United Kingdom, such significant industrial centers as Belfast, Cardiff, and the Glasgow-Clydeside belt. If we are to find crime modernizing anywhere, it ought to be there. And second, on a more prosaic note, my pursuit becomes attractive because the history of crime in England has received considerable, if far from exhaustive, attention.[6] There are gaps in our knowledge, both chronological and thematic. Most of that knowledge, certainly before national criminal statistics were produced in the nineteenth century, comes from the analysis of local, normally county, samples of material. But despite the many drawbacks, it is now possible to reconstruct much of the history of crime in England from the fourteenth to the twentieth centuries.

Before entering into the substance of this essay, I should make one further preliminary comment. I have always been a little unhappy with the concept of "modernization," and it was never as widely adopted in Britain as it seems to have been in the United States a decade or two ago: indeed, the English Marxist historian Edward Thompson once referred to modernization theory as "a pseudo-knowledge that has prestige on a few American campuses."[7] It seems to me that if we accept "modernization" as a useful shorthand term, it is another way of stating the main lines of development formulated by classical sociology: Marx's concept of a transition from feudalism to capitalism, Weber's notion of the transition from a "traditional" to a "rational" society, or that other old friend, the shift from *Gemeinschaft* to *Gesellschaft* traced by Tönnies. All of these thinkers (and, one suspects, a number of others who were influential in the decades around 1900 but who are now more or less forgotten) were concerned with exploring the problematic of the great transition from a stable, rural, preindustrial society to an unstable, urban, and industrial one. The modernization of crime in England is, therefore, a subject of relevance to any one of a number of strands of social science thinking.

◆ ◆ ◆ ◆

The idea of crime "modernizing" involves a number of elements. Initially, I should like to single out one of them, the idea that between the late Middle Ages and the nineteenth century, England experienced a shift from a "feudal" criminality based on violence, so vividly illustrated, as we have seen, by the conduct of the Grames up in Westmorland about 1600, to a "modern" criminality based on property offenses. That we are willing to posit such a shift, of course, depends heavily on our knowledge that English society became more capitalist, commercial, industrial, and urban over the period in question. Various other components can be fed into the model. One is the idea that as class structures altered, late medieval criminality involving a bastard feudal baron's retainers gave way to a criminality involving an urban "criminal class." There is an additional complication, the idea that burgeoning commercialization left more scope to what we would call "white-collar" crime: certainly the law relating to fraud in England as it developed over the eighteenth and nineteenth centuries would repay close study. More immediately, however, our discussion might most usefully turn to such statistical evidence as has been constructed about the incidence of crime.

This creates problems. Even today, when police forces and government departments are anxious to collect criminal statistics, the implications of those statistics remain debatable and their meaning contentious. Although archives may survive from which statistics can be drawn, the precise weight that can be afforded to the quantification of materials from three or six centuries ago remains problematic.[8] Nevertheless, a number of historians have turned their energies to constructing and interpreting such statistics, and we have evidence, at least in isolated samples, over a fairly long span. There is a good study for the first half of the fourteenth century,[9] then something of a gap until the sixteenth. From about 1550 records survive that have permitted a number of historians to quantify the prosecution of serious crime over the later sixteenth and seventeenth centuries,[10] and this process has been continued over the eighteenth.[11] Since the nineteenth century the creation of annual criminal statistics has facilitated the discussion of long-term trends in criminal statistics on a national basis,[12] while a number of local studies of crime, with a core of statistical evidence, have also been produced.[13]

On the face of things, then, we would seem to have a reasonable basis for entering a discussion of long-term changes in crime in England. There is, however, a major complication. Much of the study of the history of crime in England has concentrated, understandably, on serious offenses, usually that class of crimes known as felonies, which by about 1600 were normally tried at the assizes. But then as now the overwhelming bulk of crime, statistically speaking, was petty crime. This leads us into another quagmire, the problem of how to define crime. If we are to take a broad view (as I argue we should) and include the petty offenses coming before the quarter sessions, and that small change of delinquent behavior coming before the local ecclesiastical or manorial courts, still active in many areas over the seventeenth century, we get a more complex idea of what "crime" was and also a rather different notion of its statistical dimensions. Thus surviving assize and quarter-sessions records reveal that between 1600 and 1640 twenty-four indictments were brought for larcenies, burglaries, and cases of breaking and entering in the Essex village of Kelvedon Easterford. Over the same period 756 presentments against inhabitants of the parish were made in the court of the Archdeacon of Colchester, the two largest categories of offense being sexual immorality (234 presentments) and failure to attend church services (224 presentments). So there was a constant undercurrent of petty offenses, their prosecution often dependent on local initiatives, complementing the serious offenses that have attracted so much attention from historians.[14] In the fifteenth century such offenses might go to the manorial court, in the early seventeenth to the ecclesiastical court, by 1700 to the justices meeting in petty sessions. The records of such prosecutions are, despite the essentially piecemeal nature of their survival, massive, and as yet have been little studied. Before they are, it is probably premature to speak too confidently of macrochanges in English crime.

Let us set such reservations aside, however, and turn to surviving evidence for serious crime, concentrating on two types of offense, homicide and property offenses (larceny, burglary, breaking and entering, pickpocketing, robbery).[15] Beginning with homicide, we are able to tell a story that provides comfort for the advocates of modernization.[16] We have a number of samples of homicide statistics from the Middle Ages. These show massive variations in homicide rates (it should be noted that our estimates for medieval populations are only approximate, which makes the construction of crime rates an imperfect science) from 5 per 100,000 population in thirteenth-century Bristol to 110 per 100,000 in fourteenth-century Oxford. A cluster of samples, however, suggests a typical thirteenth-century rate of around 18 to 23 per 100,000. We then have more samples to suggest that the rate dropped a little, perhaps to 15 per 100,000 in 1600, and then fell dramatically over the middle of the seventeenth century.

This drop, which has been noted in all of the relatively few areas for which relevant evidence survives, remains inexplicable. It does, however, constitute a marked and sharply focused shift between "medieval" high levels of homicide and "modern" low ones. Research by J. M. Beattie has taken the story, for at least two English counties, through to the end of the eighteenth century. In the period 1660–79, homicide indictments were running at 8.1 per 100,000 in urban Surrey (essentially Southwark, a large built-up area directly south of the Thames from the City of London), 4.3 in rural Surrey, and 2.3 in the largely rural county of Sussex. By the period 1780–1802 the rates had fallen in all three areas to 0.9 per 100,000, at which level it was to stay nationally over the nineteenth and much of the twentieth centuries.[17] J. S. Cockburn has also carried out a long-term study of homicide in Kent, where he has traced a fall from around 6 homicides per 100,000 population in the late sixteenth century to less than 1 in the twentieth.[18] There may well be regional variations, but the overall pattern seems clear.

The pattern with property offenses is less unequivocal. Clearly, they were already the most frequently indicted felonies in the fourteenth century: Hanawalt's figures demonstrate that between 1300 and 1348 such infractions regularly constituted between two-thirds and three-quarters of felonies indicted in her sample of assize courts.[19] They remained so in the second half of the sixteenth: to take an extreme case, Middlesex, which already in that period included suburbs of London, on surviving documentation experienced 7,158 indictments for property offenses between 1550 and 1625 as opposed to 400 for homicide.[20] Over roughly the same period, 1559–1625, the mainly rural county of Sussex experienced 1,664 assize indictments for property offenses as opposed to 219 for homicide.[21] Taking a longer time span, Cheshire's Court of Great Sessions between 1580 and 1709 tried 2,875 property offenses as opposed to 623 homicides,[22] the relatively high ratio of homicides here being possibly a sign of a regional variation. What is more surprising is the chronology of indictments: in brief, there was no linear move toward higher levels of indictment of property offenses. Such indictments were, of course, prone to short-term fluctuations. In Essex, for example, sharp rises in the level of prosecuted property offenses occurred during the years of bad harvest in the late 1590s, the period 1629–31 when a trade depression hit the county's cloth industry, the years 1648–52 and 1661, again periods of bad harvests, and the years of dearth at the very end of the seventeenth century.[23] The long-term trend, however, was for property offenses to decline over the seventeenth century. The same trend was demonstrated in Cheshire, the archives of which county's Court of Great Sessions are probably the best series surviving for any English county. There property offenses were running at an average of 30 a year in the 1590s, peaked at an average of 50 a year in the 1620s, but then fell rapidly in the late seventeenth century to around 7 a year in the first decade of the eighteenth century.[24] The great decline in homicide in the seventeenth century was not accompanied by a rise in property offense prosecutions, but rather by their diminution.

Beattie's work on Surrey and Sussex allows us to take the story into the early nineteenth century. In urban Surrey indictments for property offenses were running at 60 to 70 a year in the late seventeenth century and, despite the odd isolated peak, were not to increase much over this until the final two decades of the eighteenth century, reaching about 200 in 1800.[25] As in the seventeenth century, property offenses tended to fluctuate in the face of harvest failure and trade depressions, although an additional factor was now present: the impact on criminal statistics of the discharge of large numbers of soldiers and sailors in the aftermath of the century's wars.[26] Population increase, and the disruption caused by the early stages of industrialization and the growth of urban centers, meant that totals of prosecuted crimes, above all of larceny, increased rapidly over the first forty years of the nineteenth century. The situation is still not totally clear, yet current research suggests that this increase was as marked in rural areas as it was in the industrializing ones, while increases in prosecutions of property offenses were still linked closely to periods of bad harvest.[27]

As the nineteenth century progressed, however, criminal statistics point toward a changing situation. Deficiencies in recordkeeping make it difficult to talk of national patterns before 1857, but from that date national statistics are available for analysis.[28] They indicate a very stable situation in indictable offenses between that date and the outbreak of the First World War. Combining larcenies (always more than 90 percent of offenses) with crimes such as burglary produced an annual average total of some 50,000 to 55,000 indictments, rising toward 60,000 over the Edwardian period. These property offenses overwhelmingly outnumbered crimes against the person, by over 23 to 1 in the years 1857–60. But it is, however, the very stability of the situation suggested by these statistics that causes problems for a simplistic notion of "modernization." England and Wales were a lot more "modern" in 1914 than in 1857, and certainly had a higher population, yet in the late Victorian and Edwardian periods the crime rate, for both property offenses and crimes against the person, had fallen, in both cases by 43 percent. Moreover, there had been no increase in the ratio of property crime against crimes of violence. As we have seen, this stood at over 23:1 in 1857–60: in 1906–10 it stood at just over 22:1; in 1911–13 at just under 19:1. On a simplistic reading of these statistics, crime in Victorian England, if we accept rising crimes against property and Zehr's use of a rising Theft/Violence Ratio as indicators, became as modern as it was going to get around 1860. Certainly, there is a strong contrast between the first half of the century and the second: indeed, according to Vic Gatrell, whose work has done so much to illuminate the history of crime in the period, it was 1842 that was "the year of the most intense judicial activity against crime in the century."[29] It was the period of transition toward an industrial society, not the period in which that society matured, that created a severe law and order problem; this problem existed in reality, and, to an even more marked extent, in elite preoccupations.

Once more, however, we must remind ourselves that more complex patterns emerge when we turn from felony to minor offenses. These have not been much studied outside the sixteenth and seventeenth centuries, but the evidence here gives a clear demonstration of some of the difficulties. The first of these was the long-term rise, varying regionally in its chronology, of what might be described as regulatory offenses: infringing the statutes regulating the economy, keeping an unlicensed alehouse, bearing or fathering an illegitimate child, being a vagrant, following a trade without having been apprenticed to it, and so on. These offenses were essentially created by an intermittent legislative drive that, from the 1530s, aimed at creating a more disciplined set of subjects for England's rulers. The imperatives of Tudor state-building interacted with the moral imperatives of the Reformation to create a new model of the citizen of the godly commonwealth: hardworking, sober, chaste, and with the values of the current religious settlement fully internalized. It proved difficult to produce such subjects; but attempts at moral, personal, and economic regulation through the course created distinctive patterns of prosecution in the early modern period. So from an early date our study of crime statistics is bedeviled by what the British criminologist Jason Ditton has described as "control waves"[30] created nationally by central government, or locally through county magistrates, urban authorities, or, indeed, even by godly parish elites.[31]

Tracing the progress of such regulatory prosecutions is complicated by the presence of a multiplicity of courts. Broadly, the objectives of these courts (the quarter sessions, local borough sessions, manorial courts, ecclesiastical courts, and, after the 1630s, petty sessions) were to punish and curb those nuisance offenses that were steadily being redefined as characteristic of the poor: petty theft, sexual immorality, bastard-bearing, drunkenness, vagrancy, or such community disorders as scolding or petty assault. In the fifteenth century, persons committing such offenses might come before a jury of their more substantial neighbors at the local manorial court.[32] In the later sixteenth and early seventeenth centuries, as the manorial courts declined, those same substantial neighbors might petition about nuisance offenders to the quarter sessions in hopes of having them bound over to keep the peace, or present them before the archdeacon's court. From the later seventeenth century they would appear before two or three local justices at petty sessions, or perhaps just be fined or sent to the house of correction by a single justice on summary conviction. The impact of these varied ways of dealing with petty offenses on crime statistics would be enormous, and would also raise a few problems about tracing modernity. Thus, combining indictments and presentments, 3,514 offenses came formally to the notice of the Essex quarter sessions between

1628 and 1632. These included 144 thefts and 48 assaults. They also included 480 prosecutions for allowing roads or bridges to fall into decay, 229 for keeping a disorderly alehouse, and 684 for failing to attend church.[33]

Another area that needs investigating is the nature of the criminals. Over the middle of the nineteenth century, debate on this issue was dominated by the concept of the "criminal class."[34] The existence (and novelty) of such a stratum lay at the center of Victorian debate on crime and punishment, and in the shape of "deviant subcultures" or "criminal areas" has survived into twentieth-century criminology. Popularized by such media as television and the press, the concept is still prevalent among the general public. If we return to the Middle Ages we apparently see a different pattern (although there is, of course, the possibility that we have been misled by a few well-documented cases) with heavy noble or gentry involvement in violence or extortion, and with occasional references to organized robbery or extortion headed by elite people.[35] This pattern had obviously disappeared by the late eighteenth century, when (apart from a few acts of violence and the odd fraud) the upper classes were extremely unlikely to be perceived as the perpetrators of serious crime. The whole issue is, however, complicated greatly by the problem of what we would describe as "white-collar" crime, whose history, as we have noted, awaits detailed investigation. If we are allowed to set this complication aside, it is obvious that some real changes had occurred.

Linking all this to socioeconomic change is a matter that should not be oversimplified. Yet whatever qualifications we make, it is evident that such links did exist. Let us return to the eighteenth century. By that era, England was enjoying an increasingly commercial and capitalist economy, and by its end was experiencing the fruits of a massive overseas trade and the early stages of what we have christened the Industrial Revolution. In the course of that century we can see a number of developments that might be interpreted as symptomatic of a criminality that was developing in keeping with economic change. The issue is not so much statistics of prosecution but levels of organization. By a happy coincidence, the rise of the country's first great criminal entrepreneur, Jonathan Wild (1683-1725), coincided roughly with that rise in capitalist speculation that abruptly ceased when the South Sea bubble burst.[36] In the localities, it is possible to see both smuggling and poaching becoming better organized in response to a growing demand for semiluxury items.[37] Thus despite the persistent image of the poacher as a "social criminal," taking the odd rabbit to feed his family, it is clear that poaching in the eighteenth century became an increasingly commercialized and organized activity responding to a demand for game among a more numerous, prosperous, and socially aspirant urban bourgeoisie. There are, therefore, some suggestions that as we try to uncover levels of organization of crime we may find some links with economic advance, and hence modernization.

The problem of organized crime, gentry-led medieval robber bands apart, has so far received little attention from historians. One place where some organization did exist was London, again suggesting a link between levels of economic and criminal organization. By the late sixteenth century London was demonstrating two symptoms of "modern" organized crime, namely organized prostitution and the organized receiving of stolen goods. One writer has postulated the existence in the capital of types of thieving that corresponded to the artisanal nature of the prevalent mode of industrial production. The main problem here, however, is that in the eighteenth century as in the late twentieth, most forms of crime, and certainly most criminals, were neither "organized" nor "professional." Court records for London have so far received little attention, and those for provincial towns have hardly been touched. Yet it remains inherently probable that for every "professional" criminal making a living from organized crime there were numerous petty opportunistic thieves, and that for every prostitute in a high-class brothel there were many casual or part-time ones. The search for the emergence of "organized" crime or of a "criminal class" obscures much of the reality of the experience of crime in the past.

We might also pause to consider whether those general developmental models that, as was suggested earlier, underpin the very notion of "modernization" might not need questioning. These main elements in these models are familiar enough: the move from a "traditional" or "preindustrial" world where the community and the extended family exercised a powerful social control, to an industrial society based on class, commerce, and individualism. This model has been questioned by a number of people taking a long view of English socioeconomic development, of whom perhaps the most radical is Alan Macfarlane.[38] Macfarlane's argument is that fundamental continuities have characterized English life since (at least) the thirteenth century (which is as far back as relevant records go). These continuities, all of them from an early date showing "modern" characteristics, are to be found in economic life, in the family, and in attitudes to property. They are also, Macfarlane has argued, present in the criminal behavior of the English.

Macfarlane's work on violence in English society, published in 1981, depended not on statistics (although he surveyed such secondary literature as was available when he wrote) but rather on a detailed case study concerning the activities of a criminal gang operating in the extreme northwest of

England in the later seventeenth century.[39] From this case study (we may safely dispense with discussion of the comparative project also present in the work) Macfarlane was able to demonstrate convincingly that even in a "backward" area of England crime was fairly "modern" in the period in question. He argued that if we accepted the standard preconceptions about "premodern" crime, "We should expect certain features in a country like England, if it was really going through the widely believed transition from a peasant/feudal society to a capitalist/modern one in the three centuries from about 1450 to 1750. We should find bandits, something akin to mafiosi, youth gangs, family feuds and vendettas, a high level of physical violence, but low level of theft, wandering bands of vagrant beggars."[40] In fact, he argued that we find nothing of the sort. Homicides were rare, as were rape, arson, and large-scale cattle rustling. Conversely, Macfarlane argued, "what might be termed 'capitalist crimes,' those to do with money and private property, are more numerous," among them counterfeiting coins and premeditated thefts, burglaries, and highway robberies.[41] If we accept Macfarlane's reading of the records, English crime did not need the mass industrialization and urbanization of the nineteenth century to modernize.

Macfarlane's conclusions may seem overstated, and they are certainly based on a limited sample of documents. Yet they are in keeping both with such statistical evidence as we have and with the sense that is left with us after we read more qualitative materials. Discussing the "modernization" of English crime is complicated by the fact that much of it looks very modern from a fairly early date. There are two main factors at work here. First comes England's early possession of a more effective monarchy and a more effective system of royal law than most comparable European states (experts on Anglo-Saxon history would claim pre-Conquest origins for this; I would feel more confident in directing the reader's attention to the eleventh-century reforms of Henry II). Second, although we need not enter Macfarlane's debate about the nonexistence of an English peasantry, there does, from an early date, seem to have been a peculiar social structure in rural England. This meant that, under the demographic pressures of ca. 1530–1640, rural England was already set en route for its classic nineteenth-century pattern of absentee landlord, prosperous tenant farmer, and landless agricultural laborer. A century before the Industrial Revolution, a large proportion of England's workforce was, in effect, proletarianized. This proletariat was, of course, largely agricultural, but many of its members were already looking fairly "modern" in their relationship to the means of production.

This has, of course, serious implications for the history of crime in England. From the late sixteenth century, when the archives allow us to be definite on the point, a large number of people being tried for theft and other property offenses were clearly antecedents of what the Victorians were to characterize as a criminal class. They were laborers, live-in servants drifting between employment or thrown out of it for petty delinquencies, unmarried women servants who had lost their jobs because of pregnancy, artisans suffering seasonal unemployment, a small hard core of criminal vagrants: that vast body of the poor who found working, begging, and stealing equally attractive means of putting a few pence in their pockets. These were the flotsam of a changing system, as individuals normally pathetic cases, collectively an irritant rather than a threat to society, yet (like the industrial proletariat in its formative years two centuries later) a source of real fear to the propertied, a threat from below, a "many-headed monster" that might overthrow social hierarchies.[42] How far back such people formed the bulk of England's criminals is unclear. But, despite the model of a feudal criminality based on violence, there are clues that the lower orders constituted the main target of law enforcement agents as far back as the fourteenth century. Hanawalt's figures, showing sharp increases in criminal prosecutions in response to bad harvests in the years 1300-48, suggest that then, as in the seventeenth century, most property offenders came from the lower peasantry, agricultural laborers, or poorer artisans.[43] As far as petty crime is concerned, the types of control being exercised by richer villagers through the manorial courts in the early fourteenth century (a period of acute demographic pressure) seem very similar in their concerns to those that activated village elites in the early seventeenth.[44] While we may be nervous about accepting a Macfarlanesque stress on social structural continuities, it is nevertheless a little difficult to establish when modernity established itself in English crime.

◆ ◆ ◆ ◆

It would, of course, be otiose to claim that nothing has changed with English crime since the Middle Ages. Indeed, living as I do in a period when law and order is a constant area of social concern, and where law and order problems can be closely linked to socioeconomic changes, makes studying crime in the past seem a very relevant activity. We look backward with considerable interest from late twentieth-century Britain, with its rising crime rates, its penal crisis, its decaying inner cities, and its emergent underclass, to earlier periods of transition when rising levels of prosecuted crime and rising levels of concern over law and order were linked symptoms of a more general feeling that the times were out of joint. Yet considering these early periods performs two initial essential functions for the historian. First, it helps avoid simplification. The deeper we penetrate into the history of crime in the past, the more our easy stereotypes, whether of a violent feudal criminality or of the idyllic and stable village community, begin to disintegrate. Second, we really do need to take a long-term view of the subject. Here as elsewhere, attaining universal knowledge is an impossibility; but studying crime and criminals in relatively distant periods is a useful, if sometimes uncomfortable, corrective to conventional wisdom.

The issue, however, takes us beyond amassing criminal statistics and cataloging elite fears about a disintegrating social order, interesting and important though these processes may be. It also involves shifts in individual psychology. After over a century of criminology it seems there is still little consensus over why criminals commit crimes, and a plea for a longer-term perspective on this problem may seem quixotic. Yet one avenue toward understanding how crime modernized must be to set the question in the wider context of how the personal comportment, psychological framework, and expectations about interpersonal interactions of individuals altered. The process of examining this problem has scarcely begun, at least as far as England is concerned.[45] Even so, the propensity to commit various types of crime must surely be an important element in that "civilizing process" to which a number of historians are currently turning their attention. At the very least, the declining taste for violence that logic suggests underlay the long-term decline in homicide prosecutions would seem to be amenable to investigation along these lines.

On safer grounds, I would suggest that another medium through which the process of the modernization of crime in England might be approached is the relationship between the community (a term that is, I realize, not unproblematic) and crime. Whether crime has modernized or not, the means of repressing it certainly have. The prison, the professional police officer, that whole "penal-welfare complex" to which David Garland refers[46] is evidence enough of this. Yet before the nineteenth century many petty offenses were tried in an essentially local context: before the manorial court in the fifteenth century, in the parlor of the local justice of the peace in the eighteenth (this shift itself is important). Thus the treatment of crime, assumptions about criminals, and patterns of prosecution were sometimes very different in the early modern period from those currently existing. Indeed, there were some offenses (notably scolding and witchcraft) that seem in many ways to have been connected intimately to late medieval or early modern village and small-town communities. Modernization of crime involves changes not only in the individual, the community, and the state, but in the relationship between them.

This provokes the not very surprising conclusion that to understand crime in the past (as in the present) it must be placed in the context of a number of other phenomena: the level of economic development and the complexity of the social structure, of course, but also the family, religion, perceptions of community, the nature of the apparatus of law enforcement, and the personnel staffing that apparatus. Despite the best efforts of social theorists, I am resistant to the notion that these entities changed in close step with each other. Tracing the long-term changes in these (and other) phenomena, and clarifying the nature of the connections in changes between different phenomena, should be fairly close to the top of the historian's agenda. This chapter has pointed to at least some of the complexities that emerge when the history of crime is approached along these lines.

Notes

1. Joseph Bain, ed., *The Border Papers: Calendar of Letters and Papers Relating to the Affairs of the Borders of England and Scotland Preserved in Her Majesty's Public Record Office* (Edinburgh, 1896), 2:686–88.

2. Howard Zehr, *Crime and the Development of Modern Society: Patterns of Criminality in Nineteenth-Century Germany and France* (London, 1976), 11.

3. Michael R. Weisser, *Crime and Punishment in Early Modern Europe* (Hassocks, 1979), 107.

4. Zehr, *Crime and the Development of Modern Society*, 125.

5. This is a point made forcefully by J. C. D. Clark, *English Society, 1688–1832* (Cambridge, 1985); see also J. A. Sharpe, *Early Modern England: A Social History, 1550–1760* (London, 1987), 147–51.

6. Most of the recent publications in the field are discussed in J. A. Sharpe, "The History of Crime in England c. 1300–1914," *British Journal of Criminology* 28 (1988): 254–67.

7. E. P. Thompson, "Happy Families," *New Society* 41 (1977): 499.

8. For discussion of some of the difficulties in using criminal statistics derived from historical periods, see: J. A. Sharpe, *Crime in Early Modern England, 1550–1750* (London, 1984), chap. 3, "Measuring Crime, Measuring Punishment"; Clive Emsley, *Crime and Society in England, 1750–1800* (London, 1987), chap. 2, "The Statistical Map."

9. Barbara A. Hanawalt, *Crime and Conflict in English Communities, 1300–1348* (Cambridge, Mass., 1979), chap. 3, "The Crimes: Definitions, Patterns and Techniques."

10. Joel Samaha, *Law and Order in Historical Perspective: The Case of Elizabe-than Essex* (New York, 1974); J. S. Cockburn, "The Nature and Incidence of Crime in England, 1559–1625: A Preliminary Survey," in *Crime in England, 1550–1800*, ed. J. S. Cockburn (London, 1977); J. A. Sharpe, *Crime in Seventeenth-Century England: A County Study* (Cambridge, 1983); C. B. Herrup, *The Common Peace: Participation and the Criminal Law in Seventeenth-Century England* (Cambridge, 1987).

11. The outstanding study of this period is J. B. Beattie, *Crime and the Courts in England, 1660–1800* (Oxford, 1986).

12. Another outstanding piece of historical scholarship, this time dealing with nineteenth-century crime statistics, is V. A. C. Gatrell, "The Decline of Theft and Violence in Victorian and Edwardian England," in *Crime and the Law: The Social History of Crime in Western Europe since 1500*, ed. V. A. C. Gatrell, B. P. Lenman, and G. Parker (London, 1980). This piece represents further thinking on themes introduced by V. A. C. Gatrell and T. B. Hadden, "Nineteenth-Century Criminal Statistics and Their Interpretation," in *Nineteenth-Century Society: Essays in the Use of Quantitative Methods for the Study of Social Data*, ed. E. A. Wrigley (London, 1972). For a shorter guide, see Emsley, *Crime and Society*, chap. 2.

13. The best regional study of crime in the nineteenth century is provided by David Philips, *Crime and Authority in Victorian England* (London, 1977).

14. J. A. Sharpe, "Crime and Delinquency in an Essex Parish, 1600–1640," in *Crime in England*, ed. Cockburn, 109.

15. In considering homicide, arguing from assault statistics is difficult. First, the technical legal definition of what constituted as assault meant that assault indictments at the assizes or quarter sessions are imperfect guides to acts of violence. Second, where such jurisdictions were still active, well into the seventeenth century assault cases might be tried, sometimes in large numbers, at the local manorial court leet. These problems are discussed in Sharpe, *Crime in Seventeenth-Century England*, 117–18; idem., *Crime in Early Modern England*, 26.

16. The literature on the history of homicide in England is reviewed by Lawrence Stone, "Interpersonal Violence in English Society, 1300–1983," *Past and Present* 102 (1983): 22–33.

17. Beattie, *Crime and the Courts*, 107–13.

18. J. S. Cockburn, "Patterns of Violence in English Society: Homicide, 1560–1985," *Past and Present* 130 (1991): 70–106.

19. Hanawalt, *Crime and Conflict*, 237.

20. Sharpe, *Crime in Early Modern England*, 55.

21. Cockburn, "Nature and Incidence of Crime," 55.

22. Sharpe, *Crime in Early Modern England*, 55.

23. Sharpe, *Crime in Seventeenth-Century England*, 198–201.

24. Sharpe, *Crime in Early Modern England*, 60.

25. Beattie, *Crime and the Courts*, figure 5.4, 214.

26. Ibid., 202–36; Douglas Hay, "War, Dearth and Theft in the Eighteenth Century: The Record of the English Courts," *Past and Present* 95 (1982): 117–60.

27. Emsley, *Crime and Society,* 29–33.

28. These calculations are based on data provided by Gatrell, "Decline of Theft and Violence," 282.

29. Ibid., 283.

30. Jason Ditton, *Controlology: Beyond the New Criminology* (London, 1979), especially chap. 2, "Crime Waves or Control Waves? A Recipe for Atheistic Statisticians."

31. The classic study of the interrelationship among social, economic, and cultural changes in a community and the problem of the control of crime and delinquency is Keith Wrightson and David Levine, *Poverty and Piety in an English Village: Terling, 1525–1700* (New York, 1979); see also Keith Wrightson, "Two Concepts of Order: Justices, Constables and Jurymen in Seventeenth-Century England," in *An Ungovernable People: The English and Their Law in the Seventeenth and Eighteenth Centuries,* ed. J. Brewer and J. Styles (London, 1980).

32. This is a theme discussed in Marjorie K. McIntosh, *Autonomy and Community: The Royal Manor of Havering, 1200–1500* (Cambridge, 1986).

33. Sharpe, *Crime in Early Modern England,* 49–50.

34. The nineteenth-century concept of a criminal class is described in Emsley, *Crime and Society,* chap. 6, "A Mid-point Assessment: The Criminal Class and Professional Criminals."

35. For an introduction to this subject, see Barbara Hanawalt, "Fur Collar Crime: The Pattern of Crime among the Fourteenth-Century English Nobility," *Journal of Social History* 8 (1975): 1–17. For a well-documented example of a deviant medieval gentry family, see E. L. G. Stones, "The Folvilles of Ashby-Folville, Leicestershire, and Their Associates in Crime, 1326–1341," *Transactions of the Royal Historical Society,* 5th Series, 7 (1957): 117–36.

36. Wild's career and significance are discussed in Gerald Howson, *Thief-Taker General: Jonathan Wild and the Emergence of Crime and Corruption as a Way of Life in Eighteenth-Century England* (New Brunswick, 1985).

37. Smuggling has attracted little attention from serious historians; for some initial comments, see Cal Winslow, "Sussex Smugglers," in Douglas Hay et al., *Albion's Fatal Tree: Crime and Society in Eighteenth-Century England* (London, 1975). Poaching is described in P. B. Munsche, *Gentlemen and Poachers: The English Game Laws, 1671–1831* (Cambridge, 1981). This should be read in conjunction with Douglas Hay, "Poaching and the Game Laws on Cannock Chase," in Hay et al., *Albion's Fatal Tree;* and D. J. V. Jones, "The Poacher: A Study in Victorian Crime and Protest," *Historical Journal* 22 (1979): 325–60.

38. Alan Macfarlane's oeuvre is extensive, but I feel that his general approach is best represented in two works: *The Origins of English Individualism* (Oxford, 1978) and *The Culture of Capitalism* (Oxford, 1987).

39. Alan Macfarlane, *The Justice and the Mare's Ale: Law and Disorder in Seventeenth-Century England* (Oxford, 1981). Macfarlane's views on this subject are restated in his *Culture of Capitalism,* chap. 3, "Violence: Peasants and Bandits."

40. Macfarlane, *Justice and the Mare's Ale,* 185.

41. Ibid., 186.

42. This subject has not received the attention it deserves. For an initial discussion, see Christopher Hill, "The Many-Headed Monster in Late Tudor and Early Stuart Thinking," in *From the Renaissance to the Counter Reformation: Essays in Honour of Garrett Mattingley,* ed. C. H. Carter (London, 1966).

43. Hanawalt, *Crime and Conflict,* 243–50.

44. For some initial comments on this point, see J. A. Sharpe, "The History of Crime in Late Medieval and Early Modern England: A Review of the Field," *Social History* 7 (1982): 202–3.

45. Robert Muchembled, *L'Invention de l'homme moderne: Sensibilités, moeurs et comportements collectifs sous l'ancien régime* (Paris, 1988), is a suggestive example of how such a study might be conducted.

46. David Garland, *Punishment and Welfare: A History of Penal Strategies* (Aldershot, 1985).

2

Criminality, Social Control, and the Early Modern State: Evidence and Interpretations in Scandinavian Historiography

Eva Österberg

◆ The Problem and the State of Research

People in the Icelandic sagas—and the narratives themselves—are impelled by powerful human passions: love, hate, pride, envy. This is vital in stories intended to captivate their audience, to spellbind listeners of both sexes and all ages with the excitement of eternal existential problems.

Yet there are other features in the sagas that modern cultural analysis has considered less dependent on the requirements of the literary genre and thus a more revealing expression of the Scandinavian mentality. These include the legalism that pervades the sagas.[1] One is struck by the extent to which people think and argue in legal terms. This applies to men in conflict, to men demonstrating their power and influence. But it also applies within the family, in the most sensitive situations of domestic life and sexuality, where both men and women know very well what they have a right to demand. We see this, for instance, in the way the marital conflict between Thorkell and Asgerd is solved in the Saga of Gisli, when Asgerd threatens with legal arguments to seek a divorce if Thorkell in his wounded pride does not stop excluding her from the marital bed. It is also clear from Gudrun's and Thord's discussion of male and female obligations in Laxdaela Saga.

When reading the sagas it is impossible to ignore the role played by law as an accepted system of norms and by the thing, the Icelandic judicial assembly. The *thing* is the hub of events. It is where people come to obtain satisfaction, where reconciliations are made, where little men seek out the strongest and wisest for advice about how to pursue the judicial process.

What is remarkable about Icelandic society, as it is described in the sagas, is that it lacks a state. We find a society held together by forces other than those of the state. One of these forces—perhaps the most important—is the law. In Kirsten Hastrup's words, it was "part of the general Scandinavian heritage that a society was defined through the law; there was no concept of society apart from this one in the early Middle Ages." The law was the society and at the same time a part of the social system; the legal system "can thus be seen both as a kind of meta-communication about society, and as a part of the whole web of institutions and social definitions of which society was constituted."[2]

In short: the picture of early Scandinavian society in modern cultural analysis is strongly colored by the presence of the law, by people's legal consciousness, and by the *thing* as a meetingplace where conflicts are resolved. It is a society permeated by law and legalism. Justice is administered without formal experts or professionally delivered judgments, but with judicial forums functioning as generally recognized and utilized social arenas for the resolution of conflict.

Let us now move forward several hundred years, to the society of the eighteenth and nineteenth centuries. In an analysis inspired to a greater or lesser extent by scholars such as Elias, Foucault, and Habermas, we find another picture of law and the administration of justice. The law is increasingly specialized, justice is more formally administered, and the courts are increasingly professional.[3] Law and justice are closely linked to—and dependent on—the state. To be sure, we do not need to see law and justice purely as instruments either of the state or of a particular class's interests. We can avoid such simple reductionism and instead view the law as the ideological cement holding society together, not only by appearing to be just, but sometimes by actually being just.[4] Even with this view, however, justice is not only a social arena where people resolve their conflicts. It is also a theater of power, where the authorities communicate with the population, legitimize themselves, and present themselves to their subjects.[5]

Both the first picture and the second one are generalized ideal types. They do not correspond to any real microsociety. Yet they generate questions and facilitate our attempts to understand by providing a starting point for the method that Peter Laslett terms "understanding by contrast."

Between the period of early Icelandic and early medieval Scandinavian society as a whole and the eighteenth century, the early modern state emerged as a centralized and bureaucratic system of power. This raises a number of questions about the significance of the state for changes in the administration of justice and in social control. Are there changes through time in the criminality that is brought before the courts, and can such changes be explained as a result of the court's increasingly becoming a theater of power rather than a social arena for the people? Do the major changes in criminality lie in variations in frequency within the same category of crime, or in the creation of entirely new categories of crime? What role is played by the state in this process? How does the state initiate changes both as an authority that passes laws and administers justice and as a general force to transform society? We must ask whether court practices in the sixteenth and seventeenth centuries should be understood within the framework of a new discourse between the state and the citizens, as for instance Natalie Davis has argued for France.[6]

Let us assume that the functions of justice—as they can be revealed by an analysis of court proceedings—change through time. Does this have anything to do with the transfer to the courts of the tasks carried out by other institutions or networks in society, or is it the other way around, that the latter take over functions previously discharged by the courts?

What is striking in Scandinavian historiography is that questions of this kind have not been seriously asked until the last decade. Yet both historians and historians of law have long been aware of the judicial sources that are available in the Scandinavian countries.

Continuous series of court records from both town and country generally go back no farther than the start of the seventeenth century. Even after 1600 there can be considerable differences in quality and quantity, but they do not prevent systematic analysis. In the late eighteenth century and the nineteenth century there are increasing numbers of criminal statistics compiled at the national level. It is more problematic, however, to find sufficient material to study prior to the seventeenth century.

In short: the material has its evident defects, but at least from the seventeenth century it is no more badly preserved than several other series of a fiscal or demographic nature. It is therefore surprising that court sources have long been used only for two main purposes: First, some historians have selected isolated cases to illustrate how different—cruel, peculiar, bizarre—people's behavior was in former times. This is a way to render bygone times exotic, which is common, for example, in works of local history. In the second approach, other scholars have discussed the witch trials of the seventeenth century as a Scandinavian and European phenomenon. This is a genre that has been increasingly influenced in Scandinavia by international theories of anthropology and cultural sociology.[7]

In the 1970s and 1980s, however, Scandinavian historians also tried to reconstruct the fluctuations in overall criminality over longer periods. The witch trials, which are in fact unique in judicial development, are then left in the background. The focus has instead been on more common categories of crime: violence, theft and other economic crime, sexual offenses, defamation, disorder and disobedience, and so on. The starting point has generally been an operational definition of crime as acts that are classed by the law as criminal, can be punished, and are thereby recorded in judicial sources. When I speak of criminality here, it is thus a matter of recorded criminality.[8]

The analyses have, broadly speaking, taken three forms:

1. Social historical correlation analysis, where the curve describing various kinds of criminality is compared with other statistical series, such as harvest yields, wages and prices, or alcohol consumption. Examples are works by Sundin, Fällström, and Hofer.[9] The intention is to find causes for human behavior in statistical correlations, for example, those of an economic kind.

2. Analysis of the conditions of workers and craftspeople, where a particular workers' or apprentices' culture is believed to explain some crimes that were common until the trend was reversed by the disciplining of the workers by the bourgeoisie. Examples are found in publications by Horgby and Magnusson.[10]

3. What for want of a better term is called cultural historical macroanalysis. This includes attempts to link criminality with major phases in societal development in a more qualitative way. Here it is no longer a question of statistical correlations, and not solely of workers' and craftspeople's conditions. Instead there is a discussion of the way great societal processes, such as a civilizing process, in the sense used by Elias,[11] or capitalism affect not only people's behavior but legislation, justice, and social control.[12]

Studies of type 1 have generally dealt with the nineteenth or twentieth century. Anne-Marie Fällström, for example, studies the period 1800–1840 in Gothenburg and finds variations in criminality that coincide with fluctuations in the economic cycle.[13] When Gothenburg was able to profit from the interruption of trade between England and France during 1809–14 and experienced an economic boom, there was a rise in the number of crimes against order (like drunkenness) and against trade restrictions. By contrast, when wages fell and prices rose in the following period, there were more thefts. For the years 1830–56 Jan Sundin similarly shows that there is a correlation between poor harvests and the frequency of thefts.[14] This applies particularly to agrarian regions where the system of landless laborers (*statare*) was generally in effect.

Examples of studies of type 2 are two analyses of conditions in Swedish towns in the nineteenth century. Björn Horgby focuses on Norrköping, which was a large industrial town for the time, with a considerable working-class population.[15] He observes that thefts, crimes of violence, and alcohol consumption increased in the first half of the nineteenth century and declined thereafter. His interpretation is that the latter half of the nineteenth century was a time when the workers were disciplined and had adapted to society's norms of respectability and order. An increase in offenses involving drunkenness and violence during the first part of the nineteenth century is also seen by Lars Magnusson in his analysis of the unruly craftspeople's culture in Eskilstuna.[16] As Birgit Petersson has shown, the start of the nineteenth century was a time when intellectuals and other "upper-class" groups in Sweden were extremely concerned about "the dangerous lower classes";[17] without having any idea about the real extent of criminality or who was committing the crimes, they had a sense of danger and the approaching dissolution of society.

Studies of type 3 arrive at results that can be interpreted in terms of macrohistory or the history of civilization, although not all scholars have painted such perspectives themselves. It is also here that we find studies that go farther back in time and aspire to cover the preindustrial period as well.

Knut Sveri's work of 1974 can be described as the first effort of this kind in Sweden.[18] On the basis of fairly small numbers of data he tentatively sketched the lines along which criminality developed in Sweden from the Middle Ages to the present day. In his opinion the whole of the preindustrial period was typified by crimes of violence, while theft and other property offenses were less frequent. The period ca. 1850–1940 in Sveri's sketch functions as a sort of transitional phase with a relatively limited amount of crime. After that the picture changes when an increasingly regulated reform society takes over: murder and manslaughter make up a smaller proportion of the total criminality, while thefts and other "modern" crimes (such as tax evasion) become more common. Sveri is thus an early proponent of the *de la violence au vol* thesis that has long been current in international research.

In Norway the historians Sverre Steen and later Hans Eyvind Naess have, like Sveri, painted quite a dark picture of criminality in early times. They find that violence, for example, increased considerably toward the end of the sixteenth century and the first decades of the seventeenth century. The local officials had good reason to complain about violence and immorality in the country. Naess argues, however, that from the 1640s and 1650s criminality declined in Norway and was at a much lower level around 1700. According to this view, then, the latter part of the seventeenth century was a civilizing period in Norwegian local society.[19] This is a dating of the decline in criminality that is paralleled in Lars-Olof Larsson's discussion of violence in southern Småland in Sweden.[20] Larsson likewise believes that the change took place between the early seventeenth century and the start of the eighteenth; it was then that the people of Småland were disciplined by the crown and the church into letting their weapons and their aggressions rest.

For Finland, however, historians have argued for a somewhat different chronology. In an essay from 1976 Heikki Ylikangas outlined the development of Finnish criminality over several centuries.[21] In a later work he has returned to the period from the latter half of the eighteenth century to the early nineteenth century,[22] when one area of Finland distinguished itself by its unusually high rate of violent crime.

According to Ylikangas, the general reason for criminal behavior was inequality regarding the possibility of achieving welfare and social status. This explains why violent crime is usually associated with the lowest classes in society. Violence can quite simply be seen as an expression of social protest, a kind of unconscious, crudely articulated rebellion. Yet in his studies from Finland, Ylikangas cannot demonstrate any link between a high rate of violent crime and increasing poverty. On the contrary, his material suggests that violent crime decreased from around the middle of the sixteenth century and remained at a low level in the following centuries, despite economic problems among the Finnish peasantry. Ylikangas's explanation is that the lower classes, at the same time as they were becoming poorer, found themselves increasingly dependent on the landowners and state officials. In other words, the lower classes had reason to protest through violence, but they simply were not able to—they were far too weak. Instead they gradually adapted voluntarily to the norms of the authorities and the upper classes.[23]

In his interpretations of the nineteenth-century wave of violence in southern Ostrobothnia, which differs from the general picture for Finland, Ylikangas similarly combines economic development, which in turn led to uneven economic growth, with regional value systems that were breaking up the informal social control. It was only when the increasing social polarization coincided with an individualistic competitive mentality that violence arose.

Ylikangas's explanations thus have two elements: arguments on the one hand about which economic factors can lead to criminality and on the other hand about how criminality is also influenced by the form and efficacy of social control. This duality in the interpretative framework is also found in publications of other scholars.[24] Recorded crime cannot be analyzed solely as a question of behavior, which is in turn a result of economic, political, or genetic factors; it must also be understood in light of the form taken by official judicial control and the various kinds of informal social control that existed in different periods.

This is an approach that has consequences for the way scholars discuss the "dark figure" in crime statistics. The dark figure can theoretically consist of offenses that were never discovered; offenses that may have been discovered and brought to court but were not registered in the extant judicial sources because, for example, the parties settled their dispute out of court; or behavior that may have been defined as criminal by the law but was not viewed thus by the people, who therefore kept it outside the scope of formal justice. The issue of the dark figure is thus transformed from a technical-statistical problem into an interesting historical topic. For instance, when does certain behavior graduate from being "social crime," and thus part of the dark figure, to become recorded crime? To what extent are the courts used to resolve conflicts between individuals, groups, or generations? In what conditions does this instead happen in other forums of social interaction?

In order to test explicitly a civilization perspective inspired by Elias, in 1983 I made the first attempt to join Swedish findings with international research. I combined my own results from some rural areas of Uppland with Larsson's conclusions from Småland. This led to a critical discussion about violence in preindustrial society.[25] Although crimes of violence were, in my analysis, common in Sweden in the sixteenth century and the early seventeenth, violence in general was usually fairly mild: petty brawls at weddings and christenings, impetuous slaps dealt in anger, and the like. The interesting question was therefore why such trivial violence reached the courts at all. Certain figures also led to the hypothesis that the more serious violence may have increased in connection with Sweden's many wars in the early seventeenth century. In a later article I developed this reasoning in a preliminary synthesis of seventeenth-century Sweden as "a civilizing process with obstacles." In symbiosis with the church, the Swedish state certainly tried to educate and discipline the people, who may have become more "civilized" in some ways. Ordinary people learned to read and write to an extent that is surprising in a European perspective; the small Swedish nobility imitated as best it could an elite culture of European style; extramarital sexuality was vigorously combatted; and so on. Yet there was another side to the coin. More and more soldiers were enlisted in the wars and died in the filth and misery of military camps. The soldiers became a significant group among the perpetrators of serious violence, and homicide tended to increase in some areas during Sweden's period as a great martial power, 1611–1718.[26]

In these early articles I examined other categories of crime, without drawing any conclusions about the total crime profile. I returned to this, however, in a larger work written with Dag Lindström, in which we analyzed the towns of Arboga and Stockholm from the latter half of the fifteenth century to the start of the seventeenth century.[27] The main findings include: (1) Violent crime—especially petty violence—was still a predominant category of crime at the start of the seventeenth century; it is largely explained, however, in terms of a culture of honor and pride. (2) Thefts made up a small proportion of the total volume of crime throughout the period; this is understood as a result of a combination of the Swedish social structure, with a predominance of freehold peasants and few towns, and popular value systems. (3) In the wake of the state-building process of the sixteenth century there came new categories of crime and an increase in cases concerning commercial restrictions, order in the towns, and sexuality.

Our findings have to some extent provided comparative material for works that have only recently been published or are not yet published.

Scandinavian historiography in the field of criminality and social control is thus changing and expanding quickly at the moment. It is therefore bold to synthesize the different findings—published and unpublished—right now. Moreover, it is difficult, since the various researchers have adapted the methods of calculating criminality to suit their particular questions. There are thus very few directly comparable results. To be able to make comparisons, we sometimes have to recalculate the figures.

Another problem arises in comparing findings from early times with those from the nineteenth and twentieth centuries. Estimates for the medieval and early modern period come from individual towns and from population figures that often are just in the hundreds. Both the absolute figures for crime and the total population figures are frequently small. Arboga, for example, had only about a thousand inhabitants at the end of the sixteenth century; Stockholm had around ten thousand. From the nineteenth and twentieth centuries we have figures from official statistics for the whole country. In this sense there is a lack of congruence in the figures in the three tables in this chapter. This is also the reason why I do not try to attach any great significance to minor variations in the figures. What is important is to discern broad tendencies extending over centuries, in a way similar to that attempted by T. R. Gurr and Lawrence Stone in their challenging analyses of historical trends in violent crime.[28] For this purpose I think that the existing Swedish studies are sufficiently useful. As I will discuss in greater detail below, what is striking is that case studies of the Middle Ages and the early modern period give results that are largely unambiguous in comparison with modern crime statistics, regardless of the areas covered by the studies and the criteria selected by the researchers.

My intention here is to present a preliminary synthesis. What does the available Swedish material, supplemented for some points with Norwegian and Finnish evidence, say about the major tendencies through time regarding crimes such as violence and theft? What does the evidence say about new categories of crime, about the criminalization of behavior that, unlike homicide, has not been so self-evidently prohibited from earliest times? How can the broad changes be explained? Did people really change their values and behavior, or is it rather the system of social control and the role of the courts in this system that changed?

◆ Constant Categories of Crime: Violence and Theft

In the Scandinavian societies, murder, manslaughter, assault, and theft have always been considered serious crimes, for which the law has prescribed penalties that have in many cases been extremely severe. The categories of violence and theft are in this sense continuous and independent of time. It may therefore be meaningful to draw up statistics for these crimes that cover several centuries. The data are taken from the various local studies that have been mentioned above and, for recent centuries, also from nationwide crime statistics. To obtain comparability the figures have been recalculated as means per year per 1,000 inhabitants. The calculations have been made with varying degrees of certainty and exactness, depending on the quality of the basic material. The tables must therefore be analyzed with great caution.

Table 2-1 requires some comments. For the period from 1750 the statistics are based on exact population figures, where criminality is calculated per 1,000 inhabitants aged 15–69. Data for the Middle Ages and the sixteenth and seventeenth centuries do not have the same precision, since rough estimates of population have to be used. In addition, the ages of the offenders are generally not stated in the sources. Nevertheless, for the earlier periods as well the crimes were no doubt committed by people aged about 15–69. Children were not taken to court in early times either, and criminality among the aged must have been negligible. For the major changes through time, then, these limitations probably have no significance.

Table 2-1. Murder and Manslaughter Calculated as Mean Values per Year per 1,000 Inhabitants, Sweden

Town	Countryside	All of Sweden	Means
Arboga 1452–61			0.10
Arboga 1462–71			0.60
Arboga 1473–82			0.40
Stockholm 1475–79			0.45
Stockholm 1480–84			0.32
Arboga 1493–1502			0.10
Arboga 1516–25			0.10
Arboga 1534–43			0.10
	Långhundra hd. 1545–60		0.14
Stockholm 1545–49			0.20
Vadstena 1580–89			0.60
Stockholm 1590–94			0.36
Vadstena 1602–10			0.77
	Västra härad 1610–19		0.08
Stockholm 1615–19			0.36
	Vendel hd. 1615–30		0.14
Stockholm 1620–24			0.32
	Konga hd. 1614–29		0.40
	Vendel hd. 1631–45		0.26
Linköping, beg. of 17th c.			0.30
	Västra härad 1660–69		0.10
	Västra härad 1720–25		0.03
		1761–65	0.0072
		1771–75	0.0059
		1781–85	0.0070
		1801–5	0.0067
		1821–25	0.0131
		1841–45	0.0177
Stockholm 1841–55			0.030[a]
		1881–85	0.0089
		1916–20	0.0057
		1966–70	0.0078

a. Approximation

Sources: Österberg 1983: 25ff.; Larsson 1982; Österberg and Lindström 1988: 43ff., 79ff.; Sundin 1992; von Hofer 1985; Bi SOS Rättsväsende 1830–56; Thunander, "Lagbrytare i bondesamhället," 1988.

What the figures show above all is that the frequency of serious crimes of violence (murder and manslaughter) is generally lower in the period from the middle of the eighteenth century to the present than it was in the period from the fifteenth century up to the mid-seventeenth century. Sometime between the middle of the seventeenth century and the middle of the eighteenth century there was evidently a dramatic change.

What can also be read from the table is that a little town like Arboga, with the exception of the figures from the 1460s and 1470s, generally had a pattern of serious violence that was scarcely different from that of a rural region at the same time. By contrast, the figures from Stockholm appear to show that there was slightly more violence there. At the same time, however, the figures from Vadstena, which was hardly bigger than Arboga, show that there may also have been considerable differences from place to place. Jörn Sandnes makes a similar observation when analyzing violence in Norwegian towns in the sixteenth century. He calculates the number of murders and manslaughters per 1,000 inhabitants in Bergen as 0.83 in the 1560s. This is clearly a higher figure than for other Norwegian towns, and even more than for Stockholm at the same time. The likely reason for this apparent uniqueness of Bergen is that the town was an international trade center with a mobile population, a meetingplace for several nationalities and ethnic groups.[29]

Yet another observation may be mentioned for table 2-1. Within the two main periods—from the 1450s to the 1660s and from the 1760s to the 1960s—there are also variations through time. In particular we see higher values in the 1460s and 1470s and in some areas around 1600. Both periods are characterized by political unrest: the 1460s and 1470s as a consequence of an internal power struggle and friction within the Scandinavian union; toward the end of the sixteenth century and the start of the seventeenth century because of both internal conflicts and the Swedish mobilization for the war in Europe.

It is difficult to judge from table 2-1 the extent of the decline in violence between the early period and the eighteenth century. Behind the national mean figures for the 1760s on, there can be large local variations. Conversely, it is possible that the mean figures for larger regions would have reduced the dramatic impression of the case studies from the fifteenth or sixteenth centuries. Rudolf Thunander's studies of violence in the whole province of Småland in 1635–44, with a total population of about 145,000, would indicate this.[30] Nevertheless, the mean figure for murder and manslaughter annually per 1,000 inhabitants in the province amounts to about 0.07, which is still far more than the figure for Sweden in the 1760s.

In the nineteenth century it is the peak in violent crime in the 1840s that must be emphasized. This is in line with the general unruliness Lars Magnusson and Björn Horgby have demonstrated for Eskilstuna and Norrköping at roughly the same time.[31]

If we look at Finland, we find that Ylikangas has calculated the frequency of murder and manslaughter in southern Ostrobothnia for 1806–15 as 0.057 and for 1816–25 as 0.094.[32] These figures may be striking in comparison with the national means for Sweden at the same time, and they are indeed viewed as a distinctive feature of the area known as "the land of the knife-fighters." Nevertheless, they are below the figures calculated for Swedish towns in the fifteenth and sixteenth centuries.

In other words, nothing in the findings that are currently known dispels the impression that murder and manslaughter became a less common category of crime in the long term. The exact chronology can be debated. I will content myself with observing that in the case of Sweden the swing occurred between the mid-seventeenth century and the mid-eighteenth century at the latest. I have here arrived at the same main conclusion as Lawrence Stone with his findings from England.[33] In a slightly shorter perspective one notes the tendency toward an increase in serious violence in the first half of the nineteenth century, an interesting phenomenon that nevertheless does not reverse the overall trend.

However, murder and manslaughter never reach high absolute figures in any period. It is therefore important to extend the analysis to include other, less serious crimes of violence, as shown in table 2–2.

The figures in table 2–2 largely confirm the picture already obtained in table 2–1. Minor crimes of violence also appear to have been fewer in the late nineteenth century than in the fifteenth and most of the sixteenth centuries. Not even the figures recording the considerable violence in Norrköping in the mid-nineteenth century exceed the figures from Arboga in the fifteenth century.

On the other hand, the statistics for minor violence do not show any undeniable increase at the start of the seventeenth century, as has previously been claimed for murder and manslaughter in some areas.[34] The significance of the wars and conscription of soldiers in Sweden's period as a great power should evidently not be exaggerated.

The main findings appear to agree also with new information obtained by Johan Söderberg and Jan Sundin.[35] Söderberg calculates various categories of crime as a proportion of the total court cases and concludes that violent crime was already receding, relatively speaking, in the sixteenth century. However, the shifts in the relative figures are due to the increasingly

Table 2-2. Minor Crimes of Violence Calculated as Mean Values per Year per 1,000 Inhabitants, Sweden

Town	Countryside	All of Sweden	Means
Arboga 1452–61			7.8
Arboga 1473–82			15.7
Stockholm 1475–84			6.0
Arboga 1516–25			8.5
Arboga 1534–43			5.0
	Långhundra hd. 1545–60		1.1
Stockholm 1570–79			2.3
Vadstena 1580–89			3.9
Vadstena 1602–10			6.7
	Vendel hd. 1615–30		2.6
Stockholm 1623–24			8.2
	Vendel hd. 1631–45		1.3
		1841–45	2.33
Norrköping 1845			3.60[a]
		1851–55	2.01
Norrköping 1855			5.00[a]
		1861–65	1.27
Norrköping 1865			2.90[a]
		1871–75	0.86
Norrköping 1875			1.90[a]
		1881–85	1.03
Norrköping 1885			1.80[a]
		1891–95	1.13
Norrköping 1895			2.90[a]
		1901–5	1.15
Norrköping 1905			1.70[a]
		1911–15	0.86
		1921–25	0.48
		1941–45	0.67
		1961–65	0.56

Note: The figures from Norrköping refer to the number of people brought to court for the offenses.
a. Approximation
Sources: Österberg 1983; Österberg and Lindström 1988; von Hofer 1985; Horgby 1986.

composite crime structure in the course of the sixteenth century. Now, and more so later on, the courts had a greater variety of duties, which changed the relation between different categories of cases. More important is that Jan

Sundin's ongoing research confirms the decline in crimes of violence (serious and minor crimes combined), calculated as mean values per 1,000 inhabitants. For example, in the city of Linköping, violence reached the figure of 6.0 in 1600–1650. During the years 1680–1729 it was no more than 2.2.[36]

If the overall trend is toward a decline in violent crime—with the exception of a certain increase in violence in the early nineteenth century—what is the situation regarding thefts? Do we see clear enough evidence of a contrary development to justify the thesis of a shift *de la violence au vol*?

At first sight, the results in table 2–3 are not unequivocal. The little town of Vadstena, for example, has more thefts at the start of the seventeenth century than Stockholm, which was ten times larger, and the figure for Gothenburg for 1815–19 is extreme. Yet if we ignore this for the moment, a few crucial findings do crystallize.

Table 2–3. Thefts Calculated as Mean Values per Year per 1,000 Inhabitants, Sweden[a]

Town	Countryside	All of Sweden	Means
Arboga 1452–61			1.1
Arboga 1473–82			0.5
Stockholm 1475–79			0.93
Stockholm 1480–84			1.1
Stockholm 1490–94			0.98
Arboga 1516–25			0.3
Arboga 1534–43			0.3
	Långhundra hd. 1545–60		0.65
Vadstena 1580–89			1.1
Vadstena 1602–10			3.0
Linköping 1600–1650			1.4
Stockholm 1615–19			1.04
	Gullberg hd. 1600–1650		0.3
	Vendel hd. 1615–30		0.27
Stockholm 1620–24			0.6
	Vendel hd. 1631–45		0.34
Linköping 1680–1729			1.2
Linköping 1790–1839			3.4
Gothenburg 1805–9			3[b]
Gothenburg 1810–14			2[b]
Gothenburg 1815–19			9[b]
Gothenburg 1820–24			3[b]
Stockholm 1830			2.7
Eskilstuna 1843–47			2.5

Norrköping 1850		2.9[b]
	1841–45	1.59
	1846–50	1.62
Norrköping 1860		2.4[b]
	1871–75	0.79
Norrköping 1880		1.1[b]
	1881–85	0.64
Norrköping 1890		0.80[b]
	1891–95	0.60
Norrköping 1900		0.70[b]
	1901–5	0.64
Norrköping 1910		0.60[b]
	1916–20	1.44
	1941–45	1.45
	1956–60	3.14
	1961–65	3.75
	1966–70	4.85
	1971–75	5.21
	1982	5.80
	1984	6.07

Note: The figures from Norrköping refer to the number of condemned thieves.

a. Jan Sundin's research concerns urban and rural parishes in Östergötland from the seventeenth century up to the twentieth. Kenneth Johansson analyzes one härad (a judicial district comparable to the English "hundred") in Småland from ca. 1600 until ca. 1850. Of the copious material from Småland, Rudolf Thunander is studying cases that were referred by the hundred courts to the newly established courts of appeal. Johan Söderberg has examined judgment books from different härads in Sweden spread over the sixteenth century and the first half of the seventeenth. Jörn Sandnes (1990) has published a major study of criminality in Norway in the sixteenth century, where he compares the findings from the Norwegian towns with those obtained for Arboga and Stockholm (Österberg and Lindström 1988).

b. Approximation

Sources: Österberg 1983; Österberg and Lindström 1988; von Hofer 1985; Magnusson 1988: 30; Fällström 1974; Horgby 1986: 172ff.; Sundin 1992.

The primary point to note is that thefts were never a major category of crime in early times. Compared with the frequency of violence in general, theft was an uncommon offense in, for example, fifteenth-century Sweden. Conditions were similar in Norway.[37] To be sure, Bergen, with its trade and international contacts, had 2.1 thefts per 1,000 inhabitants in 1567, but otherwise thieves were relatively infrequent. In what was still a fairly agrarian society, with small-scale family farms and freehold peasants predominating in large regions, people were evidently not tempted to steal to the same extent as in more commercialized or feudal parts of Europe.[38]

Another finding concerns comparisons through time. It should be noted that the national figures from the nineteenth century onward in table 2–3 refer to thefts excluding robbery. If robbery were also included it would further reinforce the tendency that is evident from the figures.[39] The towns in particular had problems in the first half of the nineteenth century. The sensationally high value for 1815–19 can be explained by the depression that occurred as a marked contrast to the boom in the preceding years in the commercial town of Gothenburg.[40] The main impression is nevertheless the steady rise that has occurred since the 1950s. In other words, industrialization in the latter part of the nineteenth century was scarcely of decisive importance for bringing about a shift from violence to theft. It is primarily in the commercial town of Gothenburg in the early nineteenth century and in the postwar welfare state that thefts are rife.

◆ "New" Categories of Crime

Certain categories of crime cannot be analyzed over long periods in this way because they arise in part as a result of new legislation. The question here is whether there are any interesting links between these new crimes and the emergence and consolidation of the early modern state.

This is a problem that unfortunately has not yet been sufficiently analyzed in Scandinavia. Some thought-provoking findings can nevertheless be presented. The evidence from a few Swedish towns in the fifteenth, sixteenth, and seventeenth centuries suggests that there were times when there was a clear increase in offenses against economic restrictions and state regulations of trade and production. This is particularly true of the mid-sixteenth century and the early seventeenth. Normally such offenses were on a level of less than 1 per year per 1,000 inhabitants in Stockholm and Arboga in the fifteenth and sixteenth centuries. But in 1553–56, for example, the figure rose to an average of 5–6 annually per 1,000 inhabitants in Stockholm, to nearly 3 per year in Vadstena in 1602–10, and to nearly 4 per year in Stockholm in 1606–10.[41] Both these periods can be associated with activity on the part of the Swedish state. The crown intervened in commerce and other urban trades, tightened control to prevent illegal trading, and fought on all fronts to increase its fiscal revenue.

State intervention is also seen in the treatment of sex crimes in the late sixteenth century and throughout the seventeenth. After the Reformation the church and state combined their efforts to tighten the control of sexuality. This is noticeable both in the harsher penalties and in the more energetic way in which the guilty were hunted down. In the Middle Ages sex crimes were generally punished by fines and humiliation. According to the regulations from 1563, 1577–78, and 1608, the punishment was to follow Mosaic law, and the death penalty was imposed for several kinds of fornication. More and more people who were guilty of adultery or premarital sex were brought to court and threatened with harsh punishment.[42] In the present state of research it is hard to say how long this close control persisted. We must reckon with regional variations in the pattern. According to Jan Sundin it was especially from the late seventeenth century and up to the end of the eighteenth that judicial control of extramarital sex was most intensive in Sweden.[43]

In Stockholm and certain rural areas, for example, so-called crimes of disobedience also became one of the major categories of crime at the end of the sixteenth century and the start of the seventeenth.[44] Such crimes could include disregard of official rulings, default in payment of taxes and other duties, refusal to show up in court to answer charges, and so on. There are also other crimes indicating conflicts between crown officials and the people at the beginning of the seventeenth century.[45]

◆ The Overall Work of the Courts: To Chastise or to Resolve Conflicts?

Scandinavian historians in recent years have begun to study how much the courts occupied themselves with cases other than those involving criminal law. As a consequence of this, there have been analyses of the total business of the hundred courts in Sweden.[46]

The findings have a somewhat surprising unanimity. They show that the courts increasingly became organs for dealing with conflicts of ownership and cases involving debts. Criminal cases still predominated in the sixteenth century and at the beginning of the seventeenth—for example, violence, disobedience, sexual offenses, and defamation. Some way into the seventeenth century, however, there is a change in the proportions, and this is even more evident in the eighteenth century. The work of the parish assemblies underwent a parallel development. Elsewhere I have summed up the tendencies as follows: "Both courts and assemblies obviously devoted a greater proportion of their time and attention to problems of criminality, discipline, and order in the seventeenth century. By contrast, in the eighteenth and nineteenth centuries they were more occupied with economic disputes, conflicts of ownership, and poor relief. This finding deserves to be underlined—as a sign of processes in society which have repercussions in both central and local sources."[47]

◆ Main Findings and Interpretations

This analytical historiography and the combinations of statistics presented here give rise to the following reflections:

1. The amount of Scandinavian research is still not extensive enough to allow us to draw sure conclusions about the pattern of development. Mean national figures are generally not available until the nineteenth century, and there have not been many local studies yet. We need more analyses of the eighteenth century and the beginning of the nineteenth in particular.

2. Despite the reservations, we must make the most of the impressions left by the existing studies. When interpreting them it seems necessary to work with a combination of both great long-term changes and short-term fluctuations. Neither of these is more interesting per se than the other. It all depends on the approach that is chosen: the macroperspective of civilization history or the microperspective of social history. What I want to do here is focus on some major long-term tendencies. They give us the opportunity of critically discussing the link between processes such as state formation, civilizing, or modernization, on the one hand, and criminality on the other hand.

3. The importance of the early modern state for social and judicial control must be discussed on several levels: the state as an agent for changes in legislation and the creation of new categories of crime, as an actor in the courts, as a controller through its officials, as a motive force behind a civilizing process, and so on.

4. Criminality is generally greater in the towns than in the country when we come closer to modern times. This is less evident in the sixteenth century, when the figures from small towns can be both higher than and just as low as those from the countryside. We should remind ourselves here just how small all the Scandinavian towns were at this time in comparison with those of, say, southern Europe. Not even the international trading towns of Bergen or Stockholm, which were big by Scandinavian standards, had populations exceeding 10,000 in the sixteenth century.[48]

5. The thesis of the transition *de la violence au vol* has played a major role in international research. The Scandinavian evidence suggests that the thesis has some validity if we look at the changes in a long-term perspective. It is at least evident that the rate of violent crime (murder, manslaughter, assault, minor violence) has consistently been lower from the late nineteenth century until the present day than it was in the fifteenth century, for example. On the other hand, it is not so self-evident that development from the sixteenth century to the mid-nineteenth century describes a falling curve

everywhere. For instance, southern Ostrobothnia in Finland and the Swedish towns of Norrköping and Eskilstuna show a distinct increase in violent crime at the start of the nineteenth century.

6. Assuming that we accept *de la violence au vol* as a crude but adequate description of development from the fifteenth to the twentieth century, we must then ask when the turning point occurred. When did violence definitely start to decline and thefts to increase? We may wonder whether these two changes occurred at the same time, so that chronology could provide a single explanation for both phenomena. Or does one of the changes happen first and require an interpretation of its own, while the other change must be understood in a much later period and in a completely different societal context? Judging by the findings presented here, violence was already decreasing in the sixteenth century in parts of Scandinavia, and in Sweden, by the mid-seventeenth century at least. Most scholars have interpreted this as a result of the aspiration of the crown and the church to train people to be obedient and peaceable.

Without doubt Sweden as a great power in the seventeenth century sought to modernize society and to increase control of the population. True, Sweden was still a peasant society, where about 95 percent of the people belonged to the agrarian population, but during the reign of Gustav Adolf (1611–32) great changes began: many new towns were founded, the administration was modernized, the fiscal and ideological control of the citizens became more efficient. Toward the end of the seventeenth century every Swede was registered by the clergy, who visited each household to supervise people's knowledge of the Bible and other religious writings. At the same time, Sweden was involved in wars during much of the century: wars against Russia, Denmark, Poland, the Catholic allies in Germany, and so on. In 1630 Sweden intervened with over thirty thousand men in the Thirty Years' War and was then a major force in the international power game until the defeat of Karl XII by the Russians at Poltava in 1709. Modern research has calculated that roughly every fourth adult man died in connection with wars in the period 1611–1718, although they died as often of disease as in battle.[49] Women and old people had a greater responsibility for production and social life at home. It is a general observation in all criminological research that crime in all cultures is mainly committed by young men—not by women or old men. The decline in violence in the latter half of the seventeenth century and at the start of the eighteenth can possibly be explained as a combination of the desire of the church and state to instill morality and demographic hard facts.

As for the increased disorderliness at the start of the nineteenth century, I would hypothetically view it as a mere short-term variation. It was due to the clash of early capitalism with the craft culture, or to a polarization between landed peasants and a growing stratum of unpropertied people, as well as between the generations. While the peasants increased from about 186,000 to 207,000 between 1750 and 1850, the number of unpropertied people rose from 48,000 to 203,000. No doubt this resulted in social and cultural conflicts. At the same time, the authorities grew worried and tightened their control, leading to waves of enforcement. In line with this, some towns in the early nineteenth century anticipated the modern pattern with increased registered thefts. However, thefts do not appear to have become stabilized at a really high level until after the Second World War.

In other words: the chronology does not allow us to assume that there was only one turning point and to adduce the same change in society as an explanation for both the fall in violence and the rise in theft. The early modern state may have had some role in the reduction of serious violence, in the tighter control of sexuality, and in the increase in commercial offenses. For the major variations in the frequency of thefts, however, it was evidently not a significant factor. Thefts do not increase significantly until postwar society, very late in Swedish history.

7. If we look at the total number of cases brought before the Swedish courts, we see an interesting gradual shift. In the sixteenth century and the early seventeenth the courts were still largely occupied with purely criminal cases. Gradually, however, disputes over property and debts came to dominate. This unequivocal trend can be observed in most regions in the eighteenth and nineteenth centuries.

The problem now is how these main findings are to be interpreted. I start with the assumption that crime statistics are not an immediate reflection of human behavior. This means that it is not easy to study criminality in order to draw conclusions about a civilizing process, if this is defined as actual changes in individual behavior. Only such actions as are equally forbidden both by law and in the popular conception of justice, such as murder, can be discussed for such purposes. Variations in other categories of crime can instead express changes in social control. My analytical framework thus demands that crime statistics be seen in a wider qualitative and social context. The court as a controlling institution must be balanced against alternative forums for social control. The administration of justice is not just a matter of orders from above and efficiency on the part of the officials. It also concerns the extent to which people are willing to use the law and the courts to resolve their conflicts. The concept of a civilizing process can thus be used heuristically, to direct attention toward a complex of societal measures to achieve more refined and peaceful social relations.

If we go back to the general explanatory models propounded by Scandinavian historians, we find that individually they explain much—but not everything. In my earlier discussions of Norbert Elias I have argued that the thesis of a civilizing process may capture something essential about changes in violent crime in the long term, but that it does not explain later temporary peaks of violence. I was referring especially to the increase in serious, mortal violence that appeared to take place in certain areas in the early seventeenth century, not least among soldiers. In the present state of research we have greater reason to emphasize the increased criminality in the first half of the nineteenth century. This too goes against Elias's ideas about the way people have been gradually disciplined, like butterflies emerging out of their pupae—unless we confine Elias's conception to a model for the diffusion of ideas that did not reach the lower strata of society until much later.

Let us instead turn to Heikki Ylikangas, the Scandinavian historian who has most consistently propounded a coherent explanation on the basis of economic and criminological theory. As I have already pointed out, his interpretive instruments are the same throughout: economic factors and social control. Material problems but strict control of the lower classes are adduced to explain the decline in violent crime in the course of the sixteenth century in Finland. Economic inequality, social polarization, and insufficient informal control are the suggested reasons for the increase in violent crime in the nineteenth century. However, Ylikangas's reasoning is not enough to explain why, for example, the fifteenth-century towns had an even higher rate of violent crime. It can scarcely have been harder to exercise informal control and to supervise one's fellow humans in a little medieval town, where people lived close together, with members of the family and servants sharing the same room, than it was in the emerging industrial towns of the nineteenth century or in the increasingly mobile agrarian society. Nor is there any reason to believe that the socioeconomic polarization of peasant society was greater in the fifteenth century than in the proletarizing process of the nineteenth century.

It nevertheless seems obvious to me that we must take inspiration from both Elias and Ylikangas if we are to interpret the main findings presented above. What is essential in Elias and in Ylikangas is, in my view, that variations in criminality are not just ascribed to people's psychological constitutions or individual responses to economic stimuli, but also to changes in the societal system. Elias may base his reasoning on a psychoanalytic phase model when he describes the way medieval people, who like children seek to satisfy their primary needs and cannot control their impulses, are transformed into civilized beings with self-discipline and an ability to sublimate. Ylikangas's knife-fighters may be impelled by their reaction to economic injustice and an individualistic competitive mentality. At the same time, however, Elias's civilizing process is far from being only a matter of the individual's learning process. On the contrary, it is an interplay between personal education on the one hand and the early modern state's monopoly of violence and stricter systems of control on the other hand. In a similar way, social control for Ylikangas is a question of the societal systems that unite the central state and the local community and keep the local communities together.

As I see it, then, important inspiration can be derived from the approach of scholars like Elias and Ylikangas. Yet to this I should like to add a few other ideas and assumptions.

In 1989 John Braithwaite published a fascinating book about criminality, in which he seeks to build a new theory that can be used on both the individual and the societal levels.[50] The key to reduced criminality is, according to Braithwaite, to be found in cultural patterns based on "reintegrative shaming." Criminality tends to diminish if shame is a living force in society. Yet shame can also defeat its purpose if it drives the offender to join a criminal subculture instead of being reintegrated into the circle of responsible citizens. Shame can thus function as either a reintegrative or a stigmatizing force. The conditions that make it easier for shame to work to reintegrate and thus combat criminality are "interdependency" and "communitarianism"; these create close networks in society to ensure mutual aid and mutual confidence.

Social control in a society can theoretically be divided into formal control (the state's official systems for direct surveillance, such as the police), semiformal control (as exercised by authorities and officials for whom control is not the primary task, such as teachers and priests), and finally informal control, for example, the way neighbors and members of the family keep watch to see that everything is as it should be.[51] All these forms of control influence the fluctuations in criminality and can, in my view, communicate reintegrative or stigmatizing shame with varying efficacy.

What happens in the courts is always part of the formal system of control. I would argue, however, that the courts in some societies and periods may also have dealt with many of the matters that would otherwise have been subject to semiformal or informal control. The distinctions between formal, semiformal, and informal systems need not be maintained absolute and independent of time. They may depend, for instance, on when the difference between private and public becomes more distinct and when the state becomes interested in drawing the boundaries between the different control systems.

What is dealt with in the courts is thus not an immediate reflection of what happens in society. It also shows to what extent the courts are allowed to play a greater or lesser role as a social arena or a theater of power, how much the court is used to convey reintegrative shame.

A Model of Swedish Society

A tentative phase model of Swedish society from the Middle Ages to the present day would combine data on criminality with evidence about varying systems of control and other important societal processes.

The Middle Ages and Most of the Sixteenth Century What is dealt with in the courts is above all crimes against the person: for example, violence, defamation, and slander. The courts are thus largely an instrument for resolving conflicts between individuals. The difference between private and public is still hardly developed in society; the royal family and the state are intertwined, family life is enacted in the presence of servants and neighbors, and it is as easy to complain about one's neighbor in the court as it is in the street. My hypothesis is that the courts thereby had responsibility for many matters that were later referred to the sphere of informal control. As Johan Asplund has formulated it, the courts in former times were an expression of "social responsivity." Trials were the public face of society—everything and everybody had to be there.[52] This explains why so much petty violence between roughly equal persons was brought to court in the first place. It makes it understandable that the penalties were often reduced to much lower fines than the law stipulated, at the same time as occasional habitual criminals were mercilessly expelled. I have argued that the penalties meted out were a combination of cruelty and realistic lenience.[53] The combination is due to the fact that the courts could stigmatize and expel those who were seen as true threats to the collective and to the inbuilt "communitarianism" of society, but those same courts could apply reintegrative shame to restore peace in society, to rehabilitate the troublemaker, and to award financial compensation to restore the honor of the man who received the blow. Thus, Braithwaite's ideas are in line with the interpretations that I have made on the basis of the empirical material.

From the Latter Half of the Sixteenth Century until the Mid-Eighteenth Century The courts continue to function as an arena where people resolve personal conflicts. Yet they increasingly come to serve the interests of the early modern state, which is reflected in occasional increases in prosecutions of illegal trading, smuggling goods into the towns, or using false measures. An interesting question here is whether the loyalty of ordinary people to the courts—their feeling that the local courts were their own social arena—declined as the state increasingly tried to use the courts as its instrument. Some crimes of disobedience seem to indicate such a development. In this period the courts also collaborate as a formal control system with the church as a semiformal control system to prosecute illicit sexual liaisons and to combat violence. Both the formal and the semiformal control systems can be said to communicate reintegrative as well as stigmatizing shame.

The Latter Half of the Eighteenth Century and the First Half of the Nineteenth Century There is a sharp rise in the unpropertied groups, and social and cultural conflicts in society are heightened. The boundary between public and private becomes increasingly distinct. The semiformal system of social control (the church, now joined by the school) still plays a large role and has assumed some of the responsibility that formerly rested with the secular courts. As a consequence of the socioeconomic and cultural polarization there is an increase in crime in the first half of the nineteenth century, at the same time as landed peasants and the people governing the towns have an interest in using the courts to control the "lower classes." The number of criminal cases brought to court in the eighteenth and nineteenth centuries is lower, relatively speaking, than the number of economic disputes and cases of debts.

The Latter Half of the Nineteenth Century and the First Half of the Twentieth Century Until the time when cases of theft increase after the Second World War, the period is generally characterized by a lower rate of recorded serious crime against both person and property. However, there was sometimes an increase in behavior such as vagrancy, drunkenness, and prostitution, for instance in the 1870s.[54] There is a great distance between private and public and also between informal control and the bureaucratic system of the judiciary. The courts are less concerned with chastising people and thereby communicating reintegrative shame. Instead they are increasingly occupied with confirming economic settlements and ruling on economic matters. When decisions concerning criminal law have to be made they follow more professional procedures. The semiformal control systems are extensive and ramified: schools, child welfare committees, reformatories, and so on. New groups create their own instruments for self-improvement and discipline, through such phenomena as labor movements and educational associations.

In this perspective the notion of a shift "from a violent society to a thieving society" is too simple a model for the description of changes in criminality in Scandinavia. "From social arena to theater of power" is an equally simplified characterization of the way the courts have functioned through time. Both of these descriptions admittedly agree with many crucial observations in the evidence. For instance, the long-term change in mortal violence can probably be linked to the concept of a civilizing process in the early modern period. Similarly, there are signs that the early modern state made greater use of the courts as its instrument of control in the seventeenth century and later. However, there are other findings that complicate the picture. There is, for example, a minor but significant increase in violence at the beginning of the nineteenth century, and a high frequency of thefts is not a result of either early capitalism or industrialization but a late postwar phenomenon. Furthermore, the courts never entirely changed into a theater of power. Regardless of the efforts of the state, they also functioned as an institution of local self-government, responsible for a variety of economic and social matters concerning the local population. Thus we require interpretations that are open for a dialectic relationship between the use of justice and actual human behavior. This essay has been an attempt.

Notes

1. See Aron Gurevich, *Categories of Medieval Culture* (London, 1985); Kirsten Hastrup, *Culture and History in Medieval Iceland: An Anthropological Analysis of Structure and Change* (Oxford, 1985); Jesse L. Byock, *Medieval Iceland: Society, Sagas, and Power* (Berkeley, Calif., 1988).

2. Hastrup, *Culture and History*, 136, 207.

3. See, for example, Michel Foucault, *Discipline and Punish: The Birth of the Prison*, trans. Alan Sheridan (Harmondsworth, 1986); Norbert Elias, *The Civilising Process*, vol. 2 (Oxford, 1982).

4. See, for example, E. P. Thompson, *Whigs and Hunters: The Origin of the Black Act* (Harmondsworth, 1977), 273; Eva Österberg, "Brott och straff i svenska småstäder under medeltid och vasatid: Svensk kriminalitet i europeiskt perspektiv." in *Över gränser: Festskrift till Birgitta Odén*, ed. J. Norrlid et al. (Lund, 1987), 473–504.

5. See Jürgen Habermas, *Strukturwandel der Öffentlichkeit: Untersuchungen zu einer Kategorie der bürgerlichen Gesellschaft*, 2d ed. (Berlin, 1965).

6. Natalie Zemon Davis, *Fiction in the Archives: Pardon Tales and Their Tellers in Sixteenth-Century France* (Stanford, 1987).

7. See, for example, Bengt Ankarloo, *Trolldomsprocesserna i Sverige* (Lund, 1971); Bengt Ankarloo and Gustav Henningsen, eds., *Häxornas Europa, 1400–1700* (Lund, 1987); Hans Eyvind Naess, *Trolldomsprosessene i Norge pa 1500–1600–tallet: En retts-og sosialhistorisk undersøkelse* (Oslo, 1982).

8. See, for example, James A. Sharpe, "The History of Crime in Late Medieval and Early Modern England: A Review of the Field," *Social History* 7 (1982): 188–203; idem, *Crime in Early Modern England, 1550–1750* (London, 1984), 4; Eva Österberg and Dag Lindström, *Crime and Social Control in Medieval and Early Modern Swedish Towns* (Uppsala, 1988), 39, 71; Kenneth Johansson, "Brott, straff och rättens funktioner i Albo härad i Småland ca. 1600–1850," forthcoming; Jörn Sandnes, *Kniven, ölet og aeren: Kriminalitet og samfunn i Norge pa 1500– og 1600–tallet* (Oslo, 1990).

9. Jan Sundin, "Theft and Penury in Sweden, 1830–1920: A Comparative Study at the County Level," *Scandinavian Journal of History* 1 (1976): 265–92; Anne-Marie Fällström, *Konjunkturer och kriminalitet: Studier i Göteborgs sociala historia, 1800–1840* (Göteborg, 1974); Hanns von Hofer, *Brott och straff i Sverige: Historisk kriminalstatistik, 1750–1884* (Stockholm, 1985).

10. Björn Horgby, *Den disciplinerade arbetaren: Brottslighet och social förändring i Norrköping, 1850–1910* (Stockholm, 1986); Lars Magnusson, *Den bråkiga kulturen: Förläggare och smideshantverkare i Eskilstuna, 1800–1850* (Vänersborg, Sweden, 1988).

11. See Elias, *The Civilising Process.*

12. Examples are Eva Österberg, "Violence among Peasants: Comparative Perspectives on Sixteenth- and Seventeenth-Century Sweden," in *Europe and Scandinavia: Aspects of the Process of Integration in the Seventeenth Century,* ed. Göran Rystad (Lund, 1983), 257–89; idem, "Civilisationsprocesser och 1600–talets svenska bondesamhälle-en historia med förhinder," *Saga och sed* (1985): 13–23; Österberg and Lindström, *Crime and Social Control.*

13. See Fällström, *Konjunkturer och kriminalitet.*

14. See Sundin, "Theft and Penury."

15. See Horgsby, *Den disciplinerade arbetaren.*

16. See Magnusson, *Den bråkiga kulturen.*

17. See Birgit Petersson, *Den farliga underklassen: Studier i brottslighet och fattigdom i 1800–talets Sverige* (Umeå, Sweden, 1983).

18. See Knut Sveri, "Brottslighetens volym och struktur," in *Samhällsförändringar och brottslighet,* ed. Ake Daun et al. (Stockholm, 1974).

19. See Naess, *Trolldomsprosessene;* see also the survey of research by Sandnes, *Kniven, ölet og aeren.*

20. See Lars-Olof Larsson, *Smaländsk historia: Stormaktstiden* (Växjö, Sweden, 1982).

21. See Heikki Ylikangas, "Major Fluctuations in Crimes of Violence in Finland: A Historical Analysis," *Scandinavian Journal of History* 1 (1976): 81–103.

22. See Heikki Ylikangas, *Knivjunkarna: Våldskriminalitet i Sydösterbotten* (Borgå, Finland, 1985).

23. See Ylikangas, "Major Fluctuations."

24. See, for example, Österberg and Lindström, *Crime and Social Control*, 71ff.; Sundin, "Theft and Penury"; idem, *För Gud, Staten och Folket: Brott och rättskipning i Sverige, 1600–1840* (Lund, 1992); Johansson, "Brott, straff och rättens funktioner"; Sandnes, *Kniven, ölet og aeren*.

25. See Österberg, "Violence among Peasants"; see also Larsson, *Smaländsk historia*.

26. See Österberg, "Civilisationsprocesser."

27. See Österberg and Lindström, *Crime and Social Control*.

28. See Ted Robert Gurr, "Historical Trends in Violent Crime: A Critical Review of the Evidence," *Crime and Justice: An Annual Review of Research* 3 (1981): 295–353; Lawrence Stone, "Interpersonal Violence in English Society, 1300–1983," *Past and Present* 102 (1983): 22–33.

29. See Sandnes, *Kniven, ölet og aeren*.

30. See, for example, Rudolf Thunander, "Tusen brott i Småland," unpublished manuscript (Växjö, Sweden, 1988).

31. See Magnusson, *Den brakiga kulturen;* Horgby, *Den disciplinerade arbetaren*.

32. See Ylikangas, *Knivjunkarna*.

33. See Stone, "Interpersonal Violence"; see also Gurr, "Historical Trends."

34. See Österberg, "Violence among Peasants."

35. See Johan Söderberg, "En fråga om civilisering: Brottsmål och tvister i svenska häradsrätter, 1540–1660," *Historisk Tidskrift* 2 (1990): 229–58; Jan Sundin, *För Gud, Staten och Folket*.

36. See Sundin, *För Gud, Staten och Folket*.

37. See Sandnes, *Kniven, ölet og aeren*.

38. See Österberg and Lindström, *Crime and Social Control;* Sandnes, *Kniven, ölet og aeren*.

39. See Hofer, *Brott och straff i Sverige*.

40. See Fällström, *Konjunkturer och kriminalitet*.

41. See Österberg and Lindström, *Crime and Social Control*.

42. See, for example, Eva Österberg, "Den gamla goda tiden: Bilder och motbilder i ett modernt forskningsläge om det äldre agrarsamhället," *Scandia* 48, no. 1 (1982): 31–60; Österberg and Lindström, *Crime and Social Control;* Sundin, "Theft and Penury."

43. See Sundin, "Theft and Penury"; see also Söderberg, "En fraga om civilisering."

44. Österberg and Lindström, *Crime and Social Control*, 120–22.

45. See Marja Taussi Sjöberg, "Staten och tinget under 1600-talet," *Historisk Tidskrift* 2 (1990): 161-90.

46. See, for example, Maria Ågren, "Att lösa ekonomiska tvister-domstolarnas främsta sysselsättning på 1700-talet?," *Historisk Tidskrift* 4 (1988): 481-511; Harald Gustafsson, "Bland grevar och avskedade soldater: Sockensjälvstyrelsen på 1840-talet," *Historisk Tidskrift* 4 (1986) 484-501; Peter Aronsson, *Bönder för politik: Det lokala själostyret som social arena i tre Smålandssocknar, 1680-1850* (Lund, 1992); Johansson, "Brott, straff och rättens funktioner"; Eva Österberg, "Bönder och stats-makt i det tidigmoderna Sverige: Konflikt-kompromiss-politisk kultur," *Scandia* 55, no. 1 (1989): 73-95; Marja Taussi Sjöberg, "Tinget som social arena," in *Historia nu-18 Umeåforskare om det förflutna* (Umeå, Sweden, 1988), 243-362; Söderberg, "En fråga om civilisering."

47. Österberg, "Bönder och statsmakt," 80-81.

48. See Österberg, "Brott och straff"; Österberg and Lindström, *Crime and Social Control;* Sandnes, *Kniven, ölet og aeren.*

49. See Jan Lindegren, *Utskrivning och utsugning: Produktion och reproduktion i Bygdeå, 1620-1640* (Uppsala, 1980), and "Kriget och arbetskraften," forthcoming.

50. John Braithwaite, *Crime, Shame and Reintegration* (Cambridge, 1989).

51. See Martin Vejbrink, "En kontrollerad brottsling som historiskt fenomen," in *In Kontroll och kontrollerade,* ed. Jan Sundin (Umeå, Sweden, 1982), 159-95.

52. Johan Asplund, *Det sociala livets elementära former* (Göteborg, 1987), 47.

53. Österberg and Lindström, *Crime and Social Control,* 156ff.

54. See Marja Taussi Sjöberg, *Brott och straff i Västernorrland, 1861-1890* (Umeå, Sweden, 1981).

3

Long-Term Trends in Homicide: Theoretical Reflections and Dutch Evidence, Fifteenth to Twentieth Centuries

Pieter Spierenburg

Homicide is haunting historians. Some welcome its possibilities for a study of the long term, calling it "the one crime for which the evidence is most reliable."[1] Others, more skeptical, are trying to prove that any visible trend is only a chimera. This clash of arguments and approaches particularly concerns the period before the availability of national statistics. Evidence from that period is indispensable, if we want to make meaningful statements about the long term.

This chapter addresses the issue from a new perspective. Up to now the study of preindustrial homicide has been largely the prerogative of English historians. While admiring their efforts at collecting the evidence, I find some of their arguments defective. In looking at the subject with a fresh eye, I draw data from a country other than England into the discussion. My aims are threefold: to put the study of homicide on a firmer theoretical base; to propose refinements in method, which follow from my theoretical conclusions; and to test the hypotheses resulting from the first two exercises, using fresh empirical data. Most of the data are from the city of Amsterdam and, as a preindustrial historian, I have done my own archival work for the centuries preceding the age of national statistics.

◆ The State of the Research

In an overview of violent crime published in 1981, Ted Robert Gurr presented the first synthesis. Two years later, Gurr's article was reviewed in its turn, with a few addenda from recent studies, by Lawrence Stone.[2] The most impressive series of quantitative data they commented on concerned the crime of killing, in England, over some seven centuries, calculated as so many cases per 100,000 per year (this is a common measure and, for brevity's sake, I will speak of *the* homicide rate from now on, meaning the annual average, over a specified period, per 100,000 population, in a specified area). The homicide rate in England declined from about 20 in 1200 to about 15 in the later Middle Ages, to between 6 and 7 in the Elizabethan period, and then further down (with the most dramatic fall from the late seventeenth to the late eighteenth century), until the figure stood at 1 around 1900. Most of these figures are second-level averages, calculated from the combined rates of several towns and regions, with the greatest range in the Middle Ages. The steepness of the overall decline compensates for the relative artificiality of the figures. The homicide rate did not increase again until the contemporary period.

The obvious conclusion is that the level of daily violence in English society had diminished over the centuries, at least until recent times. In order to account for this development, both Gurr and Stone refer to Elias's theory of the "civilizing process," a central tenet of which is the relative pacification of the habits of ever broader groups of people. Stone calls this a "cultural explanation." Alternatively, he proposes a "social explanation," based on the *violence-au-vol* thesis, first developed by French historians. They argued that the feudal code of honor led to a preponderance of violent crime, while the central place of the market in bourgeois society produced a larger share of property crime. From this perspective, the decline in the homicide rate was related to the transition from a feudal to a bourgeois society.

Another conspicuous trend concerned the proportion of killings within the biological family (excluding apprentices and servants). According to Stone, this proportion was on the rise in England already during the period from the fourteenth to the seventeenth century (from 8 percent to 20 percent).[3] In a recent overview of English and French studies for the early modern period it is concluded that family homicides consistently made up a quarter or less of all homicides.[4] In contemporary England, on the other hand, their proportion amounts to about 45 percent.[5] In the Netherlands the proportion of family homicides today is somewhat less: about 30 percent.[6]

Remarkably, in the debate that followed, the homicide rates themselves were hardly at issue, apart from authors' blaming each other for incorrectly citing their figures. A discussion between Stone and Sharpe in 1985 actually seems to be about their differing perceptions of preindustrial English society.[7] Although they quibble over which author includes infanticide cases in his set of homicide figures and which author doesn't, they do not ask which of the two procedures we should prefer. Thus, they fail to pay due attention to the most problematic aspect of the evidence gathered so far by historians investigating preindustrial homicide: the diverging criteria by which they arrived at their figures. This divergence is even more consequential with respect to the type of source used. Some sets of data were based on coroner's inquests, while others were derived from indictments. As I will show, it can make a significant difference from which source homicides are counted.

In his monumental study of crime and the courts, based on Surrey and Sussex records, Beattie shows no desire to take issue with Stone or Sharpe, restricting himself to a detailed analysis of the evidence. Beattie's homicide figures confirm the remarkable drop in the rates between 1660 and 1800, which was especially pronounced in urban Surrey: from 8.1 in the 1660s to 0.9 in the last two decades of the eighteenth century. His homicide rates are based on indictments, excluding those for infanticide; he discusses infanticide separately, without giving the rates per 100,000 population. Beattie, too, argues that daily life in England became less violent in the course of the eighteenth century, but he does not venture into theory to explain this development.[8]

Cockburn, on the other hand, is primarily looking for evidence and arguments to deny such a development. Still, in his analysis of the homicide pattern in Kent from 1560 to 1985, he is bound to confirm the trend posited by Stone (with minor differences in timing and a lowering of the Elizabethan homicide rate to 4.6). Playing down his own figures as well, Cockburn concludes that the overall decline was certainly real, but that its dimensions were less spectacular than his figures would suggest at first sight. In addition, he discusses problems of methodology. English homicide rates, he argues, are biased by two historical changes that affected the definition of the crime of killing: infanticide (which he includes in his figures) came to be viewed more leniently toward 1800 and reckless driving was introduced as a possible cause of homicide in the twentieth century. Finally, Cockburn proposes to disregard all medieval evidence, because the records are unreliable and the divergence in homicide rates for specific times and places (between 4 and 110) is too great.[9]

Thus, while Gurr was able to cite only English evidence for the period before 1800, most of the research on long-term trends performed since then concerned England as well. There are a few exceptions. Swedish developments, for example, are discussed by Eva Österberg. She posits a decline in the homicide rate similar to that observed in England, with the crucial drop between the middle of the seventeenth and the middle of the eighteenth cen-

tury. In explaining this decline she refers both to the "civilizing process" and
to modernization theory. However, there are problems with the evidence.
Österberg's data up to 1645 are from a variegated array of small towns, rural
districts, and the capital, while the period of the crucial drop is not document-
ed at all. Moreover, the nationwide figures from 1761 onward are relative, not
to the entire population, but only to the inhabitants aged 15-69.[10] The evidence for Sweden's eastern neighbor and onetime colony is even more in-
conclusive. If Ylikangas is to be believed, the level of violence in Finland
underwent a rather puzzling trend. The homicide rate was "well over ten"
in the middle of the sixteenth century; it declined to 1 or 2 in the period 1754-
1809; it rose again, largely due to a habit of knife fighting in one province, to
2 or 3 during the nineteenth century; it even rose much higher during the
twentieth. In his explanation of these developments, Ylikangas focuses on
Finnish peculiarity rather than on historical trends.[11]

For the core area of continental Europe the state of research is not much
better. Some work has been done in the Netherlands; I will review the evidence when discussing my own data. Despite a great interest in the subject
of crime and justice, French historians have declined to construct homicide
rates. Muchembled's data from pardon letters, however, are suggestive. In
Artois between 1386 and 1660 an annual average of 10 persons per 100,000
population were pardoned after a condemnation for homicide. The actual
number of killings, of course, must have been higher.[12] The figures for Cologne during the periods 1468-81 and 1557-1620, presented by Schwerhoff,
also are minimum rates. They amount to about 12 and about 10 homicides
per 100,000 inhabitants in the two periods, respectively.[13] Two other sets of
data, however, indicate that the actual level of homicidal violence could be
much higher in late-medieval continental towns. The homicide rate in Florence was 152 during the years 1352-55 and 68 during the years 1380-83.[14]
In Freiburg im Breisgau in the second half of the fourteenth century it fluctuated between 60 and 90.[15]

It should be repeated that the observed lack of data for continental Europe concerns the preindustrial period only. We are much better informed,
for the whole of Europe and North America, about trends in the nineteenth
and twentieth centuries. Everything is summed up neatly in Chesnais's synthesis on violence after 1800. Basing his argument primarily on medical statistics, Chesnais shows that homicide rates continued to decline, earlier in
the more developed regions of Europe and later in the less developed regions,
until the 1930s. After the Second World War the rates in most European countries tended to converge, which implied a slight rise for some.[16] The contem-

porary, general increase in the rates in the Western world became visible only after Chesnais gathered his data. To put this increase in the right perspective, however, it is absolutely necessary that we have the preindustrial figures.

◆ Violent Crime and Historical Theory: A Reconsideration

From my review of the state of research it must be concluded that, first, the only well-documented long-term homicide trend is the English one; second, some of the studies in question can be criticized for their methodology, and their theories are not well developed. Contrary to what is customary in historical writing, I am proceeding with a theoretical discussion, so that my rendering of the Dutch evidence can be guided by it. Historians commonly present their quantitative data first and then question how to account for them. Thus, they prefer induction to deduction. It is my conviction, however, that theorizing and gathering new evidence should always go together, in a two-way process. As new empirical data necessitate our revising our theories, these very theories suggest what kind of data to collect, how to categorize them and group them together. That family homicide is identified as a separate category, for example, obviously has to do with the fact that the family is a central subject in historical theorizing. Even seemingly minor matters of methodology, such as whether or not to include cases of self-defense in the category of homicide, are influenced by our theoretical position. How we proceed is influenced by what we expect from the data.

The scarce references to theory in the works just reviewed concerned primarily the "civilizing process" and secondarily the *violence-au-vol* thesis. In my view, the explanatory power of the second has been overestimated. Let me explain its shortcomings.

Although the thesis about a shift from violent to property offenses bears directly on the subject of crime and justice, it is of limited value for my present purposes. Its greatest defect is its concern with the ratios of criminal categories rather than the absolute rates. French historians, who developed the thesis, posited a shift from violence to theft in terms of the share of these offenses in the total criminal caseload of particular courts.[17] The *violence-au-vol* thesis is meant to account for changes in the proportion of violence versus property offenses over time, but it has little to say about the actual incidence of both types of crime taken separately. Precisely that is the relevant issue here, at least with respect to violence. The percentage of a specific category of offenses among a court's total caseload is largely a function of decisions at the judicial level. Consequently, the *violence-au-vol* thesis is better

equipped to explain shifts in prosecution policy than changes in actual criminal behavior.[18] Moreover, the distinction between the two categories is not
unproblematic, because many assaults on a person's property are accompanied by violence. So this theory is better left aside. Alternatively, I am exploring the theoretical possibilities of Elias's work for a study of homicide.

One of the major advantages of Elias's theory of civilization lies in its
scope and its comprehensiveness. Certainly, Stone is not right to call it merely
a cultural as opposed to a social explanation. It is not fruitful to establish
whether a phenomenon must be explained in terms of the one or the other.
We can see this very clearly when considering the subject of honor, intimately
related to violence. Mentalities are central to codes of honor, but at the same
time these codes are embedded and acquire meaning only in a context of
social relationships.[19] This two-sidedness, the interdependence of cultural
and social developments, is a guiding principle in Elias's work. Changes in
people's propensity for aggression were interdependent with changes in social organization, notably processes of state formation. In his analysis of societal change, moreover, Elias rejects a simple dichotomy in which feudalism
is replaced by the bourgeois or market society, as the *violence-au-vol* thesis
would have it. Instead, he emphasizes the existence of intermediate phases
such as that of the court society, important in France and other countries
though hardly so in the Netherlands.

A second major advantage of Elias's approach is that he wishes to keep
his analysis as free as possible from the intrusion of moral standards or judgments. Several participants in the homicide debate implicitly assume that a
high level of violence in past communities automatically translates into a low
quality of life in these communities. Notably, they tend to equate violence and
lack of affection in personal relationships.[20] Such an equation is surely anach-
ronistic. Elias, drawing on the Freudian notion of a link between love and
aggression, claims that impulses for both affection and aggression became
subject to constraints as a result of the same overall process. Consequently,
we should not be led astray by the current assumptions of our time, according to which violent behavior is always destructive, "dysfunctional," and
devoid of meaning. Such an unrealistic view of violence can only disparage
our historical judgment of aggressive behavior in the past. Anthropologists,
too, emphasize that these modern presuppositions may be detrimental to our
scholarly appreciation of violence in other cultures.[21] In our analysis of people's propensity for killing, then, we should concentrate on the mode in
which aggression was expressed and the extent to which different modes were
socially accepted or rejected.

Here we get to the core of the problem: what exactly is it that we want to investigate when we study homicide cases? This chapter focuses on the homicide rate as (just) one means to study forms of aggression and the ways in which aggression might be regulated or repressed. It would be an exercise in purging moral judgments from our scholarly view if we asked ourselves whether it is possible to commit a "civilized" murder. The question follows directly from a primary concern of Elias's theory, that is, What kind of constraints did people impose on themselves and on others? If increasing affect control, the taming of spontaneous drives and impulses, is indeed the dominant sociopsychological trend over the last seven centuries or so of European history, a high incidence of deliberate killings today would not be incompatible with it. Such a killing requires a high amount of rational planning and restraint of momentary impulses. Elias's theory about affect control, then, would not necessarily predict that we find a declining trend in homicide rates. Instead, the proportion of "killings in affect," as a result of sudden rage, may have declined, while that of carefully premeditated murders may have remained stable or even risen.

Two alternative reactions to this proposition are possible. I will eventually opt for the second, but before I do so, I must explain why I reject the first: a separate study of murder and manslaughter. According to conventional wisdom, it is all right to lump together these two legal categories. But if we want to distinguish "killings in affect" from the "civilized" ones, it may be necessary to separate them. And yet there are no less than four reasons, two of them more theoretical and two more methodological, why it is better after all to combine the figures for murder and manslaughter into one homicide rate. The first is that precisely the affect-control component of Elias's theory is highly contested, since it is so difficult to substantiate it empirically. Did medieval people really have fewer self-constraints, or did they simply control their behavior in a manner qualitatively different from ours?[22] Second, the empirical evidence on related developments, such as the changing attitudes to slavery, punishment, and animal sports, definitely indicates that the dominant trend within the "civilizing process" moved in the direction of nonacceptance of violence, physical subjugation, and the deliberate infliction of suffering generally. If we fail to take this evidence into account, we would go too far toward the opposite extreme of what I warned against above: relying only on deduction.

The methodological objections against separating murder cases from manslaughter cases are that the definitions of these two categories may vary, historically as well as in individual instances. In several regions of Europe before the sixteenth century the criterion of premeditation hardly applied at all. A murder was a particularly treacherous homicide: because it had been committed at night, without a warning, because the body had been hidden afterwards, or simply because the victim was a pregnant woman.[23] In eighteenth-century Spain the criterion of premeditation existed alongside that of treachery and assassination by a paid killer, to define a homicide as particularly heinous.[24] Faber concludes that the judges in eighteenth-century Amsterdam paid more attention to the consequences of a violent act than to the perpetrator's intention.[25] Premeditation did not become the sole criterion to distinguish murder from manslaughter in the Netherlands until the adoption of the French *Code Pénal* in 1811.[26] Finally, we cannot be sure in individual cases: if we calculate separate rates for murder and manslaughter, we are in fact counting the outcomes of judicial trials. Notably in the twentieth century many manslaughter trials have been initiated as such because the prosecutors thought they would fail to substantiate a murder charge. The case can also be the other way around as in early modern England, where killers were almost always indicted for murder, so that they were obliged to defend themselves at the trial and reveal the circumstances.[27] Thus, our calculations have little validity, unless we combine all cases of killing into one homicide rate.

My rejection of the idea of calculating separate murder and manslaughter rates leaves us with the second device for distinguishing between different sorts of killings: to supplement the raw data with an analysis of the social context in which homicides were committed. Of course the state of the evidence has to allow for such an analysis. Judicial trials with surviving documentation on interrogations are the ideal source for this undertaking.

Homicides can be characterized according to their position on two related but distinct axes: impulsive violence versus planned or "rational" violence on the one hand, and ritual or expressive violence versus instrumental violence on the other.[28] Of course these four categories are extreme poles of a continuum. The archetype of impulsive killing is the tavern brawl where a knife is drawn and one of the fighters is stabbed to death. According to Berents, this type of homicide was overwhelmingly predominant in fifteenth-century Utrecht.[29] At the other end of the spectrum we find deliberate acts of violence. A carefully planned murder out of jealousy or revenge, for example, may be called rational, even if the perpetrator is caught. The impulsive-rational axis has to do mainly with the psychological state of the person who engages in violence. The social meaning of the act, on the other hand, is the determining factor in the ritual-instrumental axis. Ritual violence belongs to a social context in which honor and physical bravery are highly valued and linked. This context is characteristic for preindustrial societies more than for industrial societies. Whether homicidal or not, ritual violence is guided by implicit cultural codes and often its primary aim is to degrade the victim. That kind of behavior is reflected in French pardon letters from the fifteenth to the middle of the seventeenth century.[30] Its opposite is violence used in order to get something, as with mugging, rape, or loan-sharking, crimes that we associate with modern cities. It should be emphasized that these are all ideal types; in reality different aspects of violence can be intermingled. Notably ritual and instrumental aspects may be combined, for example, in acts of rape.

My assignment of the ideal types to different periods suggests that any long-term trend would be from impulsive to rational and from ritual to instrumental violence. Presently, this can be no more than a hypothesis. Still another hypothesis is derived from the identification of two axes of violence. Both the ritual and impulsive violence of past centuries often had a distinct community character. The first derived its meaning from being understood by all participants and the second was closely associated with daily sociability. Killer and victim often were residents of the same local community. In a populous place they might be strangers to each other, but they usually belonged to the settled population. Homicides were public events, at the center of community life. To a large extent, this is no longer the case today. Serious violence has retreated partly to the margins of society. A large number of contemporary homicides are connected with a property crime or with illegal economic activity such as the drug trade. This applies to instrumental as well as to rational violence; in the latter case we can think of the liquidation of competitors. According to Stone, armed robbery is the major factor explaining the recent rise in the homicide rate, at least in the United States.[31] Thus, qualitatively speaking, marginalization was one of the major long-term developments in homicide. The trend was from violence at the center of local communities to violence practiced by groups with a professional interest in crime.

The increasing proportion of killings within the biological family forms another conspicuous development. With a sharply declining homicide rate, of course, the absolute number of killings within the family still may have declined. Nevertheless, their rising share is important for a contextual analysis. If family homicide maintains a relatively stable level even today, this would be compatible with the theory of an increase in affect regulation. As affects and emotions were the subject of increasing constraints in the wider society, the nuclear family came to serve as an island where emotions were

cultivated. Historians such as Mitterauer argue that because of this development families have become more crisis-prone.[32] To be sure, cases in which
tensions get out of hand to such an extent that homicide is the result mainly
involve spouses. Stone, too, emphasizes that spouses and lovers are the majority among the victims of contemporary family homicide.[33] Cockburn, on
the other hand, is skeptical about the thesis of an increasing share of killings
within the family. In this connection, he makes two claims. First, he thinks
that homicides of spouses in the early modern period were seriously underreported and those of lovers often unidentifiable. Second, according to a
somewhat elusive argument, Cockburn posits that infanticide should be included in the category of family homicide. That operation would raise the
level of family homicide in early modern England to over 30 percent.[34] I dis-
agree with both claims and my reaction results in a proposal for methodological refinement.

The difficulty of identifying lovers as victims of a homicide, it seems to
me, would rather apply to our own period; at least if we interpret "lovers" to
be partners outside marriage. It is precisely today that homicides on partners
are difficult to identify, for the simple fact that many partners are not registered as such. A classic case, in the 1960s, in which long pent-up tensions
between two people living together culminated in murder and suicide, is
portrayed in Stephen Frears's 1987 film *Prick Up Your Ears*. It tells the story
of the English playwright Joe Orton, whose male partner killed Joe and then
himself. Undoubtedly Joe Orton does not figure in the statistics as the victim of a family homicide. The case suggests that the biological family and legal
spouses have received too much attention from historians studying homicide.
Understandably, they have looked for a factor that could be easily quantified.
From a theoretical point of view, however, the crucial question is not whether killer and victim were related by blood or marriage, but whether they had
an intimate relationship. It is only in the latter case that we suspect the killing to have been the outcome of built-up tensions. In the categorization of
killer-victim relationships, then, intimates should be kept separate from acquaintances and total strangers as well as from nonintimate relatives.[35]

It follows that the question whether or not to rank infanticide with the
family homicides is largely irrelevant, because in any case, it should not be
included in the category of killing an intimate person.[36] The children in
question never were granted the time to become intimates and their premature death was not the outcome of a protracted conflict between the perpetrator and the victim. It might be objected that it was precisely the mother's
internal struggle during several months of unwanted pregnancy that gener-

ated tensions and a conflicted intimacy vis-à-vis her unborn child. Even if we adopt that view, it is plain that this tense and intimate relationship is qualitatively different from that prevailing between a husband and a wife or, for example, between two sisters. Whatever we decide, there is a third argument leading to the conclusion that infanticide should be kept entirely separate, from both familial and nonfamilial homicides. Infanticide rates tell us little about people's propensity for aggression and a lot more about shame and desperation. When a mother kills her infant child, there is neither a fight nor a robbery. Moreover, the perception of the act by the killer and those prosecuting her may be radically divergent: from its being "something many women might be so unfortunate as to have to do one day, because no other option is available" to "an inexcusable assault on Christian morality." The tremendous differences in the social contexts of infanticide and homicide make the former into a distinct category. Again, an objection is possible: this line of reasoning exceeds the bounds of a historian's neutrality, since infanticide obviously involves the killing of a human being. However, so does the death of a soldier at the hands of an enemy. Historians are constantly classifying, including some acts in a specific category and excluding others, according to their evaluation of the social context. This is fine, as long as the process of categorizing is made visible. Hence, we should always construct homicide rates with and without the killing of infants.

◆ Implications for Classifying the Data

The acknowledgment of the significance of different aspects of violence and the introduction of the concept of homicide on intimates were interpretive exercises. Now we must consider the implications of the preceding discussion for gathering, classifying, and counting cases. The period before 1500 presents the greatest difficulties. For that period we may have data on officially recognized feuds (and the reconciliations through which they might be ended) next to legally prosecuted homicides.[37] Elias's theory posits a negative correlation between people's inclination toward aggression and the degree of monopolization of violence in a particular society. Should we take the data on feuds as additional evidence for either a high amount of aggression or an absence of monopolization of violence? Obviously, the figures cannot be used both ways, since that would imply a circular argument.[38] Elias tried to solve this problem by considering the feuds as symptoms of a low level of pacification and looking for independent evidence that medieval people not only fought but took pleasure in fighting. However, such evidence as he found to substantiate that claim is somewhat problematic.[39] The best solution for us is to consider the occurrence of officially recognized feuds as a symptom of a low level of state formation and to reserve for the construction of the homicide rate only those killings that even the relatively weak authorities of this period considered illegal.

The early modern period no longer witnessed officially recognized feuds, except in peripheral areas of Europe.[40] A measure of internal pacification had been reached, but violence still was socially accepted to some extent. The methodological problem is whether this can be inferred from the homicide rate. The homicide rate refers to activities that were not tolerated per definition, since they were liable to criminal prosecution. Consequently, the cases we are collecting belong to unaccepted violence. The solution is to consider the homicide cases as representing the extreme pole of a continuum that begins with accepted violence: quarrels that are laughed about; fistfights in which bystanders encourage the participants more or less indiscriminately; a teasing with knives that everyone takes lightly; a beating within the family that the community does not consider serious. In the overwhelming majority of instances such acts of violence do not result in the death of a participant. Viewed from this angle, homicide occurs only when things get out of hand. Homicides are "casualties." The frequency of these casualties is an indication of the frequency of relatively minor and common forms of violence. In the sixteenth through eighteenth centuries lethal fights were not accepted, but moderate forms of violence were considered relatively normal. If we observe a decline in the homicide rate, and thus in the number of casualties, in the course of this period, it means that the level of routine violence has declined. When this process continues, there must be a qualitative shift at some point: acceptance of moderate violence turns into a rejection among most members of society; as routine aggression becomes rarer, the number of casualties becomes insignificant; the residual homicide rate largely consists of extreme or marginal cases, in either the sphere of erupting tensions or a criminal underworld. That is in line with the evidence on the contemporary proportion of homicides on intimates and killings related to other illegal activities.

Also with respect to the more technical side of reconstructing the long-term trend, problems lessen if we take theory into consideration. It might be argued, for example, that in our time the cowardice of people who are mugged lowers the homicide rate artificially. Unlike two or three hundred years ago, nowadays most victims choose not to resist, thereby allowing the instrumental violence accompanying the robbery to be limited to a light form or even just the threat to use it.[41] However, it is doubtful whether in earlier centuries many cases of resistance to an assault on one's property resulted in the death of the victim or the robber. More important is that, if most victims today prefer to hand over their wallets, this is precisely because they are unaccustomed to violence (additionally, they are often insured). So this is in line with the general trend. A similar argument applies to killing in self-defense. When a case is acknowledged as such, it is a lawful act, so we might argue that it should be excluded from the homicide statistics. Such an argument is unconvincing. Had the outcome of the event been the reverse, it would have been a regular homicide; either way there has been a fight. Manslaughter and killing in self-defense are two possible casualties arising out of the same situation.[42] Still another disturbing factor consists of the cases that remain entirely unknown. Historians generally assume that homicide is the crime most easily detectable, since it is so difficult to hide the body. Nevertheless, there are people who disappear permanently and some of them may have been murdered. Does this happen more frequently today than in earlier centuries? Reliable statistics are lacking. Whatever is the case, hidden bodies point at planned, rational violence rather than killing in affect.

Two other disturbing factors are peculiar to the twentieth century. In Kent reckless driving with lethal consequences apparently was prosecuted as a homicidal act, but this is not customary in Dutch judicial practice. In Dutch medical statistics, death in a car accident is normally listed as a traffic casualty, no matter how guilty the driver was. Although some traffic casualties may be deliberate murders, I cannot imagine these cases to be very frequent. Modern means of transport also affect the contemporary figures in the form of fast ambulances taking seriously injured victims to an operating room. Most scholars agree that increased medical skill and organization play a role only from about 1900 onward. On the whole, it is probably safe to say that all factors affecting the homicide rate were fairly constant until the end of the nineteenth century.

There may be one exception to this confident statement: poisoning. In this case the dark figure is not a constant; the chances that the crime remains undetected increase the further we go back in time. For the overall homicide trend this does not matter much, because inclusion of the dark figure would only reinforce it. But the unknown figure biases our conclusions about homicide on intimates, since wives offering their husbands poisoned food are the alleged majority of perpetrators. We may still ask whether the stereotypes of the preindustrial period are leading us astray. For a long time poisoning was seen as akin to harmful sorcery, since both activities were performed secretly and seemed to work equally mysteriously. Whereas women would kill hated persons, including neighbors, by either one of these means, men would do so in a fight. Was killing through poison really frequent in the old days or was it merely the great fear of preindustrial men? It is hard to tell, so as scholars we are left with a choice. Should we resign in dismay, complaining that we will never get our figures right, or should we acknowledge that there are two different long-term trends, which are connected but each of which can be studied in its own right as well. On the one hand we have the family and male-female relations; historical shifts in the nature of the tensions between spouses; and changes in the way these tensions were expressed in specific conflicts and different outcomes in extreme cases. On the other hand we have the history of aggression in human face-to-face relations, taking place mainly in a male world. Whatever trend we observe in other fields, this history appears to be characterized by a gradual increase in psychological constraints.

Two classification rules, finally, follow from the demand of comparability of figures. The first is that the victims rather than the killers should be the basic unit for constructing the homicide rate. It can make a difference, even if we have the complete evidence on both. There were instances in which one assailant killed several victims simultaneously as well as those in which one victim was killed by several persons simultaneously. Especially in the latter case the urge to assign individual responsibility to the actual killer and his accomplices may vary over time. Moreover, in coroner's inquests and medical statistics, we count bodies, that is, victims. The second rule is always to exclude attempted murder/manslaughter from the homicide rate. The definition of what constitutes an attempt on a person's life greatly varied over time.[43] Naturally, mere attempts are absent from medical statistics on the causes of death.[44]

◆ Violence in Dutch History

Dutch society today is widely believed to be relatively nonviolent in comparison with other Western countries. Historians and sociologists have considered this a characteristically Dutch trait, which can be traced back over the centuries. In the early 1980s Rudolf Dekker, taking issue with Ton Zwaan, argued against this traditional opinion.[45] Neither of the participants in the debate was concerned with quantitative evidence; they focused on political violence, protest movements, and revolutions. According to Zwaan, Dutch society had been particularly peaceful from the seventeenth century onward, since it had not witnessed large-scale peasant revolts, and the revolutions that did occur took few lives. Dekker retorted that some French provinces, the size of the northern Netherlands, did not witness large-scale revolts either. Therefore, he proposed to broaden the geographic scope by including the southern Netherlands and to begin the overview of political violence in the Middle Ages. In this way he was able to point at the bloody social conflicts in medieval Flemish cities, the party struggles of *Hoeken* and *Kabeljauwen* in Holland a little later, the revolt against Spain in the sixteenth century, and the struggle for Belgian independence, also known for its many victims, in the 1830s. In the end, these diverging views of the range of events to be considered produced a conflict over the boundaries separating intrastate from interstate violence.

So the debate ended in a stalemate. To open it again, I start from the premise that intrastate political violence, including food riots and the like, is more akin to interstate violence than to violence in daily life. The level of interstate violence has always fluctuated and it certainly remains high today (though not within Europe since 1945). The field contested by Dekker and Zwaan, then, is of little relevance for the study of long-term trends. As the evidence for other countries shows, it was daily violence in particular that was subject to change over the centuries. For the Netherlands, too, daily violence offers the only possibility for a meaningful diachronic analysis, especially for quantitative study. This takes us back to the evidence on homicide. Technical problems must be solved first.

◆ The Inadequacy of Trial Figures

The Dutch evidence unambiguously demonstrates that frequency rates based on prosecuted homicide are completely unreliable. Because several historians, including myself, have studied crime and justice in Amsterdam, it is easy to construct a graph of murder and manslaughter cases tried by the city's court from the beginning of the sixteenth century to the beginning of the nineteenth. Largely overlapping articles by Boomgaard and Jüngen deal with the earliest period. The former counts 23 homicide trials during the years 1524–50 and the latter arrives at 38 for the years 1524–65.[46] In both cases the annual average is 0.9 trials. In an unpublished thesis Jüngen considered six sample years between 1560 and 1614. Homicide trials in those years numbered six altogether.[47] My own earlier work focused on public punishment, but since homicide trials in the period I studied seldom ended in a nonpublic punishment or release, my evidence is comparable with that presented by the other authors. The figures cover the period 1651–1750, with the years 1706–

9 missing. A public penalty, usually death, was imposed for manslaughter (68), semimanslaughter (5), murder (22), causing an accidental death (2), and infanticide (3).[48] This adds up to an annual average of exactly one homicide trial. The work of the legal historian Sjoerd Faber, finally, partly overlaps with my own. He used the jailer's records, covering the period 1732–1811, as his source. Faber produces no exact figures, saying that there were usually one or two homicide trials per year and in some years none.[49]

This leads to a surprising conclusion: the average annual level of prosecuted homicide in Amsterdam tended to remain constant, at about one, over the entire period from 1524 to 1811 (although in the short run there were peaks and quiet decades). The city's population, however, rose dramatically from 15,000 in 1500 to 100,000 in the early decades of the seventeenth century, until it reached 200,000 around 1670 or 1680. Thereafter the population remained almost stable in the period in question, reaching 217,000 in 1795. Thus, a graph of homicide trials per 100,000 inhabitants would simply be the inverse of the population curve. The figure would be less than 0.5 per 100,000 throughout the eighteenth century. It is highly unlikely, although not impossible, that this graph would bear any resemblance to the real incidence of killing in Amsterdam.

The evidence on default procedures, discussed by Faber and by Marijke Gijswijt-Hofstra, is one indication that the real incidence of killing in Amsterdam was higher than the prosecution records suggest. The authors present two sets of figures: one derived from twelve sample years between 1680 and 1790 and another from a separate register containing all cases from 1751 to 1801.[50] From their data I calculate that the rate of homicides with identified killers (i.e., default procedures and prosecuted cases combined) lay between 1.5 and 2.1 during the period 1680–1790 and that it was 0.7 during the period 1751–1801.[51] These figures may indicate a declining trend, but the total number of homicides committed must have been higher than the rate of homicides with identified killers. Gijswijt-Hofstra discovered eight fugitive killers from Amsterdam in the registers of the sanctuaries at Culemborg, Vianen, and IJsselstein and she was able to trace only one of them in the Amsterdam default procedure records.[52]

Outside Amsterdam, too, the available data indicate that homicide rates based on records of criminal prosecution are inadequate. The next-longest period is covered by an ongoing project on criminal justice in Leiden during 1533–1811. The sentence registers of that town contain cases involving arrested killers as well as default trials. Peaks in the absolute numbers, however, are always due to increased efforts in sentencing fugitive suspects. When the number of homicide cases is low, there are almost no default trials.[53] In another project the court records of seven sample jurisdictions, mostly small towns and rural regions, are analyzed from 1700 to 1811. In those seven jurisdictions there were only 98 homicide trials altogether, including default cases, during that period. The frequency declined after 1750.[54] In Haarlem eight homicide trials were conducted during the years 1740–95, while default procedures apparently were not registered.[55] With a population of 25,000, this amounts to a rate of prosecuted homicide of 0.7 per 100,000 per year.

Two widely diverging figures for the city of Utrecht also illustrate the problem. According to Berents the average absolute number of homicide trials was 6.4 per year in the first half of the fifteenth century. Although the author does not make it clear, this figure presumably includes default cases, because otherwise it would be incredibly high. The count is based on the number of killers; the number of victims, the author says, was only a little lower.[56] With a population of 12,000, the homicide rate in the city of Utrecht in the first half of the fifteenth century comes at 53.3. If we allow for the slightly lower number of victims, the rate is about 50. In the register of criminal sentences of the city during the period 1550–70, however, the average number of murder and manslaughter trials is a mere 0.25 per year. With a population of 25,000 this amounts to a rate of prosecuted homicide of only 1 per 100,000.[57] It cannot be doubted that this immense drop within a hundred years is largely due to changes in the registration of killings.

While these data from prosecution and default procedure records are suggestive, the conclusive evidence is provided by the body inspection records discussed below. Jüngen was the first to recognize their importance and concluded that in sixteenth-century Amsterdam the chance of a killer's being caught and tried was about 7 percent; the ratio of detected to prosecuted killings was 9:1. The obvious superiority of lists of body inspections (or coroner's inquests, as the English called them) as a source for establishing the incidence of homicide lies in the fact that these records include cases in which the killer remained unidentified. To conclude, there are three types of sources, each successively yielding a higher number of homicides: court cases involving arrested killers; records listing all cases with identified killers (including fugitive suspects); and lists of body inspections. Figures derived from the first two types of sources should be taken into consideration only when they are relatively high, because in that case the actual number of killings must necessarily be at least as high.

◆ Homicide in Amsterdam, 1431–1816

Amsterdam certainly meets the methodological requirement of studying a relatively populous area over a relatively long period of time. The earliest reliable and relevant data are presented in a 1992 study by Jan Boomgaard.[58] Information is available for eleven fiscal years during the period 1431–62. The names of 54 killers were known. Exactly a third of them were dealt with judicially, which resulted in 17 financial settlements and only one death sentence. Thus, the average annual level of prosecuted homicide (1.7) was slightly higher than the number recurrent in the early modern period. Thirty-four killers had fled Amsterdam; one had died in the brawl and the fate of one is unknown. In six instances the victim was killed by two men and in two instances by three men, which means that the total number of victims was 44. These figures amount to an average of 5 killers per year and 4 victims per year. Amsterdam's population by the middle of the fifteenth century may be estimated at 8,000 or 9,000.[59] Consequently, the homicide rate was approximately 47 or 59, depending on whether we count the victims or their aggressors. We should not succumb to Cockburn's skepticism about the figures prior to the sixteenth century. Although one victim more or less would make a difference of a whole point, a sample of eleven years is acceptable and a town of almost 10,000 inhabitants is not too small. Moreover, the actual rate possibly was higher still, as there might have been cases with unidentified killers.

The Amsterdam court records of the sixteenth century include the inspections, carried out at the orders of the judiciary, of the bodies of persons who had died under suspicious circumstances. During the years 1524–65 they numbered 646 altogether, subdivided according to the following causes of death: act of violence, excluding enemy action and political murder (53.3 percent); suicide (2.9 percent); drowning (32.6 percent); accident (9 percent); unknown disease (1.3 percent); not mentioned (0.9 percent). The first category, with an absolute number of 344, consists of all homicides committed and detected within the city. Comparing this figure with the number of court cases, Jüngen calculates that the chances of a killer's being caught and tried lay between 6.4 percent and 7.7 percent.[60] Hence, in the period 1524–65 the ratio of detected to prosecuted homicide was 9:1. The average absolute number of the former was 8.2 per year. With a population of almost 30,000, this amounts to a homicide rate of around 28. In an unpublished thesis Jüngen supplements these figures with data from four sample years: 1560, 1570, 1580 and 1590. In the inspection reports of those years an annual average of 10 homicides and 1.5 uncertain cases was found. Around 1575 the city's population was probably about 47,500, which results in a homicide rate for the period 1560–90 that lies between 21.1 and 24.2.[61] This suggests that the rate was declining during the sixteenth century.

Around 1600 the Amsterdam court stopped the practice of inserting body inspection reports in the registers of criminal sentences. Possibly, they began to list these reports separately right away, but in that case the earliest lists have not been preserved. So there is a gap in our information until the 1660s. Five separate registers of body inspections carried out at the orders of the Amsterdam judiciary are extant.[62] Faber already consulted this source in order to count infanticide cases.[63] Because most of the inspections involved an autopsy, I will refer to them under that name. Together, the registers cover the period 1666–1817, with gaps for the years 1680–92 and 1727–51. When a register did not begin in January or end in December, I discarded the first and/or the last year. In this way, evidence is available for three periods: 1667–79, 1693–1726, and 1752–1816. In my tables the second period is split into two subperiods and the third into four. Because the autopsy reports were written in a bound register in chronological order, it is unlikely that cases have been lost. The problem is rather that there are too many.

Not every inspected body was actually dead. Around 1700 the registers include visitations of wounded persons, while throughout the period there are a few reports in which a person's state of mind or the condition of a woman's genitals were the issue, the latter presumably because of suspected rape. These cases are easily identified. It is different with the corpses. I noted that among the sixteenth-century reports studied by Jüngen there were quite a number of accidents. Information on the cause of death was based on the registered conclusions of a court committee, which did the inspections. The registers I studied also included cases of nonviolent death. The problem is that the judicial conclusion is missing. The autopsies were performed by the city's anatomy professor assisted by two surgeons.[64] They never stepped outside the bounds of their profession, always listing the medical cause of death only. Supposedly, the *schout* (prosecutor) and the *schepenen* (judges) drew their conclusions, based on information about what had happened. It is only in some cases that this information was inserted in the registers. Thus, we know, for example, that a man found drowned was murdered because the surgeons noted that his hands and feet were tied, or that a woman whose skull was smashed had committed suicide because a clerk wrote in the margin that she had jumped out of a window.

The only way to proceed was to collect information on every variable in the records and to use this information in order to reduce the number of uncertain cases to the lowest level possible. For the bodies of persons not identified as infants, this operation had to be performed carefully. There were four possibilities: homicide, suicide, accidental death, and natural death.[65] The identification of the fourth was relatively unproblematic. In the cases concerned, the surgeons either listed some infection or disease, or, when they did not know, noted the absence of any sign of violence. The problem was especially to differentiate homicide from either suicide or accidental death. Information on the condition of the body or the circumstances of the event sometimes allowed me to assign a case with certainty to one of the three categories. I did so in one other type of situation, not with certainty but with great confidence: I classified as suicides all cases in which the cause of death was listed as strangulation (and in which it was often noted that the body had had a rope around its neck). The Amsterdam sources contain no hints that gangs of sneaky stranglers were active in the city over a century and a half.[66] For the rest, we have to make deductions from the sort of injury that the surgeons described. Persons whose deaths apparently were caused by any sort of blunt instrument could either have been killed or become the victim of an accident. They make up the majority of the cases listed as possible homicide. When a weapon had been used, an accident was unlikely, but it could have been a suicide. When a body had more than one wound or one that could not be self-inflicted, I concluded that there had been a violent death. Then there were the categories of one stab wound, one cut in the throat, and one piercing with a sword. I decided finally to list them as certain homicides, too. Although technically it would be possible to commit suicide in this way, it is unlikely that this was done by more than a handful of people. The frequency of strangulation indicates that hanging oneself was the common method for committing suicide. Some persons, on the other hand, definitely shot themselves, which led me to assign the cases of one shot wound, except when it was in the back, to the category of possible homicide. Fortunately, the use of guns does not seem to have been very popular in early modern Amsterdam. Dying from poison, finally, also was assigned to the category of possible homicide.

The resulting file of noninfants who certainly or possibly had been killed by another person consists of 1,091 victims, out of a total of 1,451 noninfant corpses inspected. Reliable population estimates for Amsterdam are available. The number of inhabitants in the seven periods, distinguished respectively, can be put at 190,000; 200,000; 205,000; 210,000; 210,000; 215,000; and 220,000. Table 3–1 presents my calculations. (Because every average was calculated directly from the total number and rounded off to one decimal, average parts sometimes do not add up to average sums.)

Table 3–1. Homicide (of Noninfants) in Amsterdam Autopsy Reports, 1667–1816

	Certain Homicide, Annual Average		Possible Homicide, Annual Average		
Period	Abs.	Per 100,000 Population	Abs.	Per 100,000 Population	Total
1667–79	5.5	2.9	1.2	0.6	3.5
1693–1709	18.0	9.0	2.4	1.2	10.2
1710–26	17.1	8.4	0.7	0.3	8.7
1752–67	3.3	1.6	1.9	0.9	2.5
1768–83	3.7	1.8	4.4	2.1	3.8
1784–99	3.1	1.5	2.4	1.1	2.6
1800–1816	2.3	1.0	0.9	0.4	1.5

At first sight it looks as if the gaps in the documentation represent the crucial years, with the homicide rate rising sharply during the first gap and declining again during the second. The figure for the period 1667–79 is especially surprising; it is very low when compared with the sixteenth-century data but also decidedly lower than the level prevailing a few decades later. It is the only figure contradicting the hypothesis of a steady decline. However, there is good reason to assume that precisely in this period cases were underreported. An urban ordinance dated 3 June 1692 explicitly says that "some surgeons and other people dare to open the bodies or inspect the wounds of persons who have been slain or who have died in an accident."[67] The magistrates expressly stated that only the official physician and surgeons of the court were authorized to do this job. Presumably, the ordinance was rigidly enforced, which would explain the subsequent rise in registered autopsies. On the other hand, such unofficial inspections of bodies as were performed in the 1660s and 1670s would have to have been enormously frequent in order to make the total number of inspections approach the figure prevailing from 1693 onward. To some extent, then, the latter period must have witnessed a peak in homicide. That is suggested by the data from criminal records (see below). In the 1710s homicide trials were four times as frequent as they had been in the second half of the seventeenth century and they may have been frequent already in the decade 1701–10, which had a three-year gap in the criminal records.[68] Although the peak in prosecuted homicide lasted for a briefer moment than the high tide in the number of body inspections, the two cannot be entirely unrelated. Possibly, when the rise in the incidence of killing became manifest, the court reacted to it by intensifying its efforts to catch suspects. If this was so, we must conclude that, even though the homicide rate of the period 1667–79 probably was kept down by under-reporting, the figure for the early eighteenth century represented a tempo-rary upsurge from a lower level which had prevailed before the 1690s.

Since the homicide level was so much lower in the register begun in 1752, we might suppose that this was due to underreporting as well. However, it is unlikely that the practice of unofficial autopsies was resumed in this peri-od. During the eighteenth century, bureaucratization definitely increased in the city, especially in the judicial realm. Moreover, a decreased homicide rate after 1750 would be perfectly in line with the observed trend in the frequen-cy of homicides with identified killers. The small peak in the "total" column in the fifth period was due mostly to an unusually high number of uncertain cases. Decline set in again toward the turn of the century. The figures in the "certain" and "total" columns are lowest in the last period.

The actual homicide rate necessarily stood between the levels indicated in the first and third column. The ratio of possible cases to certain cases is very modest up to 1726, which means that the margin of doubt is modest as well. The actual level in the 1660s and 1670s can be put at around 3¼; it represents a minimum rate, on the premise that there was underreporting. The average level of actual homicide during the years 1693–1726 was around 9. From 1752 onward the ratio of possible homicide to certain homicide lay between 0.4 and 0.7, except in the fifth period when it was over one. That period may have witnessed a relatively high number of suicides and accidents. If this supposi-tion is correct, the temporary peak during the years 1768–83 was not as marked as it seems. Thus, the homicide rate for the second half of the eighteenth cen-tury may be estimated as standing between 2 and 3. In the early nineteenth century it was somewhere between 1 and 1½. That was the overall trend.

The reports also inform us about the victim's sex and approximate age. Table 3–2 presents the most striking results. That women and children were less likely to be stabbed to death than adult men may not be surprising. The figures become especially noteworthy when compared with the frequencies of table 3–1. The correlations, negative and positive, are nearly perfect: when the homicide rate is high, the proportion of stabbings goes up and the proportion of female and young victims goes down. Information on the perpetrators is lacking in most cases, but women who killed men, especially who stabbed them, must have been a rarity. Thus, the high level of homicide in the 1690s through 1720s was due mainly to an increase in knife fighting among men.

Table 3-2. Characteristics of Homicide Victims (Noninfants, Certain and Possible) in Amsterdam, 1667-1816

Period	Percent Female	Percent Child or Adolescent	Percent Stabbed
1667-79	21.8	2.3	49.4
1693-1709	13.0	2.0	74.6
1710-26	13.2	1.3	82.8
1752-67	27.2	9.6	28.9
1768-83	35.2	7.8	20.9
1784-99	38.6	10.2	17.0
1800-1816	33.3	20.0	29.1
Total	20.6	4.7	58.1

With the group of "recently born children," as the reports call them, the uncertainties are negligible. As a rule, their bodies had been found in the water or at another place outside a private home. Infants cannot commit suicide and the circumstances of their death make an accident highly unlikely. Indeed, the inspection of an infant's body was not primarily meant to establish the cause of death. Using the lung proof, the doctors decided whether the child had been alive or not.[69] When they concluded that it had never breathed, I did not count the case as an infanticide. This is correct simply on semantic grounds. It might be argued that stillborn children disposed of by the mother should be included in my figures precisely because of the methodology outlined above. Don't they tell the same tale of shame and desperation? Although this is true, it is not the issue investigated here. I am discussing infanticide in order that the reader may know the total number of killings. Therefore, children who were not in fact killed are excluded from the table. In some cases the surgeons concluded that the child's body was "spoiled too far" to make a valid lung proof possible. The ratio of those uncertain cases to the certain ones (in which the child had breathed) was about 1:4, which makes it reasonable to combine them into one infanticide rate.

Table 3-3 shows the frequencies over time and adds them up with the figures from the third column of table 3-1. Among this group, too, violent death may have been underreported in the first period. The lung proof was in its infancy, so the magistrates often may have concluded that an inspection was useless. Among the sixteenth-century inspections there were only one or two bodies of infants.[70] Clearly, the infanticide rate did not follow the

Table 3-3. Infanticide and Total Number of Killings (Certain and Possible) in Amsterdam, 1667–1816

	Infanticide, Annual Average		Total Number of Killings, Annual Average	
Period	Abs.	Per 100,000 Population	Abs.	Per 100,000 Population
1667–79	0.6	0.3	7.3	3.9
1693–1709	2.3	1.2	22.7	11.3
1710–26	3.8	1.9	21.6	10.5
1752–67	5.6	2.7	10.8	5.1
1768–83	7.4	3.5	15.4	7.4
1784–99	1.1	0.5	6.6	3.1
1800–1816	1.3	0.6	4.5	2.1

trend in murders and manslaughters. The former remained constantly high during the hundred years from the 1690s into the 1780s. In the fourth period infanticides outnumbered even homicides and they would have done so in the fifth period as well, had not the number of possible homicides been that high. Despite all this, the general trend in the total number of killings, certain and possible, follows a pattern similar to that in table 3-1. Admittedly, the bare discovery of a dead baby does not tell much of a story. For information about the mother's state of mind we have to be content with judicial documentation. One crucial datum, however, was usually recorded in the autopsy reports. There were 406 bodies of infants found in the city and the sex of 387 of them was mentioned. Of those 387 babies, 51.4 percent were boys and 48.6 percent girls.[71] Obviously, the child's sex did not matter for the decision to kill it. That is exactly what we would expect, based on the hypothesis that the victim's identity was no major factor in the crime.

Obviously, for the quantitative study of infanticide, too, judicial trials alone are an unreliable source. It is illuminating to compare the Amsterdam data with Hoffer and Hull's figures for England and New England, based on indictments. The infanticide rates they calculated for different periods almost always remained far below one, even though the authors included killings of children up to nine years old.[72] The Amsterdam evidence suggests that the actual incidence of the crime was higher than the number of indictments indicates.

◆ The Age of Statistics

After the last recorded case, in August 1817, the Amsterdam register of judicial autopsies has dozens of blank pages. If the surgeons continued to draw up reports, these have not been preserved. Although Herman Franke's 1991 article allows me to pick up the story again in 1850, his figures are hardly comparable with mine. Until 1911 only statistics on convictions are available; they are nationwide and they include attempts. In these statistics the homicide rate fluctuated around 0.5 well into the twentieth century.[73] For the opening decade of the series, this may indicate an actual homicide rate close to the one established for Amsterdam at the beginning of the nineteenth century, on the assumption that the level of detected killings still was about three to four times higher than the level of prosecuted killings. If this was so, the national level must have declined in the course of the nineteenth century, because in the series of medical statistics, starting in 1911, the homicide rate fluctuated around 0.3 until 1965 (except during the Second World War).[74] Although judicial and police statistics on homicide in recent decades are inflated by the inclusion of attempts at murder or manslaughter and cases of abortion and euthanasia, all the evidence adduced by Franke leads him to conclude convincingly that the national homicide rate went up beginning in 1970.

Franke does not consider the statistics on the causes of death in Amsterdam separately. They are available for the period 1979–89.[75] During those years the absolute number of homicides fluctuated without a specific pattern. The average annual rate per 100,000 population was 2.1. However, this figure is not entirely comparable with those calculated from the autopsy reports, since the contemporary statistics refer to residents of Amsterdam who have been killed anywhere and the earlier reports pertain to persons, living anywhere, who have been killed in the city. For information of the latter type, we may turn to Franke's article once more. He is able to come up with reliable figures for homicides committed in Amsterdam just for the years 1987–90. The absolute numbers of persons killed in the city in those years were 40, 52, 46, and 45, respectively.[76] This amounts to an annual average of 6 per 100,000 inhabitants.

It may be concluded that Amsterdam forms no exception to the contemporary rise in the homicide rate. Moreover, no allowance has been made yet for advances in medical technology and organization, the only factor whose influence is so much greater now than it was in previous centuries. As it happens, Amsterdam sources around 1700 allow me to estimate how great this

influence is almost three hundred years later. As far as I know, no such device is to be found in historical literature so far. Reports of inspections of the
wounds of seriously injured persons are included in the second and third
registers of autopsies. In the third their number declines toward the end; the
wounded appear to have been inspected on a regular basis up to 1706. Some
victims were visited twice, first in their capacity as injured person and one
or more days later in their capacity as corpse. During the interval, they had
been taken care of in the city's hospital. They numbered 63 altogether in the
period 1693–1706, which is 4.5 per year. With an average of about 19 homicides per year in this period, those dying of their injuries in the hospital make
up 23.7 percent. This is the proportion of victims who might have been saved,
had our contemporary medical technology been available.[77] Here we have our
measure. It is a crude one, but it is based on historical evidence. In the early
modern period about one quarter of all homicide victims died "unnecessarily." Hence, the modern rates would have to be increased by one third to make
them comparable with the pre-1900 figures. For Amsterdam this would mean
a corrected homicide rate of 8 today.[78]

As we might expect, the contemporary rise does not involve infanticide.
Only one child under one year of age figured in the medical statistics of the
period 1979–89 and nowadays there are no reports on bodies of infants found
in canals. Thus, infanticide is no longer an issue. This is perfectly understandable in an age in which birth control and abortion are common and in
which there is a near-universal acceptance of having children outside legal
marriage.

◆ Contextual Evidence

Evidence on the circumstances of a homicide case and the sort of violence
involved should be called contextual rather than qualitative, because it can
be quantified in its turn. The only systematic discussion of such evidence in
Dutch historical literature is by Gijswijt-Hofstra. Her research concerns fugitive manslaughter suspects, from all over the northern Netherlands, who
were granted a safe place in one of the five sanctuaries forming enclaves within
the republic's territory from the end of the sixteenth century until 1795.[79] The
overwhelming majority of the cases whose circumstances she discusses were
quarrels with lethal consequences. The victims were strangers or acquaintances, not intimates or family. There were no premeditated murders. Every
killer claimed he had acted in self-defense and bore no guilt. This is understandable, since such excuses were a necessary precondition for obtaining

sanctuary. Besides, a suspect needed to be relatively wealthy to pay for his subsistence and his right to stay.[80] So, the cases discussed by Gijswijt-Hofstra in no way represent all homicides in the Dutch Republic.

The Amsterdam autopsy reports sometimes contain information on the circumstances of the case, but this is never given consistently. The only way to gather contextual evidence on homicide in Amsterdam more systematically is to return to the trial records. My series of sentences involving a public punishment, collected in earlier research, forms the basis. The series covers the period 1651–1750 and it includes all cases of prosecuted homicide, except those in which the suspect had successfully pleaded self-defense. Additional information on these cases, to supplement that obtained from the sentences, was gathered from the interrogation protocols. Because the period of my earlier research ended just before the great decrease in the incidence of killing, I found it necessary to extend the set of data further in time. References generously provided by Sjoerd Faber enabled me to trace the interrogations for homicide during the years 1751–1810. For a diachronic comparison I am distinguishing three periods: 1651–1700 (34 killers making 36 victims); 1701–50 (62 killers, 66 victims); 1751–1810 (29 killers, 33 victims). Just once it was clear that two people together killed one person. Trials for mere complicity or attempted murder were not included; neither were trials for infanticide. One decade, 1711–20, with 27 prosecutions for homicide largely accounts for the greater frequency in the second period.[81]

The problem of representativeness is less distracting than with Gijswijt-Hofstra's data. When we consider the collected cases as a sample of homicide in Amsterdam, the only systematic bias is that the killers were arrested. It is difficult to assess the chances of getting caught in different situations. I would have supposed that this chance was greater for those who killed an intimate, because they were easily suspect and less likely to flee. However, in 1714 the clerk reviewing the autopsy reports noted that no less than four women were said to have been stabbed to death by their husbands and another by her son-in-law. None of these reputed killers figures in the sentence books; possibly, they had fled. Some professional criminals, on the other hand, may have remained in town without being detected. Thus, different types of killers each were able to escape prosecution. More important for determining the representativeness of the cases discussed below is the one quantitative measure we have. The victim's sex is the only variable present in the trial series as well as the autopsy reports. In the former series the percentage of female victims is 36.8, which is considerably higher than in the autopsy reports. Clearly, people who killed women were more likely to get caught (and less likely to claim self-defense) than those who killed men. However, the difference between the two series is largely caused by an exceptionally high number of female victims in the third period of the trial records. They made up 25 percent and 22.7 percent in the first and second periods, respectively; this is a proportion comparable to that found in the autopsy reports. The first and second periods, then, can be considered fairly representative. The period 1751–1810, in which no less than twenty-six out of thirty-four victims (76.5 percent) were women, has to be handled with greater caution.

The number of female killers in the trial series, ten altogether, was too small to allow a meaningful comparison over time. Together they made twelve victims, eleven of whom were either the woman's own (noninfant) child or another adult female. The twelfth victim was the woman's husband.[82] It means that of all killers of spouses and lovers tried, only one was female.

Table 3–4 identifies nine possible relationships of the victim to his or her aggressor. Strangers make up the largest category. Of course some interaction precedes almost any homicide; the victim was listed as a stranger when the killer did not know him or her before the incident leading to the killing. In most of the "unclear" cases, the records did not reveal whether the two already knew each other or not; as a rule, these victims were either acquaintances or strangers, not intimates. The category of distant kin and in-laws had only one representative in each period.[83] That makes it reasonable to combine it with the three subsequent categories. The first three together make

Table 3–4. Relationship of Victim to Killer in
Amsterdam Homicide Trials, 1651–1810

Victim Is	Abs.	Percent
Spouse	10	7.4
Lover	12	8.8
Child; parent; sibling	7	5.1
Family, other; in-law	3	2.2
Occupational relationship	12	8.8
Fellow in underworld	6	4.4
Acquaintance, other	34	25.0
Stranger	42	30.9
Relationship unclear	10	7.4
Total	136	100

up the intimates. By grouping the victims in this way, we have reduced the types of relationship to four.

Table 3–5 shows the frequencies over time. With the proportion of acquaintances more or less fluctuating and that of the unclear cases slightly on the rise but remaining well under 10 percent, our attention is drawn to the two other categories. The approximate ratio of strangers to intimates changed from 4:1 in the first period, 2:1 in the second, and 1:3 in the third. In the latter period, if all unclear cases were in fact strangers, this ratio still would be 1:2. It may be objected that I just cast doubt on the representativeness of the trials in the third period. However, I am not prepared to consider the observed trend entirely an artifact. For one thing, the percentage of all three subcategories of intimates increased. A trend can be observed also with respect to the killer's age: 27.1, 30.0, and 33.4 years, respectively, in the three periods. This trend is compatible with a shift from fights among strangers to conflicts among intimates. Finally, since the number of homicide victims in the autopsy reports was much lower after the middle of the eighteenth century, the trials of the third period represent the most intensive sample. By the early nineteenth century the number of victims appearing in the autopsy reports was only three to four times as high as that found in the trials. The homicide rate had dropped considerably in comparison with a century earlier. It was hypothesized that such a drop would be accompanied by a rising proportion of homicides on intimates. That is precisely what seems to have happened, although the dimensions of the change may have been more modest than the figure for the period 1751–1810 indicates.

A few other variables are informative. That of the killer's birthplace, for example, shows a fluctuating pattern. Those born in Amsterdam made up

Table 3–5. Intimates and Nonintimates as Victims in Amsterdam Homicide Trials in Three Periods

Group of Victims	1651–1700		1701–50		1751–1810	
	Abs.	Percent	Abs.	Percent	Abs.	Percent
Intimates	4	11.1	9	13.6	16	47.1
Acquaintances	13	36.1	32	48.5	10	29.4
Strangers	17	47.2	20	30.3	5	14.7
Unclear	2	5.6	5	7.6	3	8.8
Total	36	100	66	100	34	100

29 percent, 58 percent, and 38 percent in the three periods, respectively.[84] While for the first this is about 15 percent lower than in the general population, for the second it is about 10 percent higher. A number of homicide convicts either had a previous arrest or one or more additional offenses listed in their sentences. Those killers can be considered as the group with a criminal background. They made up 53 percent, 31 percent, and 24 percent in the three periods, respectively. If the data on birthplace and criminal background are combined, the contrast between the second half of the seventeenth century and the first half of the eighteenth is especially marked: among the perpetrators of homicide a shift took place from immigrants with a criminal background to residents without such a background.

It is illuminating to consider separately the 1710s, when the frequency of trials was so high. That decade stood out from the total file of trials in several respects. The proportion of female victims (10 percent) was even lower than in the autopsy reports of that period. The killers, all male, were relatively young (25.8 years on average) and no less than 70 percent of them were born in Amsterdam. None of the trials was for killing an intimate. Indeed, no act of violence in this decade might be called a culmination of tensions. With that observation we have moved to a more interpretive evaluation of the evidence. Eighteen cases in the decade 1711–20 concerned a tavern brawl or a similar kind of quarrel; four were robbery related; three concerned resistance to one's apprehension; one man had suddenly attacked three others for no apparent reason; in one case the circumstances were unclear. An upsurge of trials apparently meant an increase in the number of impulsive killers caught. Moreover, these killers were relatively young and rooted in the community. Since the homicide rate peaked in this very period, the upsurge of trials also must have meant an increase in the actual frequency of lethal quarrels. That suggests that high homicide rates are the result of a high frequency of tavern brawls and comparable kinds of impulsive violence within the community.

The characterization of the court cases with the help of the two axes I distinguished is a hazardous enterprise. No homicidal incident simply can be labeled according to one archetype or the other. Let me briefly review the cases, restricting myself to what is relevant for the discussion of trends. Throughout the period 1651–1750 impulsive violence was overwhelmingly dominant. About three-fifths of the killings in that period resulted from conflicts arising in a tavern or street without any similar previous history. There was no planning involved; just a little took place in some cases, when a quarrel was interrupted and one of the protagonists used this opportunity to go home and get a knife. When two persons fought, a third sometimes intervened, which might make him either the killer or the victim. In other cases the killer had been provoked, because the victim was teasing him. The nonsettled population was involved in this kind of violence, too. One pickpocket stabbed another to death as they fought over the division of the spoils. Apart from these brawls, about half of the robbery-related homicides of this period had impulsive features. A man had been drinking with another, for example, and suddenly decided to try to take his companion's possessions. Or a woman killed another out of desperation, because she owed her money that she could not pay. During the period 1751–1810, on the other hand, only between a third and a half of the homicides can be called impulsive. That does not mean that the remaining cases involved rational violence. Careful planning remained rare; it was a feature only of some robberies.[85]

Less can be said about the ritual-instrumental axis. From the available documentation it is difficult to determine the extent to which tavern brawls and comparable quarrels also had expressive features. One isolated incident of ritual murder certainly was exceptional for its extremity.[86] Most cases of instrumental violence were homicides related to property crime. They occurred throughout the period 1651–1810.

The question to what extent the killing of an intimate person was an eruption of pent-up tensions must be dealt with separately. It is difficult to relate this question to the two axes of violence. A homicide resulting from a long-standing conflict can hardly be called impulsive, but neither, as a rule, is it planned in advance. Although, supposedly, this crime is more common in modern times, its nature is closer to ritual than to instrumental violence. I am calling this type of homicide on an intimate person tension-related. The opposite type, described in several Amsterdam trial records, may be termed anger-related. We encounter it notably among men who killed their wives or concubines. Characteristically, the perpetrator was said to be drunk and annoyed over a specific thing. Sometimes the incident was a beating that got out of hand. Every story of a partner killing is like that up to the 1720s. From then on, tension-related cases surface in the court records and they become more frequent in the period 1751–1810. All but a few of the cases in that period belong to one of four groups, which are about equally frequent: tension-related homicides on intimates, anger-related homicides on intimates, impulsive violence toward acquaintances or strangers, and killings related to robbery. Finally, what about poisoning an intimate person? The first recorded trial took place in 1728, when a man had poisoned his sister with arsenic in order to inherit from her.[87] Earlier, between 1693 and 1709, the surgeons doing the autopsies had found poison in the bodies of four persons and their reports contained another twenty such cases in subsequent years. This suggests that historians' concerns about an elevated dark number for poisoning, by wives or others, may be exaggerated.

It can be concluded that the contextual evidence assembled so far indicates a trend. Straightforwardly impulsive violence predominated until the middle of the eighteenth century, becoming less prominent since then. Notably the incidence of tavern brawls decreased. Around the same time there occurred a shift from the killing of strangers to the killing of intimates. From the 1720s onward more homicides on intimates were tension related. The observed trend may have continued after 1810. In his study of royal pardons in the Netherlands, Sibo van Ruller discusses 122 homicide cases from the period 1814–70. Most cases, he says, either were robbery related or involved marital/love problems. He identified 48 female and 43 male victims.[88]

◆ Conclusion

The claim of a long-term shift in the character of homicidal violence still has to be corroborated by further research and requires evidence for the twentieth century. With my conclusion on the overall trend, from the fifteenth century onward, I am on firmer ground. Homicidal violence definitely declined in Amsterdam at least until the first decades of the nineteenth century. The trend is so marked that the uncertain ties become meaningless in comparison with it. The homicide rate, defined as the annual average of violent deaths, excluding infants, in the city per 100,000 inhabitants, was 47 (or even more) in the second third of the fifteenth century. A hundred years later it stood at 28, and it declined to about 23 toward the end of the sixteenth century. It was very low, about $3\frac{1}{4}$, in the period 1667–79, but this is probably due to underreporting. In the 1690s and the first quarter of the eighteenth century the homicide rate stood at about 9. It had greatly declined by the middle of that century: between 2 and 3. In the 1800s and 1810s it stood between 1 and $1\frac{1}{2}$.

As for other parts of the Netherlands, only Berents's data can be taken into consideration. His figure, though representing a minimum level, still is quite high. The homicide rate of about 50 for the city of Utrecht in the first half of the fifteenth century converges with the Amsterdam evidence for the same period. Thus, the Netherlands also witnessed the general trend of long-term decline, first observed for England. In the Netherlands the decline was even steeper. The Dutch trend began at a much higher level than the English and it stayed relatively high well into the eighteenth century. Obviously, this statement should be qualified. The English homicide curve is based partly on indictments and it represents the aggregate rates of counties and towns of different size. Possibly, a longitudinal study of body inspections in London would produce a curve similar to the one reconstructed for Amsterdam. As suggested by the few other figures available, the "high-level start" in the late Middle Ages may have been characteristic for the continental urban experience. The smaller peak in Amsterdam at the beginning of the eighteenth century cannot simply be explained by pointing at the many taverns of the metropolis and the tavern brawls they facilitated. After 1750 the town still was bustling and in spite of this, the homicide rate had declined. One thing, finally, can be said with confidence: the evidence casts serious doubt on the thesis that Dutch society traditionally has been nonviolent in comparison with other European countries.

In our time the Amsterdam homicide rate is back at 6 (corrected rate: 8). This approximates the level of the third quarter of the eighteenth century, infanticides included. Much has been said about the contemporary rise.[89] For the moment, two crucial qualifications should be made. First, the national homicide rate today is much lower than the capital's; the former is 0.9 in medical statistics of the 1980s. Homicidal violence tends to concentrate in Amsterdam (and a few other big cities) and this may have been less so in earlier centuries. Second, within the capital a considerable share of homicides takes place in the context of a criminal underworld, notably in connection with the drug trade. This trade is rooted less in urban communities than in international networks. Violent crime generally in Dutch society is committed disproportionately by groups who are marginal from an ethnic or cultural point of view.[90] It would seem that the idea of a marginalization of homicide holds for the Netherlands. This means that the contemporary rates are not incongruent with Elias's theory.[91] There is still another way to put it: serious violence today is concentrated in "unpacified islands." Nineteenth-century national societies in Europe were particularly homogeneous. By contrast, the greater differentiation prevailing in the late twentieth century has led to the appearance of small islands within these societies where the pacification once guaranteed by the state has crumbled to some extent. In order to confirm this hypothesis, independent evidence, apart from the homicide rate, is needed. The argument presented here links recent trends to long-term developments, claiming that historical research may contribute to an understanding of contemporary problems.

Notes

I am indebted to Sjoerd Faber for helping me locate homicide trials in the period 1751–1810 and for providing me with his research notes on infanticide cases from the Amsterdam autopsy reports. Désirée Herber and Stefanie Reesink assisted with the collection of data in the Amsterdam archive. Earlier versions of this article were presented as a paper at a session on long-term trends in crime during the SSHA conference in New Orleans, November 1991, and at a seminar of the research group on historical anthropology at my department, March 1992. I am grateful to the participants in both meetings, notably to Eric Johnson, for their criticism. Herman Franke also commented on an earlier version.

1. Lawrence Stone, "Interpersonal Violence in English Society, 1300–1980," *Past and Present* 102 (1983): 22.

2. Ted Robert Gurr, "Historical Trends in Violent Crime: A Critical Review of the Evidence," *Crime and Justice: An Annual Review of Research* 3 (1981): 295–353; Stone, "Interpersonal Violence."

3. Stone, "Interpersonal Violence," 27.

4. Roderick Phillips, *Putting Asunder: A History of Divorce in Western Society* (Cambridge, 1988), 306–10. In the subcategory of spouse homicide two-thirds or more of the victims were women throughout the preindustrial period, except in rural Languedoc in the eighteenth century.

5. J. S. Cockburn, "Patterns of Violence in English Society: Homicide in Kent, 1560–1985," *Past and Present* 130 (1991): 93–96.

6. P. van den Eshof and E. J. C. Weimar, "Moord en doodslag in Nederland: Nederlandse gegevens in internationaal perspectief," *Justitiele Verkenningen* 17, no. 1 (1991): 20.

7. James A. Sharpe, "The History of Violence in England: Some Observations," *Past and Present* 108 (1985): 206–15; Lawrence Stone, "A Rejoinder," *Past and Present* 108 (1985): 216–24.

8. John M. Beattie, *Crime and the Courts in England, 1660–1800* (Oxford, 1986), 108 (homicide rates), 113–24 (infanticide), 132–39 (violence in English society).

9. Cockburn, "Patterns of Violence," 72, 76–79, 98–104. A somewhat elusive argument on physical punishment (which he calls judicial violence, a term I first employed in 1978) apparently serves as a further rebuttal to Stone. This judicial violence, Cockburn argues, was temporarily on the increase in England after 1752, but he seems to infer this mainly from the new law on dissection. Cockburn also weakens his argument by using unscholarly, value-laden terms such as "savagery" and "progress" (99, 104).

10. See Eva Österberg, "Social Arena or Theatre of Power? The Courts, Crime and the Early Modern State in Sweden," in *Theatres of Power: Social Control and Criminality in Historical Perspective,* Publications of Matthias Calonius Society, ed. Heikki Pihlajamäki (Jyväskylä, Finland, 1991), 15. The table appearing there was

reproduced, with a few additions, in her paper delivered at the Fourth IAHCCJ Conference (on urban and rural crime), Stockholm, July 1990.

11. Heikki Ylikangas, "Major Fluctuations in Crimes of Violence in Finland: A Historical Analysis," *Scandinavian Journal of History* 1 (1976): 83, 87-88, 91, 95. This article contains few concrete figures. He discusses the same subject without giving any concrete figures in "Die Gewaltkriminalität in der Finnischen geschichte," in *Theatres of Power*, cd. Pihlajamäki. Presumably, there is more detailed evidence in his Finnish publications. In the twentieth century, Finland was the most violent European country: in 1929-31 the homicide rate per 100,000 pop. was 10.1; in 1976-78 it was 3.0. The corresponding figures for the United States were 8.8 and 9.3 (figures based on statistics of the causes of death: Jean-Claude Chesnais, *Histoire de la violence en Occident de 1800 à nos jours* [Paris, 1981], 56, 61).

12. Robert Muchembled, *La violence au village: Sociabilité et comportements populaires en Artois du 15e au 17e siècle* (Turnhout, 1989), 19-21. The peaks in his graph, at the beginning of the sixteenth century and again at the beginning of the seventeenth, probably reflect an increased willingness to grant remittals.

13. See Gerd Schwerhoff, *Köln im Kreuzverhör: Kriminalität, Herrschaft und Gesellschaft in einer frühneuzeitlichen Stadt* (Bonn, 1991), 282-84. He admits that his sources, the city's "books of the dead," probably are incomplete. In fact, Schwerhoff calculates a (minimum) homicide rate of 10, but with a different population estimate the rate for the first period would rise to about 12. In both periods the absolute annual average was four homicides. Based on Banck's estimate (cited on p. 37) of 37,000 inhabitants in 1568-74, Schwerhoff put the Cologne population in both periods at 40,000. For the second period this is no doubt correct. Both Jan de Vries (*European Urbanization, 1500-1800 [London, 1984]*) and Paul Bairoch et al. (*La population des villes Européennes: Banque de données et analyse sommaire des résultats, 800-1850 [Geneva, 1988]* list 40,000 inhabitants in Cologne in 1600. Bairoch also lists 40,000 inhabitants in 1400 and 45,000 in 1500. De Vries, however, lists 30,000 in 1500. If the Cologne population was 33,000 in the 1470s, the homicide rate would be 12.

14. Marvin B. Becker, "Changing Patterns of Violence and Justice in Fourteenth- and Fifteenth-Century Florence," *Comparative Studies in Society and History* 18, no. 3 (1976): 287; John K. Brackett, *Criminal Justice and Crime in Late Renaissance Florence, 1537-1609* (Cambridge, 1992), 107, sees a "high incidence of violence" also in sixteenth-century Florence. He criticizes Becker for not adequately explaining it, but he provides no concrete figures.

15. See Peter Wettmann-Jungblut, "Penal Law and Criminality in Southwestern Germany: Forms, Patterns and Developments," paper presented at the conference *Justice pénale et construction de l'état, 12e-18e siècle*, Brussels, 19 February 1993.

16. Chesnais, *Histoire de la violence*, 40-67.

17. See, for example, Nicole Castan, *Les criminels de Languedoc: Les exigences d'ordre et les voies du ressentiment dans une société prérévolutionnaire, 1750-1790*

(Toulouse, 1980), 299–310. She speaks of a "relative decline of violence" and discusses this only in terms of percentages, such as the ratio of violent to property crime. The author of a recent article on homicide in the Lyon area in the seventeenth and eighteenth centuries (Françoise Bayard, "Les crimes de sang en Lyonnais et Beaujolais aux 17e et 18e siècles," in *Histoire et criminalité, de l'Antiquité au 20e siècle: Nouvelles approches,* ed. Benoît Garnot [Actes du colloque de Dijon-Chenove, 3–5 Octobre 1991], 273–81) is even obsessed with percentages, while he presents the absolute figures, apparently derived from trial records, in such a confusing manner that it is impossible to calculate a homicide rate from them.

18. Compare the discussion in Pieter Spierenburg, "Evaluation of the Conditions and Main Problems Relating to the Contribution of Historical Research to the Understanding of Crime and Criminal Justice—Report," in *Historical Research on Crime and Criminal Justice: Reports Presented to the Sixth Criminological Colloquium,* 1983, Council of Europe Publications (Strasbourg, 1985), 71–74.

19. See my discussion of the subject in Pieter Spierenburg, "Justice and the Mental World: Twelve Years of Research and Interpretation of Criminal Justice Data, from the Perspective of the History of Mentalities," *IAHCCJ Bulletin* 14 (Oct. 1991): 41–45.

20. Sharpe, "The History of Violence," 213–15, seems to think that a possible low level of tensions in early modern English villages would contradict the thesis of their being relatively violent. Stone, "A Rejoinder," 222–23, tries to bolster his argument with the statement that life was "not very pleasant" in these villages.

21. See Anton Blok, "Zinloos en zinvol geweld," *Amsterdams Sociologisch Tijdschrift* 18, no. 3 (1991): 189–207.

22. See the discussion by several contributors to the special issue of *De Sociologische Gids,* 1982.

23. Dirk Arend Berents, *Misdaad in de middeleeuwen: Een onderzoek naar de criminaliteit in het laat-middeleeuwse Utrecht* (n.p., 1976), 62.

24. Ruth Pike, "Capital Punishment in Eighteenth-Century Spain," in *Histoire Sociale/Social History* 18 (1985): 380–81.

25. Sjoerd Faber, *Strafrechtspleging en criminaliteit te Amsterdam, 1680–1811: De nieuwe menslievendheid* (Arnhem, 1983), 57. This leads him, too, to take all homicides together. In fact, Amsterdam sentences often describe just what had happened, without pinning a legal label on it. Thus, my distinction of murder cases from manslaughter cases (Pieter Spierenburg, *The Spectacle of Suffering: Executions and the Evolution of Repression: From a Preindustrial Metropolis to the European Experience* [Cambridge, 1984], 116–21) represents my own conclusion after reading the sentences.

26. Sibo van Ruller, *Genade voor recht: Gratieverlening aan ter dood veroordeelden in Nederland, 1806–1870* (Amsterdam, 1987), 122.

27. Beattie, *Crime and the Courts,* 80–81.

28. This distinction of two axes, it seems to me, is better suited to grasp the

complexities of violence, historically and cross-culturally, than is a mere dichotomy. The contributors to the special issue of the *Amsterdams Sociologisch Tijdschrift* on Dutch violence adhere to a dichotomy in one way or the other: Herman Franke, "Geweldscriminaliteit in Nederland: Een historisch-sociologische analyse," *Amsterdams Sociologisch Tijdschrift* 18, no. 3 (1991): 36, distinguishes instrumental from impulsive violence; Nico Wilterdink, "Inleiding [intoduction to special issue on violence in Dutch society]," *Amsterdams Sociologisch Tijdschrift* 18, no. 3 (1991): 9, adheres to the same distinction, but he equates impulsive with expressive; Blok, *Zinloos en zinvol geweld,* 194, contrasts violence called instrumental or technical from violence called expressive, ritual, symbolic or communicative. Blok is the only one who emphasizes that these are different aspects (rather than types) of violence, which can be combined in one and the same act.

29. Berents, *Misdaad in de middeleeuwen,* 65–66.

30. Natalie Zemon Davis, *Fiction in the Archives: Pardon Tales and Their Tellers in Sixteenth-Century France* (Stanford, 1987); Muchembled, *La violence au village.*

31. Stone, "A Rejoinder," 224.

32. Michael Mitterauer and Reinhard Sieder, *Vom Patriarchat zur Partnerschaft: Zum Strukturwandel der Familie* (Munich, 1977).

33. Stone, "Interpersonal Violence," 27. On spouse homicide and killings by women, see also Olwen Hufton, "Women and Violence in Early Modern Europe," in *Writing Women into History,* ed. Fia Dieteren and Els Kloek (Amsterdam, 1990), 82–84. For an analysis of a well-documented case of spouse homicide (though not in a strict sense, since the wife had her husband killed by a paid assassin) in France in 1728, see Benoît Garnot, *Un crime conjugal au 18e siècle* (Paris, 1993). The influence of divorce on the modern homicide rate is difficult to ascertain. However, if the total number of homicides on partners today is even lower than it might have been because divorce (and leaving the house by one partner in case of couples not legally married) prevents tensions from escalating to the homicide point, this can be taken as a confirmation of Elias's theory: nowadays we solve marital problems in a more "civilized" way, that is, through separation instead of murder. It should be added that informal separation appears to have been very common until the middle of the nineteenth century. That suggests that marriages had the greatest crisis-potential in terms of violence during the period 1850–1950.

34. Cockburn, "Patterns of Violence," 93–96.

35. The categorization of Eshof and Weimar, "Moord en doodslag," 20, goes a long way to meet this criterion. For the relationship killer-victim, they give the following percentages among the total of homicides committed in the Netherlands in 1989: family and in-laws (14); (ex-) partners (10); (ex-) lovers (5); rivals [in love] (5); friends and acquaintances (15); neighbors (4); criminal relationship (16); no relationship (16); and unclear (16). Another interesting observation is that, with deadly shootings where love problems or family conflicts were the issue, most killers and also 39 percent of the victims had a criminal background (p. 11).

36. For this reason it is particularly unfortunate that Peter C. Hoffer and N. E. H. Hull, *Murdering Mothers: Infanticide in England and New England, 1558-1803* (New York, London, 1981), define infanticide so as to include killings of children up to nine years old, even by nonparents. Compare the criticism of this book by Beattie, *Crime and the Courts,* 113n. For a brief but recent synthesis of the evidence on infanticide, see Hufton, "Women and Violence," 77-82.

37. See, for example, Berents, *Misdaad in de middeleeuwen,* 56-61; and J. W. Marsilje et al., *Bloedwraak, partijstrijd en pacificatie in laat-middeleeuws Holland* (Hilversum, 1990), (esp. the contributions by Blockmans and Glaudemans).

38. The argument would be like this: a prevalence of private violence means a low level of pacification; a low level of pacification causes a relatively low psychic threshold to violence in individual people; the evidence for this low threshold is the occurrence of many feuds.

39. See Benjo Maso, "Riddereer en riddermoed: Ontwikkelingen van de aanvalslust in de late middeleeuwen," *Sociologische Gids* 29, no. 3/4 (1982): 296-325.

40. This was true in Scotland, for example; see Keith Brown, *Bloodfeud in Scotland, 1573-1625: Justice and Politics in an Early Modern Society* (Edinburgh, 1986).

41. See Iain A. Cameron, *Crime and Repression in the Auvergne and the Guyenne, 1720-1790* (Cambridge, 1981), 192; Cockburn, "Patterns of Violence," 87.

42. In the Amsterdam autopsy reports, to be identified below as a superior source for homicide, there are several cases in which it is noted that the killer, though arrested, has been released as not guilty. The inclusion of such cases in a superior source is one more reason to count self-defense as homicide.

43. See the discussion in Franke, "Geweldscriminaliteit in Nederland."

44. The figure for prosecuted homicides in Amsterdam, 1650-1750 (Pieter Spierenburg, "Judicial Violence in the Dutch Republic: Corporal Punishment, Executions and Torture in Amsterdam, 1650-1750" [Ph.D. diss., University of Amsterdam, 1978], 84), includes attempts, but they are few in number.

45. Ton Zwaan, "Politiek geweld, maatschappelijke structuur en burgerlijke civilisatie: Een verkenning van de binnenstatelijke geweldpleging in de ontwikkeling van de Nederlandse samenleving, 1648-1960," *Amsterdams Sociologisch Tijdschrift* 9, no. 3 (Dec. 1982): 433-75; idem, "Politiek geweld in ontwikkelingsperspectief," *Amsterdams Sociologisch Tijdschrift* 10, no. 2 (1983): 353-68; idem, "Nogmaals politiek geweld in ontwikkelingsperspectief," *Amsterdams Sociologisch Tijdschrift* 10, no. 3 (1983): 597-601; Rudolf M. Dekker, "'Politiek geweld' en het proces van staatsvorming in de geschiedenis van de Nederlanden," *Amsterdams Sociologisch Tijdschrift* 10, no. 2 (1983): 335-52 (1983); idem, "Ontwikkelingsperspectief of gezichtsbedrog?," *Amsterdams Sociologisch Tijdschrift* 10, no. 3 (1983), 593-96 (1983).

46. Jan Boomgaard, "Het Amsterdamse criminaliteitspatroon in de late middeleeuwen," in *Misdaad, zoen en straf: Aspekten van de middeleeuwse strafrechtsgeschiedenis in de Nederlanden,* ed. Hermann A. Diederiks and H. W. Roodenburg (Hilversum, 1991), 111-12; Jean A. G. Jüngen, "Doodslagers en hun pakkans in het

16e eeuwse Amsterdam," in *Scherp Toezicht: Van "Boeventucht" tot "Samenleving en Criminaliteit,"* ed. Cyrille Fijnaut and Pieter Spierenburg (Arnhem, 1990), 84.

47. Jean A. G. Jüngen, "Een stad van justitie? Een verkenning van misdaad en maatschappij in Amsterdam in de 2e helft van de 16e eeuw" (Ph.D., diss., Free University Amsterdam, 1979), 41.

48. Spierenburg, "Judicial Violence," 84. In addition, there were five cases of attempted murder in which the accused confessed to have had the intention of killing the victim. The infanticide cases involve only actual killings, not the crime of secretly giving birth to a dead child without calling for assistance.

49. Faber, *Strafrechtspleging en criminaliteit,* 71.

50. Ibid., 94–95, 98; Marijke Gijswijt-Hofstra, *Wijkplaatsen voor vervolgden: Asielverlening in Culemborg, Veanen, Buren, Leerdam en IJsselstein van de 16e tot eind 18e eeuw* (Dieren, 1984), 156. Faber actually performed the research, but Gijswijt-Hofstra presents the exact figures.

51. During the period 1680–1790 (the 12 sample years) there were 24 default procedures for homicide and 15 in which the records give no information about the crime. Most of these 15 procedures also must have been for homicide. The only other crime giving rise to a large number of default cases was sodomy; these cases were identified as such in 1730 and other known waves of sodomy reports in the city did not occur in one of Faber's sample years. Thus, the annual average of homicides by fugitive suspects was between 2 and $3\frac{1}{4}$ per year. If we include the homicides by arrested killers, the figure is between 3 and $4\frac{1}{4}$ per year. The population averaged slightly over 200,000 during the period concerned. During the period 1751–1801 there were 28 homicides by fugitive suspects = about 0.5 per year; with inclusion of arrested killers: 1.5 per year. The population averaged 214,000.

52. Gijswijt-Hofstra, *Wijkplaats voor vervolgden,* 156. She does not indicate over which period the count was made, but according to personal communication from her it was the entire period of her research, the late sixteenth century to 1795. Since she had information only from default procedures available for the years mentioned above, this 8:1 ratio may not be significant.

53. The data are provisionally analyzed in Gijswijt-Hofstra, *Wijkplaatsen voor vervolgden,* 151–54.

54. This was also provisionally analyzed in Gijswijt-Hofstra, *Wijkplaatsen voor vervolgden,* 157.

55. Anton van den Hoeven, "Ten exempel en afschrik: Strafrechtspleging en criminaliteit in Haarlem, 1740–1795" (Ph.D., diss., University of Amsterdam, 1982), 40–41.

56. See Berents, *Misdaad in de middeleeuwen,* 66, and idem, *Het werk van de vos: Samenleving en criminaliteit in de late middeleeuwen* (Zutphen, 1985), 136, for the annual average of trials; see also Berents, *Misdaad in de middeleeuwen,* 57–60, 64, for his method of collecting the data, and idem, *Het werk van de vos,* 210n.103, for the information on the ratio of killers to victims. Basing his conclusions on older

literature, Berents estimates the population of the city of Utrecht in the first half of the fifteenth century at 10,000. According to Bairoch et al., Utrecht had 9,000 inhabitants in 1400 and 20,000 in 1500 (the latter figure confirmed in De Vries, *European Urbanization,* 271). Therefore I put the population figure in the first half of the fifteenth century at 12,000.

57. A. Graafhuis et al., "Misdaad en straf in de stad Utrecht in de tweede helft van de 16e eeuw," in *Recht en Slecht: Een registratie van misdaad en straf in de stad Utrecht, 1550–1575,* ed. Gemeentelijke Archiefdienst Utrecht (Utrecht, 1976), 41. Possibly, other cases of homicide in the city were prosecuted by the (provincial) Court of Utrecht.

58. Jan Boomgaard, *Misdaad en straf in Amsterdam: Een onderzoek naar de strafrechtspleging van de Amsterdamse schepenbank, 1490–1552* (Zwolle, 1992), 92–93 (table 4.1; I discarded the data for the years 1426–30 because they did not refer to fiscal years and most killers were unidentified). I am grateful to Jan Boomgaard for making the data available to me before he published his book.

59. De Vries, *European Urbanization,* 271, counts 14,000 inhabitants in 1500. Bairoch et al., *La population des villes Européennes* 53, count 3,000 in 1400 and 15,000 in 1500.

60. Jüngen, "Doodslagers en hun pakkans," 84–85. The margin of uncertainty is caused by the fact that, also with the trials, he wishes to consider only those homicides where the *locus delicti* was Amsterdam. In some cases the *locus delicti* was unknown. In some of the cases in which the perpetrator escaped a criminal trial, a financial settlement was concluded involving the killer, the magistrates, and the victim's relatives.

61. Jean A. G. Jüngen, "God betert: De Amsterdamse lijkschouwingsrapporten in de jaren 1560, 1570, 1580 en 1590 " (Ph.D. diss., Free University Amsterdam, 1982), 19. The period overlaps with the one he considered in his later article (Jüngen, "Doodslagers en hun pakkans") in which the data for 1560 were incorporated. The calculation of the homicide rate was complicated by the fact that the population estimates for 1600 given by de Vries (*European Urbanization*), which was 65,000, and by Bairoch et al. (*La population des villes Européennes*), which was 54,000, diverge widely. Since Amsterdam had over 100,000 inhabitants according to the census taken in 1622, the figure De Vries gives seems closer to reality. His estimate for 1550 is 30,000. Therefore, I take the population in 1575 to be 47,500.

62. GA Amsterdam, archive no. 5061, inventory nos. 640c-640g. The inventory also lists a 640h, but this collection of documents concerns diverse kinds of medical examinations from the second half of the eighteenth century and it clearly does not belong to the series of body inspections.

Diederiks (Hermann Diederiks, *Een stad in verval: Amsterdam omstreeks 1800, demografisch, economisch, ruimtelijk* [Amsterdam, 1982], 43–49), has figures on the causes of death among all persons deceased in Amsterdam (from GAA, PA: *Collegium Medicum,* a series beginning in 1776), but homicide is not listed as a separate category in these records (it must be implicitly included in the category "other," which usually amounts to some 20 percent).

A series beginning in 1777, the so-called *Haaldodenboeken* (GAA, DTB: nos. 1271–73), cannot be considered a relevant source for homicide. See Sjoerd Faber, "Kindermoord, in het bijzonder in de 18e eeuw te Amsterdam," *Bijdragen en Mededelingen betreffende de Geschiedenis der Nederlanden* 93 (1978): 237, and the literature referred to there. Apparently, no one knows exactly what this source is about and two authors preceding Faber certainly are mistaken. However, Faber's conclusion that the registers in question were kept for judicial purposes does not seem warranted either. Literally, the name of the registers means "books of the dead who were picked up." Most of these dead bodies were picked up from specific, private addresses. The absolute number averaged between 10 to 15 per month, so that it is highly unlikely that these were all cases considered potential court matters. The fact that in the archive the registers were listed among the demographic records also points at a nonjudicial origin. Moreover, Faber found that, as a rule, the infants registered in the autopsy books were also registered in the *Haaldodenboeken*. This indicates that the latter group was much more encompassing.

63. Faber provided me with his research notes, which were helpful in determining the total number of cases in advance as well as in coding variables as far as infanticide cases were concerned.

64. These individuals alternately styled themselves *de gezworen chirurgijns van den gerechte* (the sworn surgeons of the court) or *de gequalificeerden tot het schouwen der lijken der nedergeslagenen* (the committee authorized to inspect the bodies of the slain), clearly indicating that their task was to look for signs of a violent death.

65. In his thorough study of violent death in nineteenth-century Philadelphia, Roger Lane (*Violent Death in the City: Suicide, Accident, and Murder in Nineteenth-Century Philadelphia* [Cambridge, Mass., 1979]) also deals with suicide and accidents, but his homicide statistics are based on judicial records, not on medical records.

66. There were 146 cases of strangulation altogether. In one case, however, a killer was mentioned. The body of the victim in question had been found in the water. Consequently, all cases with the combination "strangulation/found in the water" were listed as possible homicides. One more indication that strangulation was normally associated with suicide comes from Zierik zee. The committee doing the autopsies in that town was said to be dealing with three types of bodies: those drowned; those who had hanged themselves; (the wounds of) those "slain." See J. A. M. Slenders, "Het Theatrum Anatomicum in de Noordelijke Nederlanden, 1555–1800," *Scripta Tironum* 17/18 (1989): 30.

67. Ordinance inserted in GA Amsterdam, archive 5061, no. 640G.

68. The autopsy reports for those three years contain five marginal notations informing us that a killer had been executed.

69. Faber ("Kindermoord," 228–29) emphasizes the lung proof's unreliability,

but I take it that errors in each direction were matched, so that the end result, in quantitative terms, is reliable. In any case, when the lung proof showed the child not to have breathed, it was stillborn, hence not murdered, in the eyes of contemporaries. The autopsy reports also contained seventeen inspections of fetuses found in the city. Considering them as cases of abortion or miscarriage, I have left them out of the infanticide file. Faber does include all bodies of infants from the autopsy records in his table of possible infanticides (p. 235). Hufton ("Women and Violence," 79) says that the lung proof was "increasingly disregarded," but she does not specify when and where.

70. Personal communication from Jean Jüngen, who did not mention this observation in his article.

71. In this case, the bodies of children who had never breathed were included in the figure. When they are left out, the percentages are 51.6 and 48.4, respectively.

72. Hoffer and Hull, *Murdering Mothers,* 183. Compare Hufton's remark ("Women and Violence," 77) about the discovery of dead bodies of children in a French city.

73. Franke, *Geweldscriminaliteit in Nederland,* 23.

74. Ibid., 28.

75. Centraal Bureau voor de Statistiek at Voorburg, Library, no. 4 F 52, series B3. The series begins in the 1960s, but the system of classification used up to 1978 does not have a separate category of homicide.

76. Franke, *Geweldscriminaliteit in Nederland,* 28.

77. Of course victims also die in the hospital today. On the other hand, some victims who might have been picked up by an ambulance today died at the spot and so were immediately inspected as a corpse in 1700. My measure assumes that these factors cancel each other out. A more serious limitation is that the measure is based on a situation in which a knife was the common murder weapon. Discussing the issue under scrutiny here, Lane (*Violent Death in the City,* 80) points at the fact that many homicides in nineteenth-century Philadelphia involved injuries that even today are hard to treat medically; supposedly, this would mean that less than a quarter died "unnecessarily."

78. On the other hand, in the early modern period Amsterdam was a city surrounded only by rural areas. It would be fair to take the entire metropolitan area of Amsterdam today as the unit of comparison. No doubt, this would lower the contemporary homicide rate.

79. Gijswijt-Hofstra, *Wijkplaatsen voor vervolgden,* 139–49. For an elaborate analysis of contextual factors in nineteenth-century northern France, see Anne Parrella, "Industrialization and Murder: Northern France, 1815–1904," *Journal of Interdisciplinary History* 22, no. 4 (1992): 627–54.

80. See my review of Gijswijt-Hofstra's book in *IAH-CCJ Newsletter* 10 (1986): 27–31.

81. Data extracted from: GA Amsterdam, archive no. 5061, nos. 308–515, 581–

98, 605–14. It should be remembered that the sentence book for the years 1706–9 is missing.

82. There were two, three, and five female killers in the three periods, respectively.

83. The cases are: a man who had had a fight with his cousin in a tavern; a man who had quarreled with his mother-in-law; a man who stabbed his wife's sister to death and then committed suicide. There is little information on the last case; the killer and his victim may have been lovers.

84. These percentages are unadjusted for missing cases. The percentage of cases with information on the killer's birthplace missing are 0, 8, and 7, respectively.

85. One case of rational violence took place already in 1664, when a hired killer shot a Jew at the request of another Jew. GA Amsterdam, archive 5061, no. 316, fol. 64 et seq.

86. In 1742 an old man managed to overpower a younger man whom he hated. He tied his victim to the wall, chopped off his head with a chisel, and skinned him. GA Amsterdam, archive 5061, no. 402, fol. 106 et seq.

87. GA Amsterdam, archive 5061, no. 611, sentence 41.

88. Ruller, *Genade voor recht,* 126–29. Since petitioning for pardon was a routine matter and many were rejected, the representativeness of van Ruller's sample is greater than Gijswijt-Hofstra's sample.

89. I generally agree with Franke's argument: while certain groups among the population are practicing violence with renewed vigor, concern about violence among the majority of the population is higher than ever (Franke, "Geweldscriminaliteit in Nederland," 18–19 and 36–40).

90. This is the conclusion of most of the contributors to the special issue of the *Amsterdams Sociologisch Tijdschrift* 18, no. 3 (1991). Generally, ethnic and racial diversities are important factors if we want to explain contemporary trends in homicide. Compare Roger Lane's findings: in the United States, where the homicide rate has always been higher than in Europe, racial tensions have been more acute as well. Due largely to economic circumstances such as being denied employment, blacks have made up an increasing proportion of American killers (Roger Lane, "Urban Homicide in the Nineteenth Century: Some Lessons for the Twentieth," in *History and Crime: Implications for Criminal Justice Policy,* ed. James A. Inciardi and Charles E. Faupel [Beverly Hills, Calif., 1980], 103–7).

91. Compare the remarks by Schwerhoff, *Köln im Kreuzverhör,* 285–86.

PART TWO

Shorter-Term Assessments: Fourteenth to Twentieth Centuries

4

The Hundred Years' War and Crime in Paris, 1332–1488

Esther Cohen

The urban-rural dichotomy posited by modern historians often presents the medievalist with a perplexing problem. Urban settlements before 1500 were frequently small, partly agricultural, and far more similar to modern rural settlements than to urban ones. Anyone wishing to delineate urban crime in the later Middle Ages, therefore, must concentrate upon the larger cities of the West. These urban centers were affected by a number of "modern" trends, such as massive immigration and mobility. They allow us to study the impact of war upon a sedentary population in a way almost impossible concerning contemporary villages. While rural populations simply fled before the armies of the time, urban ones remained in place. Thus, the effects upon people of a period of protracted warfare, such as the Hundred Years' War, can be gauged in the crime records of Paris far better than in the sparse notations of contemporary rural crime.

◆ The Hundred Years' War

Studies of the social impact of the Hundred Years' War in France have all stressed the same picture. The war, lasting off and on for well over a century, brought about the dislocation of entire sectors of the civilian population, both rural and urban. While the earlier stages of the war affected mainly western France—Normandy, Poitou, and the Bordelais—by the beginning of the fifteenth century there was hardly any part of France that had not been affected by the war. Armies on both sides lived off the countryside, with the resultant pauperization of the lower classes in the rural sector and the starvation of their counterparts in the cities.

It has been taken for granted that the war was one of the great "schools of crime" of the period. Not only did the war refugees and victims turn to theft and brigandage in order to survive, but, more significantly, the young people trained in warfare and legalized violence turned to organized crime with the cessation of hostilities. This was undoubtedly the case with the Free Companies that ranged all over southern France even after the end of the war, holding everyone, Pope and cardinals not exempt, to ransom.[1]

This development was thus not only quantitative, but also qualitative. Together with the increased levels of crime in both urban and rural surroundings there was a growing professionalization and coherence of criminal groups. If not yet organized bands, many nuclei of semiprofessional criminals do appear during the war as part of a proto-gang organization.[2]

This picture is borne out by practically all the chronicles of the period. One and all they bewail the sufferings inflicted upon the innocent by the war and warn against the criminalizing effect it had upon surviving civilians. So far, no attempt has been made to verify these impressions against the few surviving criminal registers of the period. Did the hardships inflicted upon urban populations, especially the poor among them, actually cause a significant increase in criminal activity?

The main difficulty in attempting to answer such a question is that the war was not the only factor involved. The second half of the fourteenth century and the first half of the fifteenth were also periods of recurrent plague, economic slump, and monetary devaluation. There is no way of disentangling the variables. In addition, the Hundred Years' War was not one war but several campaigns interspersed with long periods of peace in between. With lulls as long as twenty years, it is hard to gauge the immediate effects of war. In a country with continuous criminal series, such as England, it is possible to see the interchanging effects of war and truce times upon criminal activities. Indeed, as Barbara Hanawalt has shown, the significant increase in crime came at times of truce, when companies were temporarily disbanded and the soldiers found themselves unemployed.[3]

The lack of continuous series in France makes this sort of analysis impossible, but it is highly unlikely that the same pattern would recur across the Channel. One must bear in mind that the English population felt the war only at a remove. The resultant slump in the price of wool or the presence of unemployed soldiers in truce times were minor disasters compared with the devastation of entire regions in France that were forced to feed two, and sometimes three, armies. The companies of soldiers did not restrict their private activities to periods of truce and inactivity. The practice of taking hostages, not only among the rich and noble but also among the peasantry, and extorting as much as possible from them before letting them go (or killing them) was something the English had never experienced. The French, on the other hand, had to put up with this type of violence in periods of both warfare and relative peace. Requests for royal pardons during the 1380s, after two decades of truce, show time and again that local townsmen or peasants in the provinces killed violent soldiers in self-defense.

To sum up, the Hundred Years' War for the French population was a total war in more than one sense. It affected severely the civilian population, regardless of truces. By the mid-fifteenth century, it had left no region of France unscathed. But did it cause an increase in criminal activity among the urban civilian population? In order to answer this question, I have tried to follow the outlines of crime in the biggest French urban center of the later Middle Ages, Paris.

◆ Paris: Background and Sources

Paris was hardly a typical French city of the time, but it was undoubtedly the largest urban center in France. At the outbreak of the war, it numbered approximately 200,000 inhabitants.[4] Though no complete records exist, partial tax records and rental prices indicate that the population underwent sharp changes during the war. In 1380 Charles V enclosed the northern suburbs in a long-needed new wall that nearly doubled the area of the city. But between the beginning of the fifteenth century and the 1440s, when the bourgeois of Paris counted 24,000 deserted houses, the city was severely depopulated.[5] A royal ordinance of 1438 ordered the destruction or repair of all uninhabited, dangerously decrepit houses in the city. There were many such houses, the ordinance stated, due not only to the war and the plague, but also to high rents.[6] By 1467 the city was so badly depopulated that the king offered all new settlers a full pardon for any crimes, theft and murder included, barring only lèse-majesté, committed before their settlement in the capital.[7] If rental prices are an indication, though, by the end of the century the situation had improved. Rentals, which had dropped sharply in the middle years of the century, once more resumed their levels of the beginning of the fifteenth century.[8]

Paris did not suffer directly during the early stages of the war. During the fourteenth century the city absorbed refugees from the neighboring areas and from the west, but very little more. The revolt of Étienne Marcel and the Jacquerie in the 1350s were too speedily put down to harm the city in any significant way. The tax burden for the running of the war was distributed all over France. By 1360, the first large-scale stage of the war was generally over.

The picture changed drastically at the beginning of the fifteenth century. From 1405 till 1438 Paris changed hands repeatedly among the Burgundians, the Armagnacs, and the English. While held by one power, it was often besieged by another, with the inevitable results of siege warfare for the civilian population. Even after the end of the war, the city was threatened once more with siege by the League of the Public Weal in 1465.

The repeated assaults on Paris certainly had their effects. As early as 1383, and subsequently in 1411 and 1418, there were complaints voiced at the Parlement concerning the presence of soldiers and pillagers within the city. During the same years the population of prostitutes was swelled as rape victims from neighboring towns fled to the metropolis. Similar complaints were voiced during the siege of 1465. During siege periods food prices rose sky high, with the inevitable hunger riots and mass punishments in their wake. The bourgeois of Paris counted more than 1,200 people with their children who fled the city in the spring of 1431, immediately after the city's relief by the duke of Bedford. The situation did not improve after the Armagnac reconquest of 1436, for the brigands of the countryside continued to hold up all food convoys and to make incursions into the city. As late as 1438 there was famine in Paris, and Guillebert de Metz estimated that there were 80,000 beggars in the city.[9]

The city had thus been affected by war in various ways. It had attracted refugees who sought safety within its walls. It had been given new walls and fortifications by Charles V and his successors. It had been abandoned by masses of hungry people. It had been starved, conquered, and subjected to the corporate violence of armies and the individual violence of armed men. It is a reasonable assumption that such pressures over a century would affect the world of crime. One would expect to find at the end of the war more masterless soldiers, more professionally trained criminals, and more cohesive networks of crime. Furthermore, one would certainly expect a rise in the frequency and violence of crime.

The sporadic nature of the sources makes the verification of the latter assumption impossible. There is no way of telling whether the frequency of crime in Paris increased during the war years. What can be verified is the nature of crime within the city.

Of the three surviving criminal registers of the fourteenth century, only one is useful for the study of Paris. The register of the Parlement, covering the years 1319–50,[10] concerns mostly cases involving noblemen, clergy, and appellants from all of northern France. Very few simple people could afford to take their case to the Parlement, and there were other, more immediate instances to try the people of Paris. The Châtelet register of the years 1389–92 is even more problematic. Parisians were certainly present among the criminals tried on the Châtelet docket, but among them also were noblemen from the provinces, notorious traitors, and criminals from the countryside. Furthermore, the register, while undoubtedly genuine and contemporary, is likely a tendentious selection of notorious cases meant to prove the zealousness of the Châtelet authorities in prosecuting crime. It would stretch credibility too far to assume that indeed during three years only 127 criminals were tried in the central courthouse of the city, and that 87 percent of this number merited and received death sentences.[11]

The only Parisian register of the fourteenth century to throw light upon day-to-day local justice is the register of the seigneurial jurisdiction of Saint-Martin-des-Champs from 1332 to 1357. This small enclave of ecclesiastical justice within the city, one of many, possessed the privilege of high justice—namely, it could try even capital crimes within its own area. Though the area subject to the justice of Saint-Martin-des-Champs was a fairly small segment of the city, the very geographic and chronological continuity of the register enables us to reconstruct a valid picture of criminal justice.

In theory, the register of Saint-Martin should have provided exciting reading. In the 1330s the whole area was still outside the city walls. It was incorporated only in 1380, with the construction of the new wall. But before and after that date, the area bore a well-deserved evil reputation. It was probably the stablest red-light district in the city, functioning in this capacity well into the modern era. There was good reason for changing the name of the rue Trasseputain to rue Trassenonnain, but the rue Chapon was probably the epicenter of prostitution in the area. The intersecting rue Beaubourg was notorious for a variety of crimes, fencing, and gaming halls.

And yet, very little of this activity appears in the register. Most of the homicides were the result of overenthusiastic brawling, in which the victim was hit too hard and received too little care. Hardly any prostitutes appear in the register, unless they were found plying their trade outside the permitted areas, and the few rapes reported concern honest women. There were some thefts, but for every theft there were three street fights. Bearing in mind that the jurisdiction of Saint-Martin was empowered to try also capital crimes, one cannot even assume that either professional or serious crime was funneled to another court.

Other seigneurial jurisdictions within the city have left some registers from the early fifteenth century, each of them covering a few years within a specific area of the city, but none of them is as complete as the Saint-Martin register.[12] They all reflect the same type of criminal activity as the register of Saint-Martin. The late fifteenth century, however, has left perhaps the most interesting source of all—the arrest register, *registre d'écrous*, of the Châtelet of Paris for the second half of 1488. While many such registers have survived for the sixteenth century, this register is the only one for the fifteenth century.[13] It notes, on a daily basis, all the people arrested and imprisoned at the Châtelet jail, adding occupation, address, offense, duration of imprisonment, and further procedure in each case. The arrest register of the Châtelet in 1488 covers the period from mid-June to the end of the following January for both civil and criminal offenses. The two categories are often hard to distinguish, but, roughly speaking, the cases break down in half between civil and criminal.

Naturally, an arrest register is essentially different from court records. And yet, there was little difference at the time between a record of imprisonment (almost invariably pretrial) and a record of cases brought to court. Most of the entries in Saint-Martin-des-Champs note only the criminal's name, offense, and the procedure adopted, be it temporary release pending trial, permanent release, or punitive sentence. The entries of the arrest register a century and a half later note roughly the same information. In fact, most criminal registers of the later Middle Ages reflect the same attitude, which made little or no distinction between imprisonment and judicial record. Even the records of the Parlement of Paris, undoubtedly the most sophisticated jurisdiction in late medieval France, are a mixture of detention records and trial protocols. It is this essential similarity that allows us to compare judicial and arrest records in search of a development over time.

◆ The Nature of Crime

Violence was the normative method of settling personal disputes in all classes of society in 1332, as it was in 1488. Aggression, both verbal and physical, was part and parcel of normal social intercourse.[14] In this sense, legislation diverged from societal perceptions. While two drinkers in a tavern considered a brawl a suitable way of settling the question of payment, and two fishwives competing for clientele at the port thought a fistfight an acceptable means of venting their mutual frustration, the law did not agree. The result of this tension between law and norm is the full and detailed registration of quotidian violence.

The most salient feature of almost all criminal records of Paris during a century and a half is dictated by this tension. The similarity of registers is all the more striking because judicial terminology changed so little throughout the period, but beyond the formal resemblance lies a constant pattern of crimes for which people were arrested and tried by the various jurisdictions of Paris.

All seigneurial registers present a clear-cut pattern. The majority of cases concern brawls, street fights, and casual violence. Fifty-seven percent of the cases tried at Saint-Martin-des-Champs fit this category; 76.6 percent of all cases tried in the jurisdiction of the Temple between 1411 and 1420 and 53.7 percent of the cases tried before the chapter of Notre-Dame in the years 1404–6 concerned brawls.[15] All of the cases in the latter jurisdiction involved only two people in each case, indicating the small-scale nature of the fights. The same is true for Saint-Martin, where more than two-thirds of the fights involved only two people.

Thirty years after the end of the war, the picture of urban crime remained unaltered. In 1488 almost one-third of all criminal cases concerned quarrels, and almost invariably both sides were arrested, each at the other's accusation. The result is that the percentage of people arrested for brawling is even larger than the percentage of cases. More than half the people jailed at the Châtelet were brought in for brawling, and three-fourths of all brawls involved only two people. In other words, the most typical cause for arrest in 1488 was the same as in 1332—a street brawl involving two or sometimes three people.

"Brawl" is too broad a term to define the type of street violence that came before the courts. In most cases, both parties to the litigation knew each other, either as a result of propinquity or through work connections. While people resorted to violence with great ease, it was neither aimless nor detached. Emotionally motivated, it was based upon a variety of contacts and feelings. Propinquity, coprofessional loyalty, jealousy, and revenge all played a role. It could occasionally stem from nothing more than rowdiness or drinking, while at other times it might be carefully planned and premeditated; but it was almost never violence for its own sake, wreaked upon total strangers. It took place in an extremely intimate world, one far removed from any extant underworld. Even the few rape cases in the registers were perpetrated by people who had had previous acquaintance with their victims, usually the girls next door. There was little room for aimless destructiveness.

The intimate character of violence among acquaintances is most clearly seen in the register of Saint-Martin-des-Champs. The same names appear time and again, once as offenders and another time as guarantors for other offenders' appearance for trial. In one case, two men suspected of theft were released pending trial, each standing surety for the other's return. In another, equally typical, case, a man arrested for assault filed a countercomplaint against his victim, using almost precisely the same accusation that had been leveled at him.[16] It is obvious that the justice of Saint-Martin-des-Champs at the outbreak of the war dealt mainly with the quarrels and arguments of neighbors, all living within a few streets of each other, familiar with each other, and just as ready to beat each other up as to stand surety for the same.

The picture is almost identical in 1488.[17] In some cases violence assumed the form of carefully planned and executed vendettas, as in the case of the cuckolded husband who with his friends and colleagues ambushed his wife's clerical lover. But far more often the causes were trivial incidents that sparked a row. One man beat another's wife, when she came to call her husband away from a joint game of *paume*. Another had his debtor beaten up in order to speed the recovery of his debt. People in the same trade and people who lived on the same street were the likeliest to come to fisticuffs. Three *rôtisseurs* beat up a fourth in the street, and two porters fought in the midst of the grain market. Physical proximity was likely to have a similar effect. In a chain of complaints and countercomplaints three people from the rue Neuve Notre-Dame were arrested: a chambermaid started out by slapping and insulting a housewife, calling her a loose, vagrant woman and insinuating that she slept with the canons of the Notre-Dame chapter, and ended by having her victim arrested. The housewife retaliated two days later and had the chambermaid arrested, too, but not before her husband had beaten up the chambermaid. The husband was the last in the chain of arrests.

Even indoors, violence was more often conducted in the public domain of the tavern than in the home. Though domestic violence undoubtedly existed, very little of it surfaces in criminal registers. It is noteworthy, though, that the domestic quarrels appearing in the register were not necessarily violent. In more than one case, people turned to the police to restore a broken family, return an errant husband home from his mistress's bed, or separate adulterous lovers. When an irate father had his errant married daughter, her illicit lover, their landlord, and a gossipy neighbor arrested, all at one blow, the quarrel was obviously based upon long-standing relationships. In fact, only the cuckolded husband, away on a pilgrimage to Compostella, was missing.

The normative character of street violence is evidenced also by the high proportion of women involved in those fights.[18] The altercations were obviously the result, not of premeditated attacks, but of the daily clashes in street and marketplace, where women were just as likely to be involved as men. The women of Saint-Martin appear frequently in the register, and not necessarily as victims. The same is true for the tradeswomen of Paris in 1488. As in the case of men, the fights are usually based either upon propinquity or professional conflicts. Two midwives tore at each other, literally tooth and nail; prostitutes and fishwives had frequent fights. There is no clear sexual limitation; women quarreled as easily with men as with other women. As in the case of men, most of the fighting was fairly harmless, though a few serious stabbings also took place. Noticeably, though, women fought each other in daytime. As in the case of masculine disputes, many of these fights were conducted in the streets rather than in the home. The one notable difference between 1332 and 1488 is the presence of prostitutes, notably scarce in the earlier sources and visibly present in the later. One-third of all women arrested in 1488 were prostitutes.[19] Since prostitution was not a crime, the prostitutes of Saint-Martin in the fourteenth century were unlikely to turn up in criminal records unless they were caught breaking city ordinances, working after hours or in forbidden areas, or causing a public disturbance. In such a case, they would not be arrested by the neighborhood authorities but by the night watch, which would promptly incarcerate them at the Châtelet.

Often the violence was purely verbal, involving accusations of moral turpitude or simply insults. The epithets hurled at each other by the men and women of Saint-Martin also indicated mutual familiarity; a neighbor was not just a whore or a villain but was the target of far more specific accusations, such as being a perjurer or a sorceress. The same is true for 1488. One man taunted another by claiming that several whoremasters were "riding" his wife; in another case a woman added to the usual insults of "vagrant" and "whore" the colorful epithet of *Marie meurtrière d'enffens,* capping the insult with an accusation of double infanticide. A resident of a small neighborhood on the Ile de la Cité came to trial before the tiny jurisdiction of Saint-Eloi for calling his neighbor a vagrant whore who deserved to be burned for having caused hail to destroy the vineyards. The very wording of the accusations indicates mutual acquaintance.

But even when violence turned physical, it usually resulted in very little damage, rarely involving the use of "real" weapons. Beating with sticks or work implements or throwing candlesticks and cutlery were far more common than stabbings. This is as true of night-time assault as of daytime violence. On a typical night, the Paris night watch was likely to arrest a group of rowdies making noise or beating each other up after curfew, a few drunks reeling in the streets, often in the company of prostitutes in the same condition, and some more violent drunks who either threatened or attacked prostitutes. Nocturnal drinking thus often led to violence, sometimes against companions, sometimes against innocent bystanders, and sometimes against those who tried to interfere, as in the case of the woman who complained about the noise generated by an illegal brothel in her neighborhood and was beaten up by the irate clients.

Tavern brawls were as common in Paris as in any other medieval city. Legislation notwithstanding, open taverns could operate without the intervention of the night watch, as long as there was no disturbance. Even in the case of a fight, the watch was not always called in. Instead, one or the other party would complain next day at the Châtelet. One summer night in 1488 three men (one of them a policeman) and a prostitute took a fourth to drink at a tavern. When the time came to pay, claimed the latter, he had taken out his wallet and one of the others grabbed his money, hit him, and fled.

This is perhaps the greatest difference between the records of seigneurial jurisdictions and those of the Châtelet. Almost all the fights recorded in the former took place in the street, in daytime. This does not mean that the streets and taverns of Saint-Martin were peaceful at night, at least during the fourteenth century. In the first place, late-night drinkers from other parts of town would be arrested not by sergeants of the local justice, but by the city's night watch, which would have them transferred and tried at the jurisdiction of their residence. But more important, night-time drunks, unless they caused harm, were usually not brought to trial. Hence, they would appear only in an arrest register, not in a trial record. A very small proportion of the violence cases was treated as courtworthy. Thus, a plaintiff in a civil suit for debt could be an escaped assault suspect from two months earlier and could walk away from the courthouse unharmed. An old assault was a forgotten assault, and the authorities refused to waste time dealing with it. In most cases the offenders were punished with a small fine and released the following morning or a day later.[20] Students transferred to the official's court never came up to trial at all. In fact, the judges' attitudes coincided more with the popular attitude than with the legal point of view. Violence was not even deplorable. It was part of life, one of the ways one dealt with other people. Government policies and ordinances were used to curb it when it got out of hand, but there was no attempt to stamp it out. Violence was a legal not a normative crime.

. The negligent stance of the Paris authorities had to do with the character not only of the offense but also of the offenders. Occasionally vagrants and professional criminals did turn up at the Châtelet in 1488, as they had done in 1389, but with a very great difference. These were all loners, working by themselves. There is no hint of band organization, or of any attempt to pursue criminals active in the countryside. Overwhelmingly, the cases originating outside the walls were civil.[21] The brawlers within the walls were practically all local residents, trades- and craftspeople of the city, and no vagrants. Almost all those arrested for brawling had fixed addresses and occupations. Like the residents of Saint-Martin-des-Champs in the 1330s, they posed no permanent threat to the public order.

Every type of criminal activity most typical of Paris at the end of the fifteenth century was just as typical of the city one hundred and fifty years earlier. Minor proportions of thefts, rapes, and murders occurred before and after the war, but there is no clearly discernible change. Mostly, the pattern of street fights as the main preoccupation of jails and courthouses remains constant.

Where does the war come in? Surprisingly enough, there is little evidence of soldier crime on a large scale, either in the records of the early fifteenth century or in the arrest register of 1488. According to an ordinance dating from the Hundred Years' War, all sergeants and watchmen were ordered to arrest any man in armor who had no lord and did not know the watchword. A century later, the Parlement was still issuing ordinances against the "men of war, both infantry and mounted," who were responsible for a "multitude of crimes" in the Paris area.[22] The city ordinances complained time and again about the dangers presented by armed men, but the evidence of the registers shows remarkably little violence on the part of soldiers, far less than on the part of students, a permanent presence in the city.

It is possible, however, that a postwar period would find in evidence not soldiers in service but discharged bands of soldiers. The only sign of gang formation and of criminalization via army careers surfaces in the most atypical of registers, that of the Châtelet of 1389–92. The register contains the trials of a number of criminals connected in a loose network, a sort of protogang. Here one finds all the elements a historian would expect in wartime: mobility, army careers begun at adolescence, and criminalization during young adulthood. While most of the criminals connected with this network resided in Paris prior to their arrest, they committed most of their crimes in the countryside, where the chances of getting caught were much smaller. The urban surroundings might have spawned the beginnings of band connections, but professional criminal activity was not carried out within the walls. The same is true also for the individual soldier-criminals with no band connections; they might have been tried and sentenced in Paris, but their criminal careers had nothing to do with the city.

Nor is this picture typical of Paris alone. Rossiaud has noted that while the Coquillards band successfully terrorized the countryside around Dijon during the middle of the fifteenth century, the crime registers of Dijon reflect no professional band activities within the city. The city was a meetingplace for exchange of information, rest, and distribution of spoils, but the actual thefts and robberies were committed on expeditions to the countryside.[23]

◆ Interpretation

Is one to believe that a century and a half of warfare, causing one of the greatest economic, social, and political upheavals France ever suffered before World War II, had failed to affect the picture of urban crime in any way? There is a great deal of chronicle evidence that the activities of war bands in the countryside had considerable impact. Furthermore, we know that the war affected Paris directly, especially in its latter stages. What had happened to all those people who had turned to violence and theft when food prices rose outrageously as a result of the devastation of the countryside? And what had happened to all the masterless soldiers, refugees, camp followers, and the like who were bound to crowd the cities during and after the war?

The simplest answer is that the French countryside was far more affected than the cities, and received far less royal attention when it came to reconstruction. Throughout the war, chroniclers noted the suffering of the countryside. "See if your woes are equal to mine, you who live in towns and castles," wrote the prior of a religious house destroyed by the English in 1358.[24] As a rule, the Free Companies also restricted their activities to the rural area. The suffering of the big cities was far less acute, and hence the impact of the war upon their population less significant. Furthermore, the constant presence of garrisons within the capital should have helped keep the peace.

On the contrary, it might be argued that the flight of the rural population to the cities should have aggravated the food shortages and created a considerable human pool for criminal activities. And soldiers were not only remarkably inept in putting down theft and brigandage but were also quite a threat to public order in themselves. True, efforts of reconstruction centered round the cities,[25] but even so, it is unlikely that the war should have had no long-term effects upon urban crime.

In my opinion, the explanation has less to do with the reality of postwar Paris than with the perceptions of justice and crime maintained by the authorities. An early fifteenth-century allegorical-satirical poem, *Le songe véri-*

table, has Poverty searching for Truth all over Paris. At the Châtelet, Poverty found Deceit, who told her she was a fool to search for Truth at the seat of Justice.[26] Needless to say, Poverty drew a blank at all other seats of justice as well. The poem undoubtedly exemplifies the different views of ideal and applied justice. In fact, Paris judicial authorities had very little interest in abstract definitions of justice. The word had many meanings, but insofar as the lower judicial authorities were concerned, the main aim of justice, as a bureaucratic apparatus, was the maintenance of order. Crime as lawbreaking had very little to do with daily justice.

This preoccupation with maintaining order, rather than justice, appears clearly when one considers the whole spectrum of crimes for which people were arrested. In the 1330s, some people were arrested for fencing, rape, pandering, theft, and murder. All of those categories appear also in 1488, but in minute percentages. The most common reason, after brawling, for getting arrested in 1488 was the infraction of city ordinances. Walking abroad after curfew, especially if drunk, carrying weapons (an ordinance far more honored in the breach than in observance), playing dice in public on a feast day or on a workday, wearing forbidden clothing, even swimming in the Seine—all these acts earned their perpetrators a night in the cells and a fine in the morning. Obviously, seigneurial jurisdictions were not concerned with the upholding of city ordinances, but the police force of Paris was far more interested in observance and order than in the prosecution of actual crime.

The same policy can be perceived in the stationing of the night watch. If the control of crime were the object, one would expect to find the night watch stationed in the high-crime areas of the city—the waterfront, the red-light district, the city walls, and the student areas on the Left Bank. Instead, the eight stations were placed around the centers of power. Only two were placed at a notorious area of criminal activity, the cemetery of Saints-Innocents. Of the rest, two were located at the Châtelet, two on the Ile de la Cité, and two near the Hôtel de Ville.[27] The power of the law was geared to keep order so as to uphold authority.

In this sense, there was no discernible change over a century and a half. The striking similarity in criminal registers at the beginning and after the end of the Hundred Years' War says next to nothing about the social patterns of crime in the city. What this similarity indicates is a static perception of crime—not as a violation of law or justice, but merely as a transgression against the power of authority.

When considering influences on long-term trends in crime, then, one must take into account two types of factors. The external ones, such as a war and its after effects, may influence short-term trends. But in the long run the internal factor, or the perception of what crime is, may survive much longer, regardless of external influences, to dictate the patterns of crime and law enforcement.

Notes

1. See Jacques Monicat, *Les grandes compagnies du Velay, 1358–1392,* 2d ed. (Paris, 1928); P. Champion, "Notes pour servir à l'histoire des classes dangereuses en France des origines à la fin du XVe siècle," appendix to Lazar Sainéan, *Les sources de l'argot ancien* (Paris, 1912). For general surveys of the Hundred Years' War in France, see Edouard Perroy, *The Hundred Years' War* (London, 1965); Philippe Contamine, *La guerre de cent ans* (Paris, 1968); Jean Favier, *La guerre de cent ans* (Paris, 1980).

2. Robert Boutruche, "The Devastation of Rural Areas during the Hundred Years' War and the Agricultural Recovery of France," in *The Recovery of France in the Fifteenth Century,* ed. P. S. Lewis (London, 1971), 23–59; Jacqueline Misraki, "Criminalité et pauvreté en France à l'époque de la Guerre de Cent Ans," in *Etudes sur l'histoire de la pauvreté,* ed. Michel Mollat, 2 vols. (Paris, 1974), 1:535–46; Bronislaw Geremek, *Les marginaux parisiens aux XIVe et XVe siècles* (Paris, 1976), 111–53. The most recent study of crime during the reign of Charles VI is Claude Gauvard, *De Grâce Especial: Crime, état et société en France à la fin du moyen âge,* 2 vols. (Paris, 1991).

3. Barbara Hanawalt, *Crime and Conflict in English Communities, 1300–1348* (Cambridge, Mass., 1979).

4. This estimate is based upon the 1328 hearth-count. The number has been debated by several historians, on the grounds of improbability alone, and the alternative of 80,000 suggested. See Guy Fourquin, "La population de la région parisienne aux environs de 1328," *Le moyen âge* 62 (1956): 63–91; P. Dollinger, "Le chiffre de la population de Paris au XIVe siècle," *Revue historique* 216 (1956): 35–44; for a rebuttal, see Bronislaw Geremek, "Paris, la plus grand ville de l'occident médiéval?" *Acta Poloniae Historica* 18 (1968): 18–37.

5. A. Tuetey, ed., *Journal d'un bourgeois de Paris* (Paris, 1881), 192.

6. Archives Nationales, Paris, Y4, fol. 30v–31r.

7. Jean de Roye, *Chronique scandaleuse,* ed. Bernard de Mandrot, 2 vols. (Paris, 1894–95), 1:174.

8. Jean Favier, *Paris au XVe siècle, 1380–1500* (Paris, 1974), 61–62.

9. Henri Sauval, *Histoire et recherches des antiquités de la ville de Paris,* 3 vols. (Paris, 1724), 2:597; Thomas Basin, *Histoire des règnes de Charles VII et de Louis XI,*

4 vols., ed. Jules Quicherat (Paris, 1855–59), 1:14; Jean de Roye, *Chronique scandaleuse,* 1:111; *Bourgeois de Paris,* passim and 250; Guillebert de Metz, "Description de Paris sous Charles VI," in A. Leroux de Lincy and L. M. Tisserand, *Paris et ses historiens aux XIVe et XVe siècles* (Paris, 1867), 232; Auguste Longnon, *Paris pendant la domination anglaise (1420–1436)* (Paris, 1878).

10. Monique Langlois and Yvonne Lanhers, eds., *Confessions et jugements de criminels au Parlement de Paris (1319–1350)* (Paris, 1971).

11. See M. Duplès-Agier, ed., *Registre criminel du Châtelet de Paris du 3 Septembre 1389 au 18 Mai 1392,* 2 vols. (Paris, 1861–64).

12. See Louis Tanon, *Histoire des justices des anciennes églises et communautés de Paris* (Paris, 1883).

13. Archives Nationales, Y5266. All the modern arrest registers are kept at the Archives de la Police.

14. Norbert Elias, *The Civilising Process,* 2 vols. (Oxford, 1982), 1:191–205.

15. Bronislaw Geremek, "La lutte contre le vagabondage à Paris aux XIVe et XVe siècles," in *Ricerche storiche ed economiche in memoria di Corrado Barbagallo,* 2 vols., ed. Luigi de Rosa (Naples, 1970), 2:211–36; Tanon, *Histoire de justices,* introduction.

16. Louis Tanon, ed., *Registre criminel de la justice de Saint-Martin-des-Champs* (Paris, 1887), 4, 66–67.

17. The following picture is a composite based upon a number of late fifteenth-century registers: X^{2a} 56–58 (Parlement criminel), Y5266 (Châtelet), Z^{10} 19 (Officialité), Z^2 3260 (Saint-Eloi), Z^2 3190 (For-l'évêque), Z^2 3111 (Barre du chapitre).

18. Concerning female criminality and its punishment at the time, see Gauvard, *De Grâce Especial,* 304–6.

19. Ibid., 335.

20. Fines for infraction of ordinances, blasphemy, and the like usually ranged from five to twenty *sous parisis.* See Sauval, *Histoire et recherches,* vol. 3, and Jacques Monicat, ed., *Comptes du domaine de la ville de Paris,* 2 vols. (Paris, 1958).

21. By the fifteenth century the civil justice of the Châtelet had a widespread reputation for speed, efficiency, and fairness, which drew many litigants from the countryside. See Bernard Guenée, *Tribunaux et gens de justice dans le bailliage de Senlis à la fin du moyen âge* (Paris, 1963).

22. Geremek, "La lutte contre le vagabondage à Paris," 2:235 (1422); Archives Nationales, $Y6^4$, Livre rouge neuf du Châtelet, fol. 124r (1524).

23. See Jacques Rossiaud, "Prostitution, jeunesse et société dans les villes du Sud-Est au XVe siècle," *Annales* (1976): 239–325; Sainéan, *Les sources de l'argot ancien,* 87–109.

24. Christopher Allmand, *The Hundred Years' War* (Cambridge, 1988), 124.

25. See Lewis, ed., *The Recovery of France.*

26. "Adonc en Chastellet tournay / Ouquel Tromperie trouvay / Qui de demanda où j'aloye. / Je diz que Verité queroie. / Adonc me dit qu'estoie nice / De la quer-

ir entour Justice." Henri Moranvillé, ed., "Le songe véritable, pamphlet politique d'un parisien du XVe siècle," *Mémoires de la Société de l'histoire de Paris et de l'Ile-de-France* 17 (1891): 236.

27. *Ordonnances des rois de France de la troisième race,* 21 vols. (Paris, 1723–34; repr. Farnborough, Hants, 1967), 3:668–72.

5

Ecclesiastical Justice and the Counter-Reformation: Notes on the Diocesan Criminal Court of Naples

Michele Mancino

On 28 January 1600, the archbishop of Naples, Cardinal Alfonso Gesualdo, sent an angry letter from his residence in Rome to the vicar of his diocese, Ercole Vaccari. The letter concerned the case of a young Calabrian cleric named Cesare Pisano who a few days earlier had been sentenced to death by a state court for the crime of lèse-majesté. The offense was committed in conjunction with a failed conspiracy in Calabria led by the philosopher Tommaso Campanella. Though both Pisano and the papal nuncio protested that Pisano should be afforded the right to trial by an ecclesiastical court, the state court refused and he was soon thereafter put to death.[1]

Cardinal Gesualdo and the nuncio of Naples were angered by this event,[2] not so much because they resented the death penalty for Pisano—for the Calabrian conspiracy had anticlerical aspects as well as antistate ones—but because they feared that Pisano's religious transgressions would be overlooked in a state court and needed to be dealt with in an ecclesiastical one.[3] Furthermore, the clerical authorities were provoked by the manner in which the sentence of the state court was carried out. The crown hanged Pisano in his clerical habit—an act that the clerics felt defiled the honor of the clergy (*honore del clero*). This went against the church's custom of performing an elaborate ceremony in capital sentences against ecclesiastics in which the condemned was first systematically degraded and returned to the status of layman before being put to death.[4]

Cardinal Gesualdo, therefore, saw the Pisano case as a double insult. Not only was the church's jurisdiction in dealing with its own members not acknowledged, the church was also denied the possibility of distancing itself from the condemned cleric and turning him out publicly. Hence, the cardinal decided that he could not simply let the case pass and instructed the vicar to familiarize himself "skillfully" with the background of the event and, not least of all, the nuncio's role in it.[5]

The cardinal might not have been so irritated had this case been an isolated event. But it was not. For at least the last few decades of the sixteenth century, the Italian church and state had been in a kind of territorial struggle that mandated the forging of a new kind of relationship not only in the administration of criminal justice but also in the control of sexuality, the organization of work and family life, and many other fundamental aspects of human existence.[6]

This chapter focuses on the reorganization of the inquisitional and other ecclesiastical courts that this struggle involved, and demonstrates, though from admittedly rather fragmentary but still quite consistent data, that it was only beginning with this period of counterreformation after the Council of Trent that ecclesiastical justice in criminal cases started to function uniformly in regard to its objectives, procedures, and punishments.[7] Owing to the fact that the cataloging of the relevant data for this study is only now underway, my remarks will necessarily be limited to the highly urbanized diocese of Naples, then one of the most densely populated areas in Europe. Nevertheless, the recent reorganization of the criminal section of the Naples diocesan historical archive has made it possible to find ample data that provide valuable insights into the power struggle between church and state in the area of criminal justice during this important period of historical transition.[8]

◆ ◆ ◆ ◆

We can begin with the Cardinal Gesualdo's comment about the "honor of the clergy" being assaulted in the case against Pisano. Though Gesualdo believed that clergymen who had acted in a criminal fashion should be punished, he wanted the church itself to do the punishing and he vehemently opposed having the dignity and respectability of the clergy and the church threatened in any judicial procedure. Moreover, Gesualdo's goals for the Neapolitan Catholic church were the same as those in Rome. Around the turn of the seventeenth century, the Catholic church in Italy made a serious attempt to centralize under its control all criminal infractions involving Catholic clergy. This corresponds with rather clear evidence showing how at this time an increasing number of clergymen charged with criminal infractions by state courts sought to have their cases remanded over to be heard before ecclesiastical instead of state forums.[9]

The first issues I intend to deal with, then, are to what extent the documentary evidence in Naples confirms this reassertion of the church's authority, when it began, and which crimes in particular it involved. Given the present state of my research, I can initially say that almost all of the available documents pertaining to the judicial activity of the Neapolitan see in the first half of the sixteenth century involve civil suits. Second, the few existing registers and inventories involving criminal proceedings in the mid-sixteenth century show that at that time most criminal cases were handled in a rather undifferentiated fashion, whereas those that were found for the years after about 1580 seem to have been adjudicated in a more uniform and rational manner by criminal ecclesiastical forums and by the Holy Office. An example of this would be that in 1568 one of the notaries of the archepiscopal curia noted that among the forthcoming trials in his docket were cases of witchcraft, blasphemy, simony, and incest. A few years later the same offenses would be judged in two different tribunals of the archepiscopal curia, with magic and blasphemy to be dealt with in the tribunal of Neapolitan Inquisition and simony and incest to be dealt with in the diocesan criminal court.[10]

It is unclear precisely what usually happened in cases of common criminality involving clergymen in the first half of the sixteenth century. There are good reasons to assume, however, that state courts handled most of them. For example, documentary evidence shows that many clergymen were detained in state prisons in the 1550s.[11] But after the Council of Trent (1545–63) the number of clergymen tried for common offenses by the Neapolitan archepiscopal curia grew rapidly and the number of requests by clergymen imprisoned in state jails to be remanded over to ecclesiastical forums also increased quickly. Although the relative frequency of these requests in different types of offenses has not yet been analyzed, it is clear that many condemned individuals made such requests because the ecclesiastical judicial authorities were considered to be far more lenient than the state authorities, who frequently meted out death sentences for common criminal acts. Good examples can be found in cases involving counterfeiting and sodomy. During the late sixteenth and seventeenth centuries people committing such crimes usually were given the death penalty in state courts,[12] but clerics, who were tried by the archepiscopal curia, received far milder sentences, even in cases of repeat offenses.[13]

Such diverging practices often became the subject of considerable tension between church and state. In 1621, for example, four clerics were first tried by state judges for counterfeiting, and they then asked to have their cases remitted to the ecclesiastical forum. Through the intervention of the viceroy himself, Cardinal Zapata, they were handed over not simply to the archepiscopal curia of Naples but to the ecclesiastical criminal forum of Rome, the highest criminal judicial body of Catholicism. Evidence of the state authorities' displeasure at this outcome lies in the fact that before the clerics were allowed to sail to Rome they were forced to ride on horseback through the crowded streets of Naples in such a way that a mockery was made both of them and of the Neapolitan church. In response, the church excommunicated the secular captain of justice and his soldiers who were involved in this act. Thereupon the state authorities pressed for the intervention of the Pope himself, who decided to absolve the excommunicated laymen because he recognized the need to pay attention to the overall political balance between the Italian church and state, even if it was resented by the Neapolitan Curia.[14]

This is not to say that requests for remission to the church forum were less frequent in criminal cases where the penalties handed down by the state courts were less harsh. The rather lenient treatment of rapists is a case in point. Though both state and church courts usually delivered fairly mild punishments for rape offenses at this time, there were many trials begun in the secular forum that were soon broken off and later continued in the archepiscopal curia.[15] Judging by roughly two hundred cases considered by the ecclesiastical forum that have now been studied in the period, it is clear that the archepiscopal curia was quite moderate in its punishments and also was usually anxious to avoid public spectacles in carrying out its penalties.[16]

The great publicity and making of example that often surrounded the sentences meted out by the state's judges (which recurs, though to a lesser extent, in the "style" of the Neapolitan Inquisition) seem quite different from the handling of cases by the archepiscopal see. Exile was the only punishment that the latter body frequently prescribed that resembled the sentences of the ecclesiastical judges in its degradation of the condemned.[17] In such cases the ecclesiastical authorities sought to expel the wrongdoing clergyman from the group of law-abiding clergy as if it were symbolically cutting out an infected part of an otherwise healthy body to preserve its purity from possible contamination.

All the other forms of punishment that we have seen until now reflect a moderate and cautious legal logic: in serious cases a few years' imprisonment or a sentence to row in galleys, and in less serious cases a perhaps not disinterested insistence on monetary penalties.[18] The state of the present research, however, doesn't permit us to account for these trends fully, though this certainly needs to be done especially in relation to individual criminal typologies and their historical development. Nevertheless, some especially significant individual cases can be cited to help us advance more clearly articulated hypotheses. One of these cases in particular is drawn on below.

◆ ◆ ◆ ◆

In a suit begun on 3 September 1632, a twelve-year-old rape victim named Porzia Frezza brought suit against a clergyman, Don Muzio Francioso, who had raped her in April of that year. She and the rest of her poor family had moved to Naples only shortly before that time, taking refuge from the village of Ottaviano, which had been half-destroyed by the eruption of Mount Vesuvius.[19] After the girl was raped she came back to her home and complained to her mother that she felt ill. A short while later, the mother, fearing that her daughter was about to die, called in the local parish priest to have her confess. In her confession the girl revealed to the priest what had happened. The priest, sensing no doubt that she would in fact survive, advised her to confide in her mother if only so that she and her mother could determine some way that she could avoid becoming a prostitute now that she had lost her virginity.[20]

We know nothing about what happened in the case for the next three months. If indeed the girl heeded the priest's advice, one can assume that neither she, nor her mother, nor other relatives and acquaintances, nor the priest himself did all they could do to find some remedy for the grievous event. We only know that on 2 September 1632 the girl, accompanied by her mother and sister, had gone to church to speak with the parish priest. Given the family's recent move to the city and their common background, they were evidently ignorant about how they should proceed. So they simply went to the church for help and advice.

At a trial before the ecclesiastical judges, the parish priest, obviously seeking to protect a fellow cleric, first defended his own actions by pleading that he was obliged to maintain secrecy about facts revealed to him during confession.[21] But eventually it came out that he had given in to the urging of the girl's mother and other relatives and had indeed advised the raped girl to bring charges against the offending fellow priest, which led to the trial. It was also revealed that once he had obtained the girl's consent, he agreed to draft a statement about the events and send it on to the archepiscopal curia. Despite strong evidence that eventually emerged in the case, and although the offending priest was already in jail for a similar rape offense, the trial ended with a sentence of just two years' exile. Hence, in the end, the opinion of the ecclesiastical trial judges appeared basically consistent with that of the local priest to whom the women had turned originally for help and guidance. Had the convicted priest not been involved in repeated cases of rape—ones carried out with considerably more violence than was involved in this case—even the mild sentence he received would have seemed punitive by the relaxed standards of ecclesiastical justice at the time. In most other cases of rape that have been studied in Naples and elsewhere, it appears that such cases against clerics usually ended up with the release of the offender with at most the duty to compensate the raped woman with a dowry large enough to enable her to have a chance of someday finding a marriage partner, which was now considered much more difficult for her as she had lost her virginity.[22]

A final aspect of the case must be underscored, one that is of particular interest for an analysis of the different reactions of victims toward the criminal behavior of ecclesiastics at the time. Since the raped girl, Porzia Frezza, and her family had only recently come from a small country village, their life in Naples was quite precarious. Surely they did not know the legal institutions of their new city. That their appeal was brought to a priest in his role as confessor, and only in an emergency situation at that, is an important indication of the near complete isolation and ignorance in which they found themselves in the metropolis. In the earlier rape charge lodged against the priest Don Francioso, on the other hand, the mother of the girl immediately filed a petition to the archepiscopal curia initiating a case against the rapist (and only two days elapsed between the rape and the suit). Though that mother was also of provincial origins, she had lived many years in Naples and was far more worldly wise.[23]

◆   ◆   ◆   ◆

A pattern seems to emerge from the above-mentioned cases that allows us to advance provisionally the following hypothesis: beginning in the late sixteenth century, in order to redefine entirely its own presence in the city and in the diocese, the Neapolitan church reorganized and intensified its control over crimes committed by clerics. Though the procedures and results of the legal repression exerted by the archepiscopal curia's criminal forum must be investigated further, it seems that we can ascribe to it legal action inspired by caution and temperance, at least in comparison to similar procedures of the Neapolitan state courts. On general grounds, and in anticipation of analysis aimed at specific criminal typologies, we can attribute these attitudes of the ecclesiastical institution to its wish to alleviate the hardship and the damage that a crime caused the victim and to its underestimation of the repressive aspect of the punishment. We are not now in a position to assess exactly to what extent this judicial course of action was taken to maintain the "honor of the clergy" or to nip possible scandals in the bud. However, ample evidence strongly indicates that the effects of legal actions on the clergy's overall image were of great significance in determining how ecclesiastical justice was meted out.

◆　◆　◆　◆

In the previous pages we have shown that the late sixteenth century was a crucial period in the life of the church in Naples (and, generally, throughout Italy). Important pieces of evidence point to the intensified activities of the archepiscopal curia's criminal forum. But an analogous discourse may also be undertaken concerning the conduct of the Neapolitan Inquisition.[24]

In 1585, a second inquisitorial forum appeared, headed by a minister designated by Supreme Inquisitors and supporting the preexisting Holy Office's court of the archepiscopal curia. This is likely to be the clearest proof of the renewed importance ascribed by the Catholic Church's supreme authority to the presence of a strong inquisitorial structure in the city of Naples. The church intended it to supplant the authority exerted by the bishops up to then, as was happening in all of north-central Italy. Even though the move did not succeed in Naples, the powerful local archepiscopal curia was forced after that time to take account of the troublesome ministers, who were strongly defended by Rome, and to acquiesce to the strictest controls of the Congregation of the Holy Office.[25]

This situation has been mentioned here to emphasize that it could have had an impact on the criminal court of the archepiscopal curia. The fact that the judges had to account to the Supreme Inquisitors for some of their trials might have influenced the most independent legal activities—the criminal ones—that they carried out. Whatever reliability such a hypothesis might have, there are some points of contact between the reorganization of the curial criminal forum and the development of its inquisitorial structures.

In the same years in which an ecclesiastical forum attentive to the "honor of the clergy" succeeded in monopolizing the control of crimes committed by clergy, thanks to a moderate punitive procedure aimed at dressing the wounds opened by crime in the social body, an equally skillful Inquisition, after the bloody fight against heresy in the 1550s and 1560s, began implementing flexible repressive strategies that were inspired to build consent rather than to destroy dissent. The most prominent of these strategies were the renunciation of the burning of witches and of the demonizing of superstitious laypeople (particularly women), along with the development of the activities of exorcism, which were monopolized by the clergy, and with the ample tolerance guaranteed to the superstitious devotions that grew so tumultuously. It may be opportune to emphasize that, in a substantially homogeneous national picture, if we look at cases of famous clergymen involved in lucrative devotional business, the most sensational cases are recorded in Naples.[26]

In such cases, the "honor of the clergy" was not directly in question, or, at least, was not the only thing in question. If the clergy had been too heavy-handed in those cases, which were regarded as abuses only by a small minority of enlightened churchmen, they would have risked ruining the attempt to regain the Catholic masses, begun on a worldwide scale after Trent, by reinstituting religious practices (such as the cult of the saints or the emphasis of thaumaturgism and the introduction of new devotions) so long silenced by the reform's assault. Furthermore, the Holy Office did not find it hard to try or to punish strictly the clergymen as well, where the seriousness of the crimes of faith (particularly heresy or the abuse of sacraments such as Confession, Mass, or Holy Communion) demanded it. In such cases, obviously, the defense of the orthodoxy superseded the need to protect the "honor of the clergy."

Moreover, in this perspective, one may account for a finding that emerges when one compares the actions of these two courts of the Neapolitan Curia, especially during the late sixteenth century and the first decades of the seventeenth century. We are referring here to the widespread tendency, coming primarily from criminal milieux, to present false denunciations to the inquisitorial courts, in an attempt to ruin personal enemies on trial. This tendency was very strong during the late sixteenth century among clergymen as well, in particular among the monks.[27] We can also find such influences in the trials performed by the archepiscopal curia's criminal forum, although in a more limited way. Perhaps an awareness that the "honor of the clergy" was well defended discouraged the cunning inhabitants of the metropolis from the usual practice of denunciation. From the comparison with the inquisitorial series, we have indirect confirmation of the tendency of the Neapolitan Curia's criminal court toward a cautious and measured treatment of the common crimes committed by the ecclesiastics of the diocese.

Notes

An expanded version of this essay appeared as "Giustizia penale ecclesiastica e Controriforma: Uno sguardo sul tribunale criminale arcivescovile di Napoli," in *Campania Sacra* 23 (1992): 201–28.

1. The basic reference for the events of the Calabrian conspiracy and its long and restless judicial developments remains L. Amabile, *Fra Tommaso Campanella, i suoi processi e la sua pazzia,* 3 vols. (Naples, 1882). For the Pisano episode, which I specifically refer to here, adequate space is given both in the narrative section (2:43–47 and passim) and in the imposing collection of documents (vol. 3, passim). For Cardinal Gesualdo's letter see *Archivio Storico Diocesano di Napoli* (hereafter referred to as *ASDN*), Carteggi degli Arcivescovi, Cardinal Alfonso Gesualdo's Roman correspondence with his General Vicar Monsignor Vaccari, 7 January–16 June 1600, fol. 67r.

2. See the letter to Cardinal San Giorgio of 21 January 1600, in Amabile, *Fra Tommaso Campanella,* vol. 3, doc. no. 83. In it the nuncio of Naples communicates his deep "risentimento" toward the viceroy's prosecutor regarding the method of Pisano's execution. In the letters of 28 January to Cardinal San Giorgio and of 11 February to the Cardinal of Santa Severina, the nuncio refers once more to his "risentimento" directly to the viceroy himself; see vol. 3, doc. nos. 85 and 88.

3. Fears of this kind are expressed as soon as the first news about the detection of the conspiracy began to reach Rome. They go far beyond the period of the constitution of the court authorized to try the ecclesiastics involved in the conspiracy. Because of analogous preoccupations, the double trial, which the lay conspirators charged with heresy undergo, is justified. On these problems see Amabile, *Fra Tommaso Campanella,* vols. 2 and 3 passim.

4. See *ASDN,* Carteggi degli Arcivescovi, Correspondence, fol. 67r.

5. Ibid.

6. The areas mentioned are those most supported by documentary evidence both in the Neapolitan diocese's archive and in many other Italian episcopal archives for the late sixteenth century, rather than the object of precise research. From my point of view, unfortunately the inquiries on the application of the Council of Trent are still insufficient. I refer in particular to interventions in medical matters, both empirical and not, to the increase of controls on rest during feast days, and, for innkeepers, to the observance of dietary prohibitions prescribed by the church; as far as family is concerned, to the imposition of the new wedding model foreseen by the Tridentine; as far as sexuality is concerned, to the struggle against concubinage and prostitution in accord, but often also in competition, with state interventions. On these subjects, which deserve just as much attention as that given to censorship and to repressive measures of various kinds against culture and art, research appears disappointing. But recently the scholars of post-Tridentine Roman Catholicism seem to be more sensitive to some of the topics mentioned above, as shown by some contributions (for example, a few of the essays included in *Disciplina dell'anima, disciplina del corpo e disciplina della società tra medioevo ed età moderna,* ed. P. Prodi [Bologna, 1994]).

7. For discussion of Inquisition courts, see G. Romeo, *Inquisitori, esorcisti e streghe nell' Italia della Controriforma* (Florence, 1990). For ecclesiastical criminal

courts, research is only just beginning, but comparisons between the Neapolitan records and those from two other southern diocesan archives (Telese and Sant'Agata dei Goti) mark the late sixteenth century as the crucial period for the reorganization of the respective criminal courts.

8. In the only general inventory of *ASDN* published thus far (*L'Archivio Storico Diocesano di Napoli: Guida,* 2 vols., ed. G. Galasso and C. Russo [Naples, 1978–79]), criminal papers have not been registered, and the inquisitorial ones only partially registered. In October 1989, in an effort to organize the two collections, the administration of the archive decided upon a general revision of its extensive holdings of papers, many of which are still dispersed in several deposits. I am indebted to this initiative, of which I am a collaborator, for the opportunity to produce this essay. I am pleased to thank Prof. Ugo Dovere, the director of the archive, who guides its reorganization with competence and passion; I thank also my colleagues in the research group who are carrying on the initiative, and particularly my friend Giovanni Romeo, who offered many useful suggestions.

9. The issues in question are too complex to be examined here. Suffice it to mention the many harsh clashes sustained by the church of Naples in order to defend the immunity of sacred places and even of the clergymen's houses. As far as prosecuted men are concerned, it is possible, on the other hand, to point out the numerous criminal typologies (murders, counterfeiting, robberies, sexual crimes of various kinds), which testify to the "rush" toward ecclesiastical courts.

10. See *ASDN,* uninventoried papers, inventory compiled by Giovanni Porto, published by G. Romeo, "Per la storia del Sant' Ufficio a Napoli tra '500 e '600: Documenti e problemi," *Campania Sacra* 7 (1976): appendix 1, 73–75.

11. *ASDN,* Carteggi degli Arcivescovi, register of letters of the Congregation of the Holy Office, unnumbered papers, Neapolitan General Vicar Quattromani's letter to Roman authorities of 28 January 1581: here is mentioned a Neapolitan priest, Don Camillo Lantano, imprisoned more than twenty years before in the state jail for commonplace crimes (and later cross-examined by the archepiscopal curia for suspicion of heresy).

12. Without resorting to the general literature, the rich documentation of the archive of the Compagnia Napoletana dei Bianchi della Giustizia (in charge of spiritual assistance of men condemned to death) offers unequivocal evidence for this material. See G. Romeo, *Aspettando il bòia: Condannati a morte, confortatori e inquisitori nella Napoli della Controriforme* (Florence, 1993).

13. These data appear amply supported in many of the trials found up to now relative to such typologies (about fifteen between 1570 and 1650). To underscore the moderation in the punitive praxis of the Neapolitan archepiscopal criminal court, it should be noted that the canon law in particular situations consigned to the secular branch the clerics guilty of counterfeiting and sodomy. See P. Farinacci, *Praxis et theoricae criminalis, Pars Quarta* (Lugduni, 1631), quaestio 115, no. 33, p. 71 (counterfeiter clerics); quaestio 148, nos. 26 and 28–30, pp. 570–71 (sodomite clerics).

Apropos of the involvement of ecclesiastics in counterfeiting crimes, for a comparison with the contemporary Neapolitan situation, see the observations in E. Grendi, "Falsa monetazione e strutture monetarie degli scambi nella Repubblica di Genova fra Cinque e Seicento," *Quaderni storici* 66 (1987), esp. 827–30.

14. *ASDN,* Carteggi degli Arcivescovi, register of letters of the Congregation of the Holy Office, unnumbered papers, Cardinal Sauli's letter of 8 April 1621 to the General Vicar of the archdiocese of Naples.

15. See, for instance, *ASDN,* Criminalia (now being reorganized), the trial against the cleric Tommaso Spiezia (or di Spetia). The proceedings against him had been begun by state judges on 31 October 1630. On 1 April of the following year, Spiezia, having proved his clerical status, was entrusted to the archepiscopal curia.

16. A verification is offered by the murder trials. For this crime the state judges in Naples and elsewhere often exercised capital punishment, while there are no traces of it in the sentences of the Neapolitan diocesan court for the same crime. Only for bigamy and rape, as I have mentioned, the punitive choices of both ecclesiastical and secular judges show analogous aspects. In one of the very few cases followed by state judges in 1618, while the ecclesiastical sentence was being executed, with the condemned already in the galleys, the punishment of the archepiscopal curia was confirmed (see *ASDN,* Sant' Ufficio, uninventoried papers: dossier of 1651 concerning the clashes between church and state in Naples on the matter of bigamy; I am referring to the document of the proceedings against Giovanni Sabato Califre). It is worth remembering that these remarks are based on the punitive habits of the Neapolitan ecclesiastical court, which often followed canon law in a rather elastic manner.

17. A significant index of the actual punitive tendencies in the Neapolitan Curia's criminal court can be found in Libri fideiussionum, in *ASDN,* Miscellanea Curiae. Already in the earliest at our disposition, the Liber fideiussionum . . . a die 14 mensis Martii 1616, there are recorded a large number of sentences with different kinds of exile, as far as the distance (from the "civitas" or the "dioecesis," including at times the whole Neapolitan ecclesiastical province) or the length of time are concerned; moreover, instead of jail, there is a sort of compulsory stay in a place determined by the judge, which involves, if it is respected, the guilty person's "habilitatio."

18. For this aspect as well, see the above-mentioned Libri fideiussionum.

19. *ASDN,* Criminalia, 1632, Processus Criminalis de tentato stupro et alio stupro in personas virginum contra Don Mutium Francioso. The girl's suit is in fols. 39r–41v. But the whole reconstruction of the fact suggested in the book also rests on the evidence given by the rape victim's sister, Giustina Frezza (3 September 1632, fols. 42r–44v), and by the priest of S. Maria della Misericordia, Don Giandomenico Russo (28 September 1632, fols. 48r–49r).

20. Ibid., fol. 48v, Don Russo's evidence on 28 September 1632.

21. Ibid., fol. 49r.

22. In the various adjunctive sentences provided for by the canonists in order to repress rape by clerics, the dowry of the victim is regarded as an unbreakable sanc-

tion. For a review of positions, see P. Farinacci, *Praxis et theoricae criminalis,* quaestio 147, nos. 61–65, p. 560. In particular, with reference to the current praxis, one reads: "poena Clerici stupratoris hodie est arbitraria, quandoque scilicet poena pecuniaria, quandoque depositionis, et quandoque suspensionis, sed semper cum praestatione dotis puellae": ibid., no. 65. This concept is repeated in no. 107, pp. 563–64. In fact, besides the legal statements, the praxis of Farinacci is a valuable reference also for what is allowed to appear about the legal procedures in such important courts as the Roman ones, in which its author has covered such prominent tasks. Particularly, one is struck by the fact that the theoretical possibility, recognized by the judge, of supporting the obligation of giving a dowry to the raped girl along with other punishments, sometimes even corporal, is not applied either in Naples or in Rome ("Fustigationis . . . poenam, tanquam ignominiosam, numquam in Urbe vidi servatam in Clericis": ibid., no. 65). Sometimes, indeed, one realizes that, in dealing with dowry demands considered unproportionate to the damage done, by the one who must pay compensation for it, the ecclesiastical judge's attitude reveals an excessive attention to the clergyman's financial obligations, to the detriment of the raped girl's interests. A typical case of this sort is the one regarding the clergyman Antonio D'Avosso. Prosecuted on 4 August 1625 for having raped Porzia de Pastena, after long and useless attempts at mediation carried on by his wealthy family and also through ecclesiastics (there was no agreement on the amount of the reparation dowry), he was definitively acquitted less than two years later. On this case see *ASDN,* Criminalia, 1625, Processus Criminalis pro Reverendo Domino Fisco contra clericum Antonium D'Avosso Neapolitanum, passim. For a recent investigation on the oscillations of the judicial evaluation between the "penal" and "civil" sanction of simplex rape and on the role played by the post-Tridentine moral theology and casuistry in the prevailing of judicial measures aimed at agreements of economic compensation for the damage of deflowering, see G. Alessi, "Il gioco degli scambi: seduzione e risarcimento nella casistica cattolica del XVI e XVII secolo," *Quaderni storici* 75 (1990): 805–31.

23. *ASDN,* Criminalia, Processus . . . contra Don Mutium Francioso, suit presented by Tommasina Paulella, mother of Candida Celetta, a ten-year-old girl who, in her words, was raped by the priest on 1 May 1632.

24. Concerning the part of the Congregation of the Holy Office and the basic strategies enacted in the reorganization of Italian religious life, see G. Romeo, *Inquisitori,* chaps. 6 and 7.

25. See L. Amabile, *Il Santo Officio della Inquisizione in Napoli* (Città di Castello, 1892), especially vol. 1, 331ff. As to the difficult relationship between the archepiscopal court of faith and the court delegated in Naples by the Holy Office, see G. Romeo, "Una città, due inquisizioni: l'anomalia del Sant' Ufficio a Napoli nel tardo '500," *Rivista di storia e letteratura religiosa* 24 (1988): 42–67.

26. For the analysis of this aspect of Neapolitan religious life during the last decades of the sixteenth century, see G. Romeo, *Inquisitori,* chapter 7 passim.

27. J. M. Sallmann dwells upon this phenomenon in *Chercheurs de trésors et jeteuses de sorts: La quête du surnaturel à Naples au XVIe siècle* (Paris, 1986), passim. There is also a reference in G. Romeo, *Inquisitori,* 196.

6

Between Town and Countryside: Organized Crime in the Dutch Republic

Florike Egmond

Banditry as most of us know it—from fiction and the publications of social historians and anthropologists—is a distinctly rural and largely premodern phenomenon. The term evokes famous outlaws such as Robin Hood, Cartouche, and Schinderhannes, and includes Brazilian *cangaçeiros* as well as Italian brigands and other exotic figures. During the past twenty years research has shown that few historical outlaws fitted the stereotypical image of the *social* bandit—who habitually robs the rich, assists the poor, takes revenge on harsh landowners and other members of the elite, and invariably gets killed in a dramatic way. Nonetheless, bandits continue to belong outside, in the wilds, far away from towns and centers of state power. The countryside is their territory.[1] Towns, on the other hand—and in particular early modern capitals such as London and Paris—have long been known as the location of a different type of criminal association: the urban underworld, which consisted largely of thieves, specialized burglars, pickpockets, and their fences.[2] Connections between these two worlds are rarely discussed. Even Mary McIntosh's study of criminal organization in the past credits early modern societies only with rural (picaresque) bandits or an urban underworld that seems to derive most of its characteristics from the studies of eighteenth- and nineteenth-century London.[3]

Representations of historical organized crime thus reflect—as might indeed be expected—the focus on capitals and on predominantly rural early modern societies. The Dutch Republic does not fit either case. First, it boasted an exceptional number of major towns besides a capital, all of which were located close together and connected by busy roads and waterways. Second, the countryside in the western half of the Netherlands was densely populated, town dominated, and urban oriented from a very early period. This chapter considers the relevance of the peculiarly Dutch type of urbanization and of concomitant contrasts between town and countryside to the orientation, organization, and activities of organized crime in the Northern Netherlands during the seventeenth and eighteenth centuries.[4] Precisely because of its singularity the Dutch case may help us escape the above-mentioned narrow characterizations and develop different perspectives on the organization of crime in the past.

Regional differences *within* the Dutch Republic were considerable, moreover, and allow comparison between the highly urbanized and densely populated province of Holland and the rural inland province of Brabant south of the big rivers. In the province of Holland, cities like Amsterdam, Rotterdam, Leiden, The Hague, Delft, Haarlem, and Alkmaar strongly influenced the economy and infrastructure of the surrounding countryside. In Brabant, towns were few and far apart; woods and heathlands covered large areas, and many inhabitants of the poor, sandy eastern parts supplemented their income from agriculture by weaving and spinning at home or by leaving for Holland and western Brabant during the summer months to earn a living by seasonal labor. As will be seen, Dutch organized crime reflects some of these regional differences and characteristics.

◆ Urban Networks

Even in the town-dominated province of Holland, the distinction between "safe" towns and "dangerous" rural areas had not lost its significance by the late eighteenth century. Thefts committed in the countryside and threats to the safety of the rural population were considered especially serious. A sentence pronounced in 1620 by the local court of Brielle, near Rotterdam, describes some thefts and burglaries as particularly grave offenses *because* they had been committed in the (open) countryside, "where people are less able to defend themselves against thieves and violence than in enclosed towns."[5] Similarly, in 1700 the court of Bergen op Zoom in western Brabant stated that theft committed in rural areas, "where there is no more protection than the law itself," is a worse crime than theft committed in a town.[6]

Compared to the countryside, Dutch towns were indeed marked by considerable "state presence." Urban prosecutors and their assistants hardly constituted a police force in the modern sense of the term, but even small provincial towns had their own criminal courts, and in most Dutch cities the public prosecutor and chief constable of police (called *schout* or *baljuw*) were assisted by one or perhaps two deputies and some "servants."[7] Together with a somewhat larger number of night watchmen they maintained public order. They also took care of crime prevention, detection, and most other police functions. At the same time town walls, gates, and other boundary markers both symbolically and effectively helped to keep out dangers. Until the final years of the eighteenth century the city gates of Amsterdam were closed and locked every evening, while iron barriers were lowered into the canals to prevent strangers from entering the town by boat. In the countryside, on the other hand, judicial and police presence was minimal. A bailiff and a few assistants had to fulfill the same functions as their urban counterparts in jurisdictions ranging in size from one village to a quarter of a province. Except for these few constables per district there was no police. At times of unrest the rural inhabitants themselves organized nightly patrols; as far as their personal safety was concerned they generally had to rely on their own resources.

Yet, neither was urban life as protected nor were possessions in town quite as securely guarded as these opposing images suggest. It was rather a matter of different dangers confronting the respective inhabitants of town and countryside. Urban professional crime in the Dutch Republic included a wide range of both activities and patterns of organization. On the one hand, we find highly specialized thieves and burglars who generally worked alone, though obviously relying on the "criminal infrastructure" for both information and the sale of their stolen goods. During 1656–58, Engelbrecht Stroo (Straw) from Hamburg, for instance, burgled the houses of wealthy nobles and diplomats (such as the Polish ambassador) in and near The Hague. Though acquainted with a number of men involved in illegal dealings, he preferred to operate alone and invited assistance only when a specific job required it.[8] At the other end of the scale, extensive networks of urban thieves, cut-purses, and pickpockets comprised as many as thirty or forty persons. The members of these networks operated in smaller groups, staying only for short periods in each town before traveling on to the next one. Their tours might cover the whole of the Dutch Republic; occasionally they extended to the Southern Netherlands and parts of Germany as well.[9]

Between these two extremes—in terms both of size and of geographical mobility—we find groups of thieves specializing in the theft of large quantities of commercial goods from warehouses: coffee, white lead, wood, and textiles were among their favorite commodities. There were also sneak thieves; gangs of shoplifters; small groups of burglars who broke into houses and shops by prizing open shutters and windows; burglars who used ladders and entered houses through the attics; thieves who specialized in stealing silver and jewelry; and petty thieves who tried their hand at anything.

Two examples illustrate the main characteristics of organized urban crime in the Netherlands. During the late 1680s a group of three men had developed a special method of stealing. They presented themselves on the doorstep of a rich merchant's house in Amsterdam: one of them was disguised as the tutor of a young baron (played by the second); the third man pretended to be his valet. When it turned out that they had been misdirected they left. In the meantime, however, the men had made use of the confusion caused by their "mistake" to obtain a wax imprint of the front-door key. A few weeks later—generally on a Sunday morning when the inhabitants had gone to church—the same three men entered the house and removed a large quantity of merchandise from the basement. On one occasion they stole a few thousand pairs of silk stockings, valued at roughly eight thousand to nine thousand guilders. Some of their booty was illegally exported to England and sold there.[10]

A few decades earlier, during the 1650s, Andries Wissenhagen (alias, The Heathen) from Berlin was involved in several types of illegal activities all over the western half of the Dutch Republic. For most of the year Wissenhagen lived in Amsterdam, but he regularly visited Rotterdam, The Hague, Delft, and a few other Dutch towns. He and his colleagues spent much of their time in taverns frequented by a mixed company of sailors, (former) soldiers, artisans, and unskilled laborers, where they planned series of sneak thefts and burglaries. Within a period of two to three weeks Wissenhagen and his accomplices would break into several houses and shops in various towns in Holland—for instance, Amsterdam, The Hague, and Leiden—stealing silver, money, clothes, and small pieces of furniture, which were sold to their regular fences. Two or three men usually worked together on a number of "jobs." During the same period each of them also undertook other burglaries together with different sets of companions.

Like Wissenhagen's accomplices, most urban thieves in the Netherlands belonged to several overlapping networks of thieves, burglars, pickpockets, street robbers, cardsharps, confidence tricksters, and other criminals. Such networks by no means formed a single, centralized criminal organization, but together they did constitute the urban underworld. Rather than an assortment of local criminal circuits operating separately, this was indeed a single Dutch—or to be more exact Holland-centered—urban underworld. It was precisely the considerable overlap among the networks of urban thieves operating in Holland that comprised its unity. Most of the men and women involved knew or knew about each other. Moreover, certain locations and people—in particular pubs and lodging houses, innkeepers and fences—formed focal points where different types of information and people with different specializations came together.[11]

The interurban character of the Dutch urban underworld was perfectly in accordance with the prevailing pattern of urbanization in the province of Holland. Like most other inhabitants of the area now denoted as the *Randstad* (roughly comprising the area enclosed by Rotterdam, The Hague, Utrecht, and Amsterdam), men and women involved in criminal activities made use of the existing infrastructure and the excellent means of communication.[12] It was not at all unusual for a thief to take the morning barge from Amsterdam to Haarlem, spend an afternoon with some friends in a pub, burgle one or two houses in the evening, and leave the next morning for Delft or The Hague. Accordingly, urban thieves of any professional standing who operated in only one city are difficult to find in the Dutch criminal records. Their previous convictions by town courts all over Holland attest to a highly mobile existence.

Apart from the numerous interurban connections, the organizational pattern of overlapping networks, and a tendency toward specialization, three more outstanding characteristics of the Dutch urban underworld should be mentioned. Urban thieves and burglars rarely operated in large groups. The number of people involved in a theft or robbery did not usually exceed five or six. It is not difficult to imagine why. Speed (both in entering a house and in getting away in case of an alarm) and silence were of prime importance; the presence of a large group invited discovery and impeded mobility in the narrow urban streets. Second, the small size of groups of criminals jointly engaged in stealing, as well as the typical pattern of shifting coalitions, entailed a comparative lack of hierarchy as well as a virtual absence of any "leading" figures.[13] Third, urban thieves and burglars rarely committed crimes outside cities. In a professional sense—and it seems in every other respect as well—the countryside was irrelevant to them. They lived in towns; most of them rented rooms or boarded in cheap lodging houses. They spent their leisure hours in towns, drinking in pubs, visiting fairs, fighting, and showing off. Most of their (temporary) legitimate jobs were connected with the urban economy; very few of these people ever worked as casual rural laborers. And of course their main, illegal, business was exclusively urban. In short, their whole orientation was urban.

◆ Rural Bands in Holland

Whereas urban thieves rarely if ever left their own territory, the opposite was true of rural bandits and members of vagrant bands operating in the western part of the Dutch Republic. For them, town walls obviously did not represent the boundaries of an urban terra incognita. But there was just as much differentiation among rural bands as we have found among urban groups. Towns did not have the same meaning for all of them. Members of the well-known Jaco Band, for instance, committed all of their important crimes in the countryside but returned to Amsterdam after each expedition. Between 1715 and 1717 this band undertook a dozen or more large-scale armed robberies, some of which involved violence, including murder. A few of the rural dwellings that they attacked were located near Amsterdam; others were as distant as Groningen and Zwolle (in the northeastern and eastern provinces, respectively). Like urban thieves, members of the Jaco Band lived in urban lodging houses and rooms, spent much of their time in pubs, and sold all their stolen goods to urban fences; but unlike its urban counterparts, the Jaco Band was a close-knit and hierarchically organized group, as may also be inferred from the fact that it was named after its leader.[14]

Towns were much less important to the vagrant group of Dirk Verhoeven, active during the period 1757–65.[15] Members of this band spent a large part of their lives touring the countryside, crisscrossing the provinces of Holland, Utrecht, and Gelderland and adjacent German territory. They stole food, shoes, clothes, textiles, farm implements, and money at rural markets and fairs and from barns, farmhouses, and local shops. Petty theft was only one of their everyday activities, which also included casual rural labor, peddling, grinding knives, and repairing chairs, pots, and pans; some members of the group played musical instruments and performed at fairs as actors or jugglers. A set of about five men belonging to this band occasionally undertook more daring armed robberies.

Verhoeven's group—like most vagrant bands operating in the western and most urbanized part of the Dutch Republic—was less close knit than the Jaco Band, but it did have a certain hierarchy and some men acted as leaders. Unlike the networks of urban thieves, it formed a community: band members were frequently connected by ties of kinship, and not only men but women and older children toured the countryside in small groups. They met regularly at certain inns and fairs, and joined in the illegal activities that provided part of their income. Much of their life was spent outdoors, traveling on foot along the tracks, sleeping in barns and haystacks, working in the fields, and performing at fairs.

Even such rurally oriented bands frequently "made use" of towns. They sold at least part of their stolen goods in big cities, in particular clothes, jewelry, silver, and other objects that would be easily recognized by their owners when sold in a village or small provincial town. They also paid brief but fairly regular visits to towns in order to buy new merchandise, change money, see a doctor, call on relatives, go to pubs, and generally make use of services that were not available in the countryside. Towns were even more important for a third reason. The interrelated families that made up these vagrant rural bands spent a large part of the winter in the big cities of Holland. Few fairs were held between December and April, and it was too cold and wet for traveling and peddling. Some band members found temporary employment in town. Quite a few spent their time in stocking up on supplies and otherwise preparing for the summer season. All of them therefore constantly renewed their ties with urban society.

A typical rural band active in the urbanized western zone of the Dutch Republic thus showed the following characteristics. Its structure was similar to Dirk Verhoeven's band: less close-knit and hierarchical than the Jaco Band, but without the shifting coalitions characteristic of the urban underworld either. Such bands formed communities of men, women, and children. All of them toured the countryside—usually in small family groups—and spent a large part of the year out in the open. Many bands included men born outside the Dutch Republic, such as Germans, people from Flanders and Wallonia, Scandinavians, and a few English or Irish. Most of the women, however, were born in the big towns of Holland. The composition of these bands thus reflected the status of the province of Holland as an immigration area par excellence.

Petty theft committed by pairs or small groups of band members predominated among the activities of these rural groups. The women were as active as the men in this respect, but they seldom joined in large-scale burglary or armed robbery. On the whole, rural bands operating in Holland rarely used violence. They preferred to enter a house quietly, go about their business without waking the inhabitants, and leave again unnoticed. Often they chose a moment when the family had gone to church or when most of the inhabitants were working in the fields. Sometimes, however, a group of band members appeared at the front door and demanded food, drink, and money under threat of arson or murder, and a few bands did commit large-scale armed robbery using violence against the inhabitants of the houses they plundered.

Compared to their urban counterparts, members of rural bands operating in the western part of the Dutch Republic lacked specialization; they stole whatever they could use and the techniques they employed for entering houses very much depended on the circumstances. They used more violence than urban burglars, but their operations were—as will be seen—considerably less brutal than those of their "southern" counterparts. Towns were eminently important to rural bands operating in Holland, both as places to live during the winter season and as places to visit briefly for a variety of reasons during the rest of the year. No member of a rural band active in Holland was unfamiliar with urban life.

◆ Rural Bands in Brabant

There is a sharp contrast between these "urbanized" rural bands active in Holland and the bands operating in Brabant. Whereas the former incorporated both immigrants and native "Hollanders" of either urban or rural background, membership of the Brabant bands was nearly exclusively indigenous and rural. *Brabanders*—born either in Dutch or Spanish/Austrian Brabant—dominated the large bands; smaller groups included even fewer outsiders. Only a small number of these native band members came from the few towns of any importance in this province, such as Breda and 's-Hertogenbosch. The majority were born and bred in the villages of eastern and southern Dutch Brabant, or belonged to families that had been touring the countryside for decades as vagrants, peddlers, and rural laborers. Many, indeed, came from the area where their bands committed thefts and burglaries. Accordingly, local and regional ties remained strong. Band members relied on kin, local friends, former colleagues, and neighbors for information and various types of assistance. Local knowledge and a longstanding familiarity with local geography played an important part in the planning and execution of their illegal activities.

It was not only in small bands with a limited area of operations that local ties were extremely important. A case in point is the notorious band of the *Zwartmakers* (Blackeners), whose operations continued for nearly a decade (1690–99). It comprised more than 100—and perhaps as many as 160 to 180—men and women, 69 of whom were sentenced by courts in Dutch and Spanish Brabant, Gelderland, and Holland.[16] The band consisted of two main branches: a large Brabant division and a much smaller segment operating in the province of Gelderland. Various sections can be distinguished within the Brabant branch. Two of these operated chiefly in the western and central border area of Dutch and Spanish Brabant; the third was active in northeastern Brabant. Each of these sections consisted largely of local people, and the nucleus of each section was formed by a cluster of two or three interrelated local families.

These were rarely families of high status or good reputation. They still belonged to local society, but marginally. Some members of these kin groups were only remotely involved in the band's illegal activities. As farmhands, spinners, weavers, and rural artisans who spent most of their lives in the region where they were born, they remained part of village life. Others no longer had a fixed domicile. They toured the area, begged, worked as casual rural laborers during the summer and autumn, served as soldiers for a year or so, stayed with their relatives, worked as peddlers or refuse collectors, and sometimes found temporary jobs as unskilled assistants of rural artisans. The journeys of these men covered the whole of Brabant and even extended to the islands of Zealand in the west or to adjacent German territory in the east. At the end of the season, however, they generally returned to their own district or village, where they spent the winter with their mothers, wives and children, and other relatives.

The operations and structure (and to some extent customs) of the Zwartmakers Band were strongly influenced by the armies. Indeed, the Zwartmakers were by no means the only band active in Brabant between 1650 and 1800 that could be described as a paramilitary band. Both the Zwartmakers and, for instance, the much smaller Band of the Catoen brothers (1780s) were organized and behaved like army units; both had a small number of outstanding leaders, and in both bands women played a minor role. Such groups modeled their operations on military expeditions. At night a party of about six to fifteen men would go to the isolated farm, rural inn, or local shop they planned to rob. Some traveled on horseback, some on foot. Many carried pistols, a few brought ropes and candles, and all of them had knives. Having posted sentries, a handful of men would break into the house and start plundering, taking money, clothes, textiles, linen, small furniture, and of course jewelry and silver. They rarely seemed to care if they made a lot of noise. Front doors were sometimes battered in. The thieves broke open cupboards and chests. No attempts were made to avoid alarming either the inhabitants themselves or their neighbors. On the contrary, victims were often challenged, attacked, trussed up, locked in cellars, or beaten and even tortured and killed.

Rural bands operating in Brabant ranged in size and coherence from the large, segmented, and hierarchically organized Zwartmakers Band to smaller, loose-knit groups of vagrants roaming the countryside.[17] The latter groups included women and children as well as men. They were only rarely involved in armed robbery, but "less serious" activities such as begging, petty theft, and occasional burglary formed part of their everyday agenda. Now and then these bands too used violence. They occasionally attacked and killed people who refused to give them food, or they set fire to houses and barns. Most of these groups lacked both captains and a clear hierarchy, but they were much more visible than bands like the Zwartmakers because of their continuous tours in the countryside. It is these vagrant groups in particular that have come to represent the dangerous rural classes in Brabant.

The orientation of all of these bands was strictly rural. Band members spent the larger part of the year outdoors, sleeping in rural inns, barns, stables, or woods, working in the fields, traveling on foot from one fair to another, and in similar pursuits. Some of these vagrant family groups lived for months on end in the woods of western Brabant and the extensive heathlands and moorlands of central and eastern Brabant. Unlike their counterparts in Holland, they even spent the winters in hamlets and villages rather than in provincial towns or big cities. Towns played only a minor part in their existence. They visited cities like Breda, 's-Hertogenbosch, and Antwerp in order to sell booty, buy supplies, or attend a big fair or a public execution, but these were only brief stays. Towns were no more familiar to them than the countryside of Holland had been to the urban underworld.

Taken together, rural bands in Brabant consisted predominantly of indigenous people. Kinship ties were extremely important in keeping these bands together and cementing existing bonds between "marginalized" itinerant band members and certain sections of local rural society.[18] The Brabant bands were generally larger than the groups in Holland; hierarchical organization was more common, and the number of people actively involved in robberies was definitely larger than in the urbanized parts of the Dutch Republic. Finally, expeditions in Brabant tended to entail much more noise and violence.

◆ Different Models

These major differences between rural bands in Holland and Brabant indicate that early urbanization in the western provinces of the Dutch Republic had important effects not only on the structure (or pattern of organization) of urban and rural bands in Holland, but also on the types of offenses and the ways in which they were committed—in short, on criminal styles. The diverse composition of rural and urban groups active in Holland—as opposed to the largely indigenous and rural background of bands in Brabant—reflected the character of Holland as an immigration area par excellence. Military-style hierarchies and leadership were inextricably bound up both with the larger size of Brabant bands and with military traditions and military service in this region, which was (unlike Holland) the scene of most fighting of any importance in the Northern Netherlands during the seventeenth and eighteenth centuries.

The Brabant bands' larger size, the boldness with which they went about their business, and their frequent and quite often extremely brutal use of violence can likewise be interpreted largely in terms of ecology and urbanization. The wooded areas of the southern province, its heathlands, moors, and relative lack of natural barriers such as lakes, canals, and, of course, mountains allowed sizable expeditions by men on horseback. The flat countryside of Holland, on the other hand, provided little cover. Its maze of ditches, canals, lakes, and bogs prevented quick escapes and dictated more cautious approaches. Besides, in the densely populated countryside of Holland many people lived within shouting distance of each other, and there was safety in numbers.

The fate of one of the few bands that transferred its activities from Brabant to Holland illustrates to what extent bands needed to adapt their methods to regional circumstances. The operations of the Van Exaerde brothers, a band of west Brabanders (1711–13) in the area just north of Antwerp, were notable for their violence, ruthlessness, and noisy character. In Holland, however, these same men were scared away on at least three different occasions by a dog and by a man shouting "thieves, thieves" when they tried to break into some farmhouses not far from The Hague.[19] Obviously, these men had not suddenly turned into cowards. In their former territory the big farmhouses were located several miles from each other and far from the villages. The neighbors of the man who shouted "thieves," on the other hand, lived a few hundred meters away. Compared to modern circumstances, all rural inhabitants were virtually unprotected at the time, but they were much less so in Holland than in Brabant.

The Dutch criminal records thus suggest a rather different picture from the "classical" pattern of historical organized crime. Whereas the Dutch urban underworld closely resembled its Parisian and London counterparts in terms of offenses and network organization, its interurban character and the mobility of particular thieves and burglars were predicated upon an urban configuration and modes of transportation peculiar to the Dutch Republic.

The extent to which their lack of interest in the countryside should be regarded as typical of urban underworlds in general remains undecided.

Rural bands in the Netherlands did not confine their activities to peripheral regions, backward provinces, inaccessible woods, and other areas associated with Robin Hood-like bandits. On the contrary, rural bands were just as active in the urbanized countryside of the western part of the Dutch Republic as in rural inland areas. Towns were crucial to these bands, and it was precisely the sustained interconnections between town and countryside—the fact that the bands' activities and very existence were predicated on the lack of barriers and of physical and symbolic distance between towns and countryside—that was typical of these forms of rural organized crime. Evidently urbanization did not cause the disappearance of rural bands; bands simply developed new criminal styles to suit the circumstances.

Organized crime in preindustrial Europe turns out to have been much more varied than suggested by the dual model of picaresque rural bands and urban underworlds. The urban and rural bands that operated in the province of Holland may perhaps be regarded as typical of the urbanized, flat, and densely populated coastal zones of the North Sea, which include Flanders as well as southeast England and northwestern Germany. This whole zone was characterized by a lack of strong feudal traditions and by early urbanization, continuous immigration, and a strongly developed infrastructure. Brabant, on the other hand, might represent the "continental" model of band organization and activity. The larger size of bands in Brabant, their far more frequent use of violence, and their familiarity with military models fit in with what we know of banditry in central and southern Germany, "Belgian" Brabant, and Wallonia. In this way regional differences in urbanization, ecology, and infrastructure within the Dutch Republic and their consequences for the organization of crime may provide a model for the comparative study of such connections in other parts of early modern Europe.

Notes

An earlier version of this essay was presented as a paper at the IAHCCJ Conference in Stockholm, 5–8 July 1990. The essay is mainly based on archival research for my dissertation on Dutch organized crime, published as *Underworlds: Organized Crime in the Netherlands, 1650–1800* (Cambridge, 1993).

1. On social bandits and the connections between their (stereotypical) image and their activities see especially E. J. Hobsbawm, *Bandits* (New York, 1981), and A. Blok,

"The Peasant and the Brigand: Social Banditry Reconsidered," *Comparative Studies in Society and History* 14 (1972): 494–503. More recent studies on ancien régime rural banditry include (for Germany) C. Küther, *Räuber und Gauner in Deutschland: Das organisierte Bandenwesen im 18. und 19. Jahrhundert* (Göttingen, 1976); idem, *Menschen auf der Strasse: Vagierende Unterschichten in Bayern, Franken und Schwaben in der zweiten hälfte des 18. Jahrhunderts* (Göttingen, 1983); idem, "Räuber, Volk und Obrigkeit: Zur Wirkungsweise und Funktion staatlicher Strafverfolgung im 18. Jahrhundert," in *Räuber, Volk und Obrigkeit: Studien zur Geschichte der Kriminalität in Deutschland seit dem 18. Jahrhundert,* ed. H. Reif (Frankfurt, 1984), 17–42; and U. Danker, *Räuberbanden im Alten Reich um 1700: Ein Beitrag zur Geschichte von Herrschaft und Kriminalität in der frühen Neuzeit* (Frankfurt, 1988). For France see especially R. Cobb, "La Vie en Marge: Living on the Fringe of the French Revolution," in his *Reactions to the French Revolution* (London, 1972), 128–79; idem, "La Bande d'Orgères," in the same study, 181–215; idem, *A Sense of Place* (London, 1975); idem, "La Route du Nord: The Bande à Salembier," in his *Paris and Its Provinces, 1792–1802* (London, 1975), 194–210; and idem, "La Route du Nord: The Bande Juive," in the same study, 141–93; see also O. Hufton, *The Poor of Eighteenth-Century France, 1750–1789* (Oxford, 1974). For the Netherlands see A. Blok, "The Symbolic Vocabulary of Public Executions," in *History and Power in the Study of Law: New Directions in Legal Anthropology,* ed. J. F. Collier and J. Starr (Ithaca, N.Y., 1989), 31–55; idem, *De Bokkerijders: Roversbenden en Geheime Genootschappen in de Landen van Overmaas (1730–1774)* (Amsterdam, 1991); and F. Egmond, *Banditisme in de Franse Tijd: Profiel van de Grote Nederlandse Bende, 1790–1799* (Amsterdam, 1986), and idem, *Underworlds.* For England, see J. M. Beattie, *Crime and the Courts in England, 1660–1800* (Oxford, 1986); A. Macfarlane, *The Justice and the Mare's Ale: Law and Disorder in Seventeenth-Century England* (Oxford, 1981); and A. L. Beier, *Masterless Men: The Vagrancy Problem in England, 1560–1640* (London, 1985).

2. For London see M. D. George, *London Life in the Eighteenth Century* (Harmondsworth, 1985); J. McMullan, "Criminal Organization in Sixteenth- and Seventeenth-Century London," *Social Problems* 29 (1982): 311–23; J. J. Tobias, *Crime and Industrial Society in the Nineteenth Century* (Harmondsworth, 1967); and K. Chesney, *The Victorian Underworld* (Harmondsworth, 1972); see also E. P. Thompson and Eileen Yeo, eds., *The Unknown Mayhew: Selections from the Morning Chronicle 1849–50* (Harmondsworth, 1971). For Paris, see R. Cobb, *The Police and the People: French Popular Protest, 1789–1820* (Oxford, 1970); P. Peveri, "Les Pickpockets à Paris au XVIIIe siècle," *Revue d'histoire moderne et contemporaine* 29 (1982): 3–35: and I. Foucher, "Deux bandes de voleurs au XVIIIe siècle" (M.A. thesis, Paris, 1990).

3. See M. McIntosh, *The Organisation of Crime* (London, 1975), esp. 18–41; see also her "Changes in the Organisation of Thieving," in *Images of Deviance,* ed. S. Cohen (Harmondsworth, 1971), 98–133.

4. This essay focuses on nonethnic organized crime; for the important Jewish networks and Gypsy bands active in the Dutch Republic, see F. Egmond, "Crime in Context: Jewish Involvement in Organized Crime in the Dutch Republic," *Jewish History* 4 (1990): 75–100, and *Underworlds*.

5. Algemeen Rijksarchief in The Hague (hereafter ARA), Criminal Records (hereafter CR) of Brielle, 21.

6. State Archive (hereafter SA) of North Brabant (hereafter NB) in 's-Hertogenbosch (hereafter SANB), CR of Bergen op Zoom, 21.

7. Most of these men should be regarded as the prosecutor's personal staff rather than as police or civil servants. Like night watchmen, many of them had other jobs and duties as well.

8. Stroo was arrested and sentenced in 1658 for the theft of a large quantity of diamonds. He escaped from detention but was caught again and sentenced to death at Leiden in 1663. See ARA, Hof van Holland, 5656 (1658); and ARA, CR of Rijnland, 8 (1663).

9. In 1659–60 two men from the Southern Netherlands who had served in the Spanish armies were sentenced at Rotterdam. Together with a number of colleagues they had committed burglaries in towns all over the Northern as well as the Southern Netherlands. See Municipal Archive (hereafter MA) of Rotterdam, CR 248.

10. See MA of The Hague, 106 (1690).

11. Slang terms were frequently used among the members of this network. It is still unclear, however, to what extent thieves' cant constituted a real language.

12. On passenger transportation by barge in the Netherlands see J. de Vries, *Barges and Capitalism: Passenger Transportation in the Dutch Economy, 1632–1839* (Utrecht, 1981).

13. Of course, there was a difference between newcomers and experienced thieves, but thieves who had reached a prominent status were usually known for their individual skills, numerous previous convictions, and wide range of experience.

14. A relatively large number of men (up to ten or twelve) acted together during these rural robberies. For their sentences see MA of Amsterdam, CR 608 (1716–17).

15. On the Band of Dirk Verhoeven see ARA, Hof van Holland, CR 5482–84 and 5665; MA of Gorinchem, CR 38; and SANB, CR of Oosterhout, 116.

16. See MA of 's-Hertogenbosch, CR 39, 164/11, 146/13, 131/24, 83/8; MA of Breda, CR 112–13. District Archive (hereafter DA) at Heusden, CR of Heusden 34; SANB, CR Land van Ravestein, 1; Archives du Royaume de Belgique in Brussels, CR Drossaard of Brabant, 61; MA of Antwerp, CR 159; SA of Gelderland, CR Hof van Gelre, 4506, 1694/3.

17. Among the more important smaller groups were the Band of Engele Jantje (Angel John) during the 1730s and the Band of Calotte, active between 1759 and 1765. The former consisted of numerous interrelated vagrant families, who begged, stole, and set fire to several farmhouses. The Calotte band formed a loose-knit and exten-

sive network comprising more than a hundred people. Its operations covered most of eastern and central Brabant as well as parts of (modern) Limburg, adjacent German territory and the area of Liège.

18. It should be emphasized that such ties do not imply any significant measure of support for these vagrant groups and other bands from the nonmarginal rural population in Brabant.

19. On the Band of the Van Exaerde brothers, see SANB, CR of Putte, 3, 5, and MA of Rotterdam, CR 253, 145, and 176.

7

Urban and Rural Criminal Justice and Criminality in the Netherlands since the Middle Ages: Some Observations

Herman Diederiks

Town and countryside are classic topics of traditional criminology, and this may be due to the dichotomy of *society* and *community*, of *Gesellschaft* and *Gemeinschaft*, that was favored in nineteenth-century sociology. The new "social history of crime and criminal justice" has focused on this aspect much less. We may find some clues to this classic problem of urban versus rural criminality in the modernization of crime patterns. In general, modernization has subsumed urbanization, and in so doing, traditional crime patterns are simultaneously defined as rural. The urban dweller or the immigrant assimilated into towns is considered in this conceptualization to commit "modern crimes." The modernization-of-crime thesis claims that a general societal development moves from much (public) violence to a pacified society. The state slowly made effective its claim on the monopoly of violence and the citizen could calm down and become less aggressive.[1]

Another aspect of the subject of urban/rural crime and criminal justice is the interlinkage of town and countryside. How far did the town dominate the countryside in regard to criminal justice? Was the town the locus of crime or of its controllers? Did rural criminals just enter the town for its protection of urban anonymity? These questions can be easily posed, but in research and the literature little attention has been given to those problems. So, this preliminary survey is presented on the basis of scattered pieces of information derived from the literature and ongoing research without a pretense of completeness.[2] I would like to deal with the subject of the "urban/rural" contrast and the relationships between town and country on the basis of the following topics: the criminal justice system; the courts and their penalties; the kinds of criminality and the offenders.

Dealing first with the criminal justice system, we may consider the courts and then the penalties or the way these courts punished their "clients." The northern Netherlands had had a very high degree of urbanization since the late Middle Ages, especially in the western part—the provinces of Holland, Zeeland, and Utrecht. We can say that about half of the population lived in smaller or greater urban centers. The first general census, in 1795, revealed that of the 794,146 inhabitants of the province of Holland, 59 percent lived in 15 municipalities of more than 5,000 inhabitants.[3] With the exception of the municipality of Nieuweramstel, south of Amsterdam, those 15 municipalities were all towns or cities in the 1795 census. They all had courts dispensing the "high jurisdiction," implying the power over life and death of an offender brought before that court. The town of The Hague had two courts: the municipal one and the Court of Holland, the latter with jurisdiction over part of The Hague, giving the province a total of 16 courts for 467,254 inhabitants, or as the French say, *les justiciables.* That makes one court for about 29,000 urban *justiciables* on the average. If we make a distinction between Amsterdam on one hand and the rest of the province on the other, we have about 250,000 urban residents in 15 jurisdictions. This implies about 16,500 *justiciables* per urban court in the medium-sized towns in Holland. The total number of courts for the province of Holland at the end of the ancien régime has been estimated at 205.[4] So, for the rural areas there were 189 competent courts, implying for a total rural population of 326,892 in 1795 about 1,700 *justiciables* on the average for each rural court.

These rural courts were staffed by the local elite, well known to its clients; this must have brought rural courts into much closer community contact than the urban jurisdictions. In general we may assume that, informally, the presence of a criminal court and its judges was felt more in the rural areas, whereas in the urban setting the formal visibility of the court (the tribunal as part of the town hall) and the distinctive clothing of the judicial authorities compensated for their broader—and therefore less intensive—formal scope. In the towns with fewer courts, the authorities had to create a much greater distance from their clients compared to the simple, rural tribunals. One may wonder whether the use of formally correct law was different in the rural and urban courts. In a large study covering a number of selected jurisdictions in the Dutch Republic for the eighteenth century, only two jurisdictions on the fringe of the territory of the Republic provided a great number of reports containing legal advice to the rural courts.[5] Outside the major towns in one of the rural regions, Twente, at the east border of the Dutch Republic, the judicial power rested with the bailiff.[6] Twente is a part of the province of Overijssel, with the capital Zwolle, and in all cases the bailiff sought legal advice from juridical experts in the capital. In most cases this advice made up an integral part of the sentence. Thus we can follow the arguments of the jurists in respect to the definition of the crime, the juridical procedure, and the penal consequences. For other districts covered by the research project similar information is absent with the exception of another, more marginal region in the southeast of the Dutch Republic, in the province of Limburg—the court of aldermen of Heerlen. So, the rural, peripheral courts made more use of "official" or "scientific" law compared to the urban courts. The next question might be: What was the difference for an offender before a rural court compared to an offender before an urban court? We do not find in the urban sentences much "juristic" reasoning as existed in the rural sentences, because there the sentence was literally the legal advice of professional lawyers residing in the provincial capital.[7]

Another aspect of the urban-rural contrast is the problem of competence and the relations between the persons in charge, the bailiffs of the different jurisdictions. The criminal justice system up to the beginning of the nineteenth century had a local character. The urban jurisdiction really ended with the city walls, where the jurisdiction of the lord of a village or of a polderboard began. Sometimes towns extended their rights over a rural area, but usually the local people and local arrangements prevailed. In the rural province of Friesland the criminal justice system was already centralized; there the court in Leeuwarden, the capital, dealt with all criminal cases.[8] The southern provinces also contained a few exceptions. So, Bois–Le Duc, the capital of North Brabant, had the jurisdiction in the surrounding countryside, the "Meiery."[9] In the region known as the province of Limburg since the nineteenth century, there was a scattered quality mainly due to a very diversified political situation. The whole territory can be characterized as a borderland.[10]

Taking the urban-rural relationships into consideration, we can see how during the eighteenth century the court in the small town of Venlo tried to gain power in criminal cases over rural courts in the nearby district of Montfort. The local, rural courts' appeal to the Estates-General in The Hague resulted in a victory.[11]

What about a suspect fleeing from the town or from the rural jurisdiction? Was the bailiff or his servant allowed to continue the prosecution outside their own strict jurisdiction? Preliminary research in the judicial archives of Amsterdam for the eighteenth and early nineteenth centuries has revealed growing reciprocity between the authorities of Amsterdam and those in other jurisdictions. While in 1700 the Amsterdam authorities sent only 23 letters requesting information about an offender or a case, we see that in 1805 there were 171 letters such letters.[12] From this preliminary finding one may conclude that the local boundaries during the eighteenth century became less restrictive, and "criminality" and "criminals" became "nationalized." Consequently the prosecution was becoming more coordinated until the 1811 incorporation into the French Empire and the 1813 establishment of the central nation state, when the judicial apparatus became nationally organized.[13]

♦ The Visibility of the Sanctions

It is clear from the publications of Pieter Spierenburg and of Herman Franke that during the ancien régime as well as in the nineteenth century the public nature of a penalty was important, although there were considerable changes in the later period.[14]

Michel Foucault, in his well-known work *Discipline and Punish,* makes a sweeping argument about the relationship of torture to monarchy, prison to bureaucracy: the growth of state and crime are intimately intertwined. In his view the "invention" of the prison is supposed to have abolished the public "spectacle of suffering." Spierenburg concludes his analysis at the end of the eighteenth century, and for that reason he does not really discuss the Foucault thesis on the basis of empirical findings. Yet Franke describes a much slower process of change during the nineteenth century compared to the picture offered by Foucault.

To what extent was the public execution that symbolized the ancien régime an urban phenomenon? This question leads us to the place of the gallows. The gallows were not the sites of execution but rather the places where the corpses were displayed after criminals were dealt with on the scaffold. In the towns, executions normally took place in the city center and the scaffold was only temporarily erected there, while the gallows for the exposure of the executed corpses were permanently located outside the cities, visible to persons entering and leaving. For the province of Holland, twelve such places just outside the urban settlement have been found, and for the countryside the same number have been identified in the literature.[15] In the provinces of Utrecht and Gelderland the rural sites were more prevalent; outside the city gates, gallows fields were found near the city of Utrecht, Amersfoort, Rheenen, and Arnhem while there were at least eleven in rural jurisdictions.[16] One can conclude that the visibility of the hand of criminal justice represented by the presence of corpses on the gallows near cities may have compensated for the much lower density of courts and their officials.

During the nineteenth century this visibility changed and instead of gallows fields we find prisons and other institutions, such as workhouses and penitentiaries for young offenders, located in both the urban setting and the rural landscape. The dome-shaped prisons in the towns of Haarlem, Arnhem, and Breda, the first two towns being provincial capitals, must have been impressive sights.[17] The relationship between town and surrounding countryside—at least in the northern seven provinces of the Dutch Republic—can be described, therefore, as a system of separation.

The question can be raised about differences in effectiveness of the rural and urban systems of criminal justice. In this respect an analysis of the sentences pronounced in absentia may provide some clues. Are there indications of a greater or lesser effectiveness of the criminal justice in the urban context? How far can we use the uncontested number of sentences—those by default—in this respect? What was the use of a sentence in the absence of the offender?

In general we can say that such a decision of the court gave the authorities a weapon against an unwanted person in case he or she came back. Taking the figures in the eighteenth-century Dutch Republic we find a very high percentage of sentences by default in two peripheral rural areas. There, nearly 40 percent of all sentences were pronounced in the absence of the offender.[18] In rural areas near urban centers the percentage of sentences in absentia was much lower; a jurisdiction near The Hague and another one north of Amsterdam had only 14 percent of such sentences. In small towns we find the same share. We may conclude that the effectiveness of criminal justice policy in the rural districts may have been lower than in the urban jurisdictions.

◆ Town and Countryside in the Process of State Formation

Turning to the practice of punishment in the ancien régime, one may wonder whether the formation of larger political units had an impact on the way judges treated the offenders. In a locale with small communities, banishment beyond those communities might have been effective enough. With an expansion of the central state and its agencies, the territorial perimeters of banishment might have to be extended to match the scope of the state. Considering the combined figures for two small towns (Brielle and Zierikzee) for two periods (106 and 80 sentences in 1701–55 and 1756–1810, respectively), we find that in the first period 54 percent of the sentences that had banishment as a penalty involved a banishment outside the small jurisdiction, whereas in the second period this percentage dropped to 31 percent. Similar courts in cities banished their offenders farther away in the second period. The provinces of Holland and Zeeland banished 21 percent in the period up to 1755, while after that year almost half were banished out of their own provinces. The Dutch Republic as a whole did not play an important role in this respect, but the local urban barriers had been extended and concerned the whole province. Perhaps an awareness that one did not solve the problem by just banishing someone from a small jurisdiction helped determine this change in decisionmaking.

◆ Offenders

What can we learn from the birthplaces of offenders? Do they tell us about the character of a community or about the nature of the social control, or perhaps both? An urban community may be characterized more by delinquency of persons from outside that community and the rural jurisdictions may deal more with their own people. Some figures for the eighteenth century are suggestive.

Birthplaces of offenders in the eighteenth-century Dutch Republic are characterized in table 7–1, which presents figures for six jurisdictions. The first two mentioned jurisdictions, Waterland and Wassenaar, can be characterized as rural districts within the vicinity of urban centers, The Hague and Amsterdam, respectively. The second two jurisdictions, Twente and Heerlen, were located in the periphery of the Dutch Republic, Twente in the east near the German border and Heerlen in the southeast (province of Limburg). Brielle and Zierikzee were two small harbor towns, and the former had a garrison. We see in table 7–1 that the share of offenders with origins outside the Dutch Republic are rather similar for the six jurisdictions in the sample. On the other hand there are big differences in respect to persons born within the jurisdiction. More than half of the offenders in the peripheral rural districts were born there whereas the rural districts near urban centers were characterized by an exogenous delinquency. The two small harbor towns are in between these rural districts. If we take also the place of residence of the offender into consideration we find a much greater similarity in regard to indigenous delinquency. The peripheral rural districts and the two harbor towns both tallied around 85 percent of offenders with local residences. The two rural districts near the cities of The Hague and Amsterdam lagged a bit behind in this respect: there only

Table 7-1. Birthplaces of Offenders in the Eighteenth-Century
Dutch Republic

	Jurisdiction		
	Waterl./Wass.	Twente/Heerlen	Briel/Zierikz.
Within (%)	19.6	51.8	31.4
Nearby urban (%)	11.1	1.4	5.8
Nearby rural (%)	18.1	17.0	13.9
Dutch Republic (%)	28.1	8.2	25.6
Outside (%)	23.1	21.8	23.3
N	199	147	554

77.6 percent had an address within the jurisdiction and more than 14 percent came from The Hague or Amsterdam. We can say that delinquency was a local, indigenous affair, and only the vicinity of urban centers like The Hague or Amsterdam interrupted this pattern.

An analysis of the lists of sentences of the Leiden court reveals the offenders' places of birth. In the first half of the seventeenth century only about 17 percent were born in the city; after 1750 this figure jumped to 75 percent. Up to 1675 immigration into Leiden is determined by streams of persons coming from outside the Dutch Republic, a tendency reflected in the group of persons brought before the court in Leiden. If we look at the share of offenders originating from the province of Holland outside Leiden, we see that this share dropped from 33 percent during the period 1676–1700 to only 10 percent in the years 1776–1800. Within this stream of persons most of the offenders came from towns within the province of Holland with more than 5,000 inhabitants (77 percent in the seventeenth century and 64 percent in the eighteenth century). The immediate rural hinterland (within a radius of five kilometers) provided in the seventeenth century 9 percent and in the eighteenth century 16 percent of the persons condemned by the Leiden court.[19]

For the nineteenth century, the registration books of one of the new prisons have been analyzed. The records included sex, age, places of birth and residence, education, occupation, crimes, sentences, and prison career. The registers contain data for the more than 10,000 persons sentenced to a maximum of five years in that prison.[20] If we consider their places of birth and residence, we find that 36 percent of the prison population for the period 1840–86 did not live in their birthplaces. We can also distinguish the pris-

oners from cities and those from the countryside. In the cities this population is much less indigenous. The prisoners from Amsterdam were born there
in 68 percent of the cases and those from cities in the provinces of Holland,
Utrecht, and Zeeland had been born there in 59 percent of the cases. In towns
like Zwolle and Nimwegen this figure is even smaller: 53 percent. The prisoners born in the countryside also lived there. In the provinces of Gelderland, Overijssel, and Drenthe this share is 74 percent, and in North Brabant
and Limburg it is an even greater proportion, 92 percent. A comparison of
the place of the court condemning an offender and his residence leads us to
the conclusion that crime was a local affair. In the different provinces in the
nineteenth century, between 78 and 90 percent of the offenders with a prison sentence lived in the region of the court condemning them.

Another aspect of crime and location is the distance of the flight after a
crime to a place of refuge. We may assume that places of asylum were a
specific urban phenomenon, but the identification of safe havens had its roots
in the political status of the small towns concerned. From the sixteenth century until 1795, five small towns in the border territories of the provinces of
Holland, Utrecht, and Gelderland functioned as asylum towns; as far as is
known, they received about a thousand persons fleeing as debtors or as those
accused of manslaughter.[21] More than 10 percent were persons fleeing because they killed another by accident or in self-defense and were afraid of
being prosecuted. In the archives, 130 of them have been traced back. Of
these, 61 came to one of the asylum towns in the period before 1700, 51 during the first half of the eighteenth century, and only 5 in the years 1750–95.
Twenty-four came from the bigger cities of Amsterdam, The Hague, Rotterdam, or Utrecht and 81 from the rest of the Dutch Republic including smaller
towns and the countryside. One came from outside the Republic and the
places of origin are unknown for the remainder. So flight to an asylum town
and receiving a passport to stay there was not something unique to the bigger towns in Holland.

◆ Criminality

Did urban and rural patterns of criminality exist? To answer this question,
we may turn to figures presented in table 7–2. They pertain to the six sample regions in the Dutch Republic and their share of the four main crime
categories for the entire eighteenth century.

The rural-peripheral regions show the highest percentage for crimes
against persons, implying all sorts of violence, while their share of disturbance

Table 7–2. Share of the Four Main Categories of Crime in Six
Regions in the Dutch Republic, 1701–1810

	Region		
	Waterl./Wass.	Twente/Heerlen	Briel/Zierikz.
Public order (%)	32.7	24.9	19.8
Against persons (%)	17.9	27.3	11.2
Property (%)	45.4	45.0	58.7
Morality (%)	4.0	2.8	10.3
N	324	249	678

of the public order is also very high—almost 25 percent. The rural districts
near The Hague and Amsterdam nevertheless have higher figures for the
disturbance of the public order and lower ones for violence. It will be clear
that property crime is dominant in the small towns of Brielle and Zierikzee—
almost 60 percent. If we take some other figures into consideration, we find
for the town of Delft for the long period 1591–1810 a share of almost 36 percent of property crimes, with low figures for the early seventeenth century
(22.3 percent) and very high ones for the early nineteenth century (70 percent).[22] The overall figure for the town of Leiden for the seventeenth and
eighteenth centuries is 34 percent for property crimes. The figures for violent criminality for Delft and Leiden in the seventeenth and eighteenth centuries are, respectively, 11.1 percent and 16 percent.

   Taking into consideration one type of violent crime, that within the family, we see the following pattern: the sentences analyzed in the SR18 Project
contain 9.4 percent cases of "family crime" (259 of 2,750) for the period 1700–
1811. Seven sentences concern the violence of husbands against their wives
and all these cases were rural.[23] Other cases of violence involving family
members are much more heavily registered in the rural district of Wassenaar
near The Hague and in the rural district of Heerlen in the south. In a city
like Amsterdam the main court did not deal with such affairs. There smaller
and more informal courts dealt with minor cases of violence, within or outside the family.

   The patterns of crimes against morality also show a definite urban-rural
split: urban in Delft, Leiden, Brielle, Zierikzee, and Amsterdam with, respectively, 13.2 percent, 15.9 percent, 10.3 percent, and 21 percent, in contrast with
4 percent and 2.8 percent for rural Waterland/Wassenaar and Twente/Heerlen,
respectively. Up to now, rural jurisdictions have not been the subject of much

research. The impression is that, especially in the eighteenth century, rural jurisdictions were mainly subject to two types of criminality: "local" criminality, mostly made up of violence, and "imported" criminality, mainly vagabondism and begging. Especially in the rural borderland the influx of immigrants and of vagrant soldiers, an "imported" criminality, could be very burdensome.[24]

◆ Female-Male Delinquency

If we assume that rural crime was more violent than urban crime we may also assume that the share of male offenders was higher in the rural jurisdictions. During the eighteenth century in the six sample regions in the Dutch Republic the rural peripheral jurisdictions had the highest share of male offenders, 88.2 percent; the two rural districts in the western, urbanized part of the country had 81.8 percent; and the two small towns had a male delinquency of 70.5 percent. If we compute the rank order correlations between the share of male offenders per region and that of the four main crime categories (violence, crimes against the public order, crimes against morality, and crimes against property), the correlation of the share of male offenders and violence is positive, .61, and of property crime, negative, .89.

◆ Some Conclusions

The assumptions about urban/rural differences with which we started have been largely confirmed by the empirical data presented here. Most of these data concern the period of the ancien régime. The rural countryside showed more male and violent criminality. The rural courts seemed to be less effective although the "social" distance between rural court members and their "clients" was much less. While part of the rural crime was "imported" by soldiers and vagrants, the larger part of the offenses were perpetrated by local people—if not local by birth at least by residence within the jurisdiction. The same picture has also been found in regard to the inmates of one of the main prisons in the nineteenth century. State formation and centralization had already influenced judicial practice before the establishment of the centralized and unified state after 1811–13, the territory from which the offenders were banished widening in the eighteenth century. Another aspect of state unification was the increasing collaboration of the judicial authorities in rural and urban settings. Urban and rural, local and national, differences and structures experienced a long-term shift that no single event, such as national political unification, can explain.

Notes

1. See, among others, R. M. Dekker, "'Politiek geweld' en het proces van staatsvorming in de geschiedenis van de Nederlanden," *Amsterdams Sociologisch Tijdschrift* 10, no. 2 (1983): 335–52.

2. For another type of survey see Herman Diederiks, "Criminality and Its Repression in the Past: Quantitative Approaches: A Survey," in *Economic and Social History in the Netherlands* 1 (1989): 67–86.

3. See, among others, Herman Diederiks, *Een stad in verval: Amsterdam omstreeks 1800: demografisch, economisch, ruimtelijk* (Amsterdam, 1982), 6–10.

4. Florike Egmond, "Hoge Jurisdicties van het 18e-eeuwse Holland, een aanzet tot de bepaling van hun aantal, ligging en begrenzingen," *Holland: Regionaalhistorisch Tijdschrift* 19 (1987): 129–61, esp. 131.

5. For a description of the project see Herman Diederiks, "Patterns of Criminality and Law Enforcement during the Ancien Régime: The Dutch Case," *Criminal Justice History* 1 (1980): 157–74.

6. For a description of the administration of one of these towns see H. J. M. Weustink, *De Rechtsgeschiedenis van de Stad Oldenzaal en van de Mark Berghuizen tot 1795* (Assen, Netherlands, 1962), 46–61.

7. There is discussion on this point by Sjoerd Faber, *Strafrechtspleging en Criminaliteit te Amsterdam, 1680–1811: De Nieuwe Menslievendheid* (Arnhem, Netherlands, 1983), chap. 11, "Regel en rechter," 213–27.

8. S. J. Fockema Andreae, *De Nederlandse Staat onder de Republiek* (Amsterdam, 1969), 134ff.

9. B. C. M. Jacobs, *Justitie en Politie in 's-Hertogenbosch voor 1629: De bestuursorganisatie van een Brabantse stad* (Assen, Netherlands, 1986), 18–19.

10. J. A. K. Haas, *De verdeling van de landen van Overmaas, 1644–1662: Territoriale desintegratie van een betwist grensgebied* (Assen, Netherlands, 1978).

11. E. Roebroeck, *Het land van Montfort: Een agrarische samenleving in een grensgebied, 1647–1820* (Assen, Netherlands, 1967), 167–74.

12. Toon van Weel, "De interjurisdictionele betrekkingen in criminele zaken van het Amsterdamse gerecht (1700–1811)," in *Nieuwe licht op oude justitie, misdaad en straf ten tijde van de republiek,* ed. Sjoerd Faber (Muiderberg, Netherlands, 1989), 23–48, esp. 32.

13. See, among others, H. A. Diederiks, S. Faber, A. H. Huussen Jr., *Strafrecht en criminaliteit: Cahiers voor lokale en regionale geschiedenis* (Zutphen, Netherlands, 1988), 21–29.

14. Pieter Spierenburg, *The Spectacle of Suffering, Executions and the Evolution of Repression: From a Preindustrial Metropolis to the European Experience* (Cambridge, 1984); Herman Franke, *Twee Eeuwen gevangen: Misdaad en straf in Nederland* (Aula, Netherlands, 1990).

15. The urban places of the gallows (*galgevelden*) were near Amsterdam, Haar-

lem, Alkmaar, Hoorn, Enkhuizen, Leiden, The Hague (two), Delft, Gouda, Woerden, and Dordrecht; the rural sites: Amstelveen, Beverwijk, Oosthuizen, Broek in Waterland, Rinnegom, Bergen, Schoorl, Westfriese Ringdijk (polderboard), Opmeer, Den Helder, Texel, Scheveningen; see H. G. Jelgersma, *Galgebergen en Galgevelden in West- en Midden Nederland* (Zutphen, Netherlands, 1978).

16. Those in rural locations were at Zeist, Leersum, Amerongen, Rozendaal, Doorwerth, Lunteren, Renswoude, Bergharen-Afferden, Leerdam, Apeldoorn (more than one), and Zeddam; Jelgersma, *Galgebergen en Galgevelden.*

17. M. A. Petersen, *Gedetineerden onder dak: Geschiedenis van het gevangeniswezen in Nederland van 1795 af, bezien van zijn behuizing* (Leiden, 1978).

18. Herman Diederiks and Pieter Spierenburg, "Delitti e pene in Olanda (1550–1810)," in *Cheiron, materiali e strumenti di aggiornamento storiografico: Il piotere di guidicare, giustizia, pena e controllo sociale negli stati d'antico regime* 1 (1983): 85–108, esp. 98.

19. Herman Diederiks, "Stadt und Umland im Lichte der Herkunftorte der Kriminellen in Leiden im 17. und 18. Jahrhundert," in *Städtisches Um- und Hinterland in vorindustrieller Zeit,* ed. H. K. Schulze (Cologne, 1985), 191–92.

20. Herman Diederiks, "Gevangenen en gevangenis te Hoorn in de negentiende eeuw," *Criminaliteit in de negentiende eeuw, Hollandse Studien* 22 (1989): 83–94.

21. Marijke Gijswijt-Hofstra, *Wijkplaats voor vervolgden: Asielverlening in Culemborg, Vianen, Buren, Leerdam en IJsselstein van de 16de tot eind 18de eeuw* (Dieren, Netherlands, 1984).

22. H. Diederiks, "Criminality and Its Repression in the Past, Quantitative Approaches: A Survey," in *Economic and Social History in the Netherlands* 1 (1989): 72–78.

23. Cases from 1716–99; SR18 636, 702, 445, 1859, 801/805, 821, 544. The SR18 Project is an ongoing, collaborative data collection housed in the Municipal Archives of Amsterdam.

24. See, for example, Roebroeck, *Het land van Montfort,* 173.

8

For God, State, and People: Crime and Local Justice in Preindustrial Sweden

Jan Sundin

During the last few decades, legal sources—consisting primarily of books containing trial verdicts from court hearings, and other remnants of legal proceedings—have been used increasingly by historians in different countries. These scholars' goals have varied from attempting to describe the development of registered crime to producing analyses of the legal system. Others have availed themselves of similar sources in order to trace the attitudes and evaluations of past times as an *histoire de la mentalité*. I have concentrated on local justice and the crimes that were heard at Swedish district and town courts from the beginning of the seventeenth century until 1840.[1]

My aim has been to create a picture of the work sphere and functions of local justice and how they have changed during the last centuries of preindustrial Sweden. However, I have also attempted to convey an impression of the everyday life of ordinary people. The legal system was influenced by an economic, social, and political transition that was not unique to Sweden. Similar changes took place over the whole of Western Europe, which explains why results from international research have been of great help in the interpretation of the course of events.

A total of approximately fifty thousand individual notes have been excerpted and processed with the aid of a computer. These notes have come mainly from the town of Linköping and the county district of Gullberg, both situated in the south of Sweden, and from the town of Härnösand and the county district of Säbrå in the north of Sweden. Some results also have been included from the Göta Court of Appeal in the province of Östergötland, which includes Linköping and Gullberg, during specially selected ten-year periods from the middle of the seventeenth century until the beginning of the nineteenth century. In this summary an outline is given showing how the sources reflected changes in the structure of crimes over the course of approximately two hundred years. The results are then seen in relation to some questions that are currently of interest to historians.

◆ The Agenda of the Courts

First, we can take a look at how the total number of people fined varied over time in the towns compared with numbers in the rural areas up to, and including, the end of the eighteenth century. In both Linköping and Härnösand the average number per year remained relatively stable at between twenty-five and fifty up until the decade starting in 1740 (see fig. 8-1). After this there are no figures available for Linköping until 1797. Härnösand experienced a temporary increase during the 1750s. Crimes against religious rules had increased in number, but crimes of violence, disorderly conduct, and breaches of the

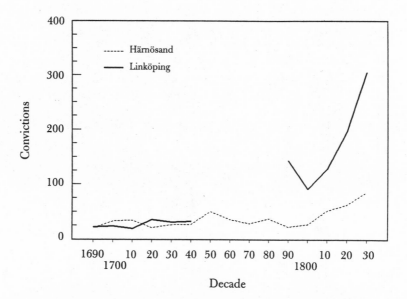

Figure 8-1. Number of convictions for all types of offenses by decade in the cities of Linköping and Härnösand, 1690–1839.

Sources: Lists of citations and fines in the Provincial Archives of Vadstena and Härnösand.

peace had increased, too (see figs. 8-2, 8-3). It is likely that during that century the campaign for better moral behavior in towns intensified.

After 1760 the total number of crimes decreased, but it increased again after 1810. The crimes involved then were acts violating special statutes on the retailing of alcohol, the management of fire, the maintaining of public health, and similar concerns—which account for a notable part of the increase—together with a large number of crimes concerning law and order. In part there was an increase in the ambitions of the magistrates concerning regularization, but it also seems as though drunkenness and other disturbances of the peace actually became more usual. The same explanation is valid to a greater extent in Linköping, where the hundred convictions per year during the decade of 1800-1809 rose to nearly three hundred during the 1830s.

In Gullberg and Säbrå, 10 to 20 persons were convicted per year up through the 1740s. Then both curves point upward, so that Gullberg is noted as having slightly less than 30 convictions and Säbrå as having about 25

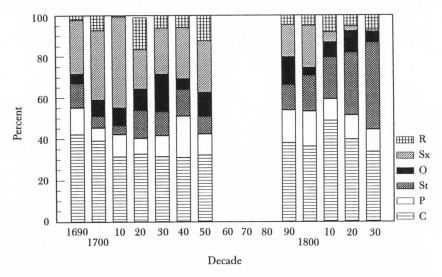

Figure 8-2. Percentage of convictions for different types of offenses by decade in Linköping, 1690–1759 and 1797–1839.

Key: R = religious offense; Sx = sexual offense; O = other; St = special statutes regarding interests of state, church, or local administration; P = property; C = personal conflicts with verbal or physical assaults and disturbing the peace

Sources: Lists of fines in the Provincial Archives of Vadstena.

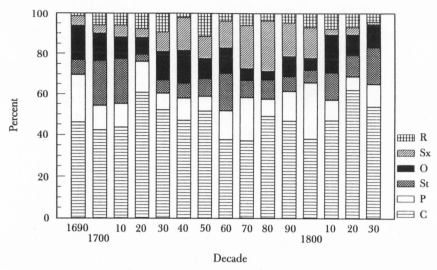

Figure 8-3. Percentage of convictions for different types of offenses by decade in Härnösand, 1690–1839.

Key: R = religious offense; Sx = sexual offense; O = other; St = special statutes regarding interests of state, church, or local administration; P = property; C = personal conflicts with verbal or physical assaults and disturbing the peace

Sources: Lists of fines in the Provincial Archives of Härnösand.

per year during the 1760s (see fig. 8–4). The increase in Säbrå was evenly distributed among different types of crime, but crimes of a religious nature increased in particular (see fig. 8–5). More categories of crime increased in Gullberg during the 1770s, too, among others, crimes against property (see fig. 8–6). The figures for all those convicted for all kinds of crimes stayed at a high level until 1839. In Gullberg the total number increased even more, so that during 1830–39 there were approximately 40 per year. These increases occurred in several categories. Compared to the towns, however, the difference between the 10 to 20 per year in the early part of the eighteenth century and the 20 to 40 per year a century later is relatively modest and is practically counterbalanced by the increase in population.

The courts in rural areas had more criminal cases to deal with during the early part of the nineteenth century than did their predecessors a hundred years earlier. Also, the legal processing of court records from hearings had seemingly become more detailed. In addition, civil disputes had increased compared to the number in previous centuries. The work burden for judges and lay judges had grown steadily, even if some of the cases still could be handled quickly and routinely. This was the case to an even greater ex-

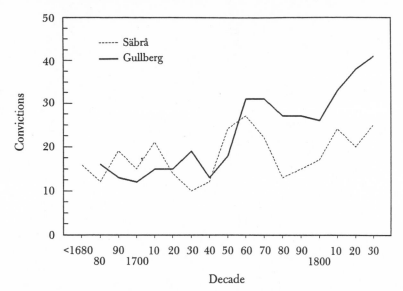

Figure 8-4. Number of convictions for all types of offenses by decade in the countryside court districts of Gullberg and Säbrå, 1680–1839.
Sources: Lists of citations and fines in the Provincial Archives of Vadstena and Härnösand.

tent in the towns, particularly in Linköping, where the number of cases per year increased approximately fifteen times from the beginning of the eighteenth century until the 1830s. The officials of the town courts became busier, timewise, than their predecessors.

From these rough figures we can discern certain trends. No unequivocal transition from crimes of dispute and order can be traced. In fact the percentage as well as the number of those convicted in relation to the population remained relatively constant. The increases in the lists of fines during the eighteenth century were caused partly by the church offensive against illegitimate births and for better behavior at High Mass, Communion services, and parish catechetical meetings. The state's increased demands also can be observed. In rural areas this increase was expressed by state intervention against those who did not participate in tax collection and obligatory duties, against the illicit distillation of alcohol, and against those who had breached the ordinances regulating the use of the forests. In the towns it was mainly a question of the illicit distribution of alcohol. A slight weakening trend can be noted during the beginning of the nineteenth century regarding the state's direct taxation, but even the control over alcohol and forests lessened in extent.

At this point church discipline and the institution of legal proceedings against fornication had become less usual elements in the secular world of

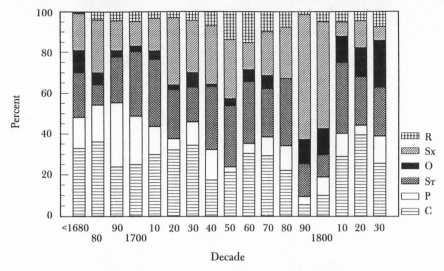

Figure 8-5. Percentage of convictions for different types of offenses by decade in Säbrå, 1680–1839.

Key: R = religious offense; Sx = sexual offense; O = other; St = special statutes regarding interests of state, church, or local administration; P = property; C = personal conflicts with verbal or physical assaults and disturbing the peace

Sources: Lists of fines in the Provincial Archives of Härnösand.

the courts.[2] Disturbances of the peace on the Sabbath were now punished mostly in connection with other crimes. In the towns, above all, local statutes multiplied in order to keep order and improve the supervision of fire and sanitation. In some areas of the courts' agenda, justice had, to a lesser degree, come to concern itself with interpersonal relationships and, to a greater extent, with repressive measures initiated by the state, the church, and later, the town magistrates. However, this does not mean that the settling of personal disputes had completely disappeared.

◆ The Judicial Revolution

"The judicial revolution" has become an accepted description of a development that took place in Western Europe during the preindustrial period.[3] Behind this concept lies the changeover from a locally dominated system of justice to one that was state dominated, followed by an increased influence of experts at the expense of laymen. Such a development took place in Sweden, too. Most cases at the beginning of the seventeenth century were decided

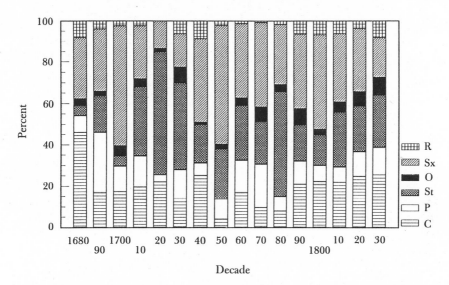

Figure 8-6. Percentage of convictions for different types of offenses by decade in Gullberg, 1680–1839.

Key: R = religious offense; Sx = sexual offense; O = other; St = special statutes regarding interests of state, church, or local administration; P = property; C = personal conflicts with verbal or physical assaults and disturbing the peace

Sources: Lists of fines in the Provincial Archives of Vadstena.

without the intervention of representatives of the state. In rural areas the lay juries had strengthened their influence during the previous centuries. The most established farmers in the area were often elected to the bench year after year and in this manner acquired great experience of the cases that were presented. Instead of ordinary judges, relatively unschooled law readers were deputized as chairmen, persons who were socially not far removed from the farmers. The situation was similar in towns. The town court judges were often laymen, recruited from among merchants and craftsmen. This class still had, at least in smaller towns, great influence over the appointment of the mayor, the chairman of the magistrates.

Most cases heard were concerned with everyday occurrences in which the central powers did not have any reason to intervene. These were civil disputes about property rights for farms and houses, borders between private properties, inheritance, and debts. When criminal law needed to be applied it was often to an unpremeditated kind of offense, such as verbal abuse or petty larceny. Basically it was a question of the necessary defense of personal honor or a person's economic situation. The greatest value regarding honor was without doubt that it reinforced an individual's accepted position in the local community. With one's honor intact it was easier to conclude a deal, borrow money, and defend oneself against charges brought in court. The borderline between civil disputes and criminal cases is sometimes difficult to identify even in the court records. It must have been of minor importance to the parties involved because in both cases they were concerned with compensation and "achieving justice," not with punishing the other party. Justice was, therefore, pragmatic and often mild for those who broke the law. However, it was not lenient because of any all-embracing humanism. Rather, leniency simply helped to create a less conflict-ridden local community.

There were, of course, exceptions. People who had already lost their honor, the poor who could not offer monetary compensation, and strangers met with greater reservation and more repression. These people were prohibited from taking the oath of innocence and faced banishment and corporal punishment more often than did their honorable and propertied neighbors. Nor was punishment always mild concerning crimes that were regarded as particularly repulsive. The death penalty was applied without mercy, for example, in cases of premeditated murder, rape, bestiality, and stealing from the church. However, while mutilation as a punishment had occasionally been exercised during the Middle Ages and the sixteenth century, it rapidly disappeared at the beginning of the seventeenth century.

The growth of central government has been put forward as the most important explanation of the judicial revolution. The crown's regulating ambitions had left traces in the court records of the capital as early as the sixteenth century. In rural areas the process was slower. Such cases constituted only a fraction in Linköping and an even smaller part in Gullberg's county district at the beginning of the seventeenth century. However, before the middle of that century certain signs of a government offensive can be seen even in those areas, an incursion that was connected with the role that secular justice had taken upon itself to defend religious criteria. For example, in the 1640s the county sheriff began to appear as prosecutor in cases of fornication, and the number of people convicted of crimes against other types of statutes increased somewhat.

An important step toward the centralization of justice was taken when the Swedish Court of Appeal was established in 1614. It soon became necessary to establish more appeal courts for the different districts in Sweden, and these appeal courts quickly became supervisors of the work of the local courts. This meant that the administrators of justice were forced, to a greater extent, to take into consideration the letter of the law. The right to reduce sentences on account of special circumstances was reserved primarily for the higher courts of justice. When the law readers were abolished during the course of the seventeenth century, the appeal courts became training centers for the prospective judges in the town and county courts. It was clearly established in the second half of the seventeenth century that it was the king and not the merchants who would appoint the mayors in towns. Slowly but surely the influence of the lay jury decreased in rural areas.

At the end of the seventeenth century, government interests left more traces in the lists of fines than was the case earlier. The percentage and number of those convicted of crimes against state statutes was greater, and more people were convicted for not paying their taxes or not having met other state obligations. This was especially clear in rural areas during the first two decades of the eighteenth century, when the expense of wars put the population under great strain. Apart from concerning itself with extracting extra contributions, horse transportation, and other obligations from the populace, the government had also increased its claims on the forests. The local courts became, more than ever before, repressive instruments against scoff-law farmers.

This trend continued until the end of this period of investigation, the year of 1839. The forest statutes became more lenient in time, but another form of regulation was extended. One of the farmers' most important sidelines, the distillation of alcohol, came into conflict with fiscal interests toward the end of the eighteenth century. Government claims in this area were, without doubt, the greatest source of conflict between state and local community ever to be brought before the district courts. Townspeople were not plagued to such an extent as before by obligatory duties (for example, innkeepers had been required to provide horses), nor was the forest an acute source of conflict. Instead, the sale of illicit alcohol became a relatively usual cause for fines, but not to the same extent as did crimes against statutes in the countryside.

At the same time the church made claims on the courts' participation in order to increase its own authority and that of religion. During the seventeenth century, criminalization of the female party in fornication was enforced, which notably increased the workload of the courts. Sin became seriously accepted as lawful grounds for sanctions. Taking oaths and swearing were, from the year 1687, secular crimes, and absence from High Mass, Communion, or parish catechetical meetings could be punished by the county court or a magistrate. If crimes against the laws governing sexual acts and other religious crimes are consolidated in research, then the curve peaks for all court districts at some time during the eighteenth century. The exact point in time depends on, above all, the number of illegitimate births combined with the court's capacity and will to punish. In reality the church's power over the law should have been at its highest during the first half of the eighteenth century. During the latter part of the century the persecution of those who had been absent from church ceremonies lessened and those who had committed fornication were less often punished by secular courts. Yet the traditional church discipline still existed. The right of the church to be responsible for church discipline was admitted in the Church Law of 1686, and it was exercised in many parishes. While the secular courts relaxed their religious zeal, some parishes continued to exercise it with lesser or greater success even in the nineteenth century.[4]

When the task of the court was, above all, to settle disputes between private citizens, the plaintiffs had to initiate prosecution, gather witnesses, bring forward other proof that was needed, and, finally, represent themselves before the court. It was extremely rare that a plaintiff had legal representation. In order for state interests to be asserted in the courts it was necessary to improve the resources for tracking down and prosecuting criminals. While the legal profession expanded extensively in England during the eighteenth century, it took a great deal longer for it to play an essential role in criminal cases in Sweden. Both the English and Swedish legal procedures during the seventeenth century were overwhelmingly procedural, that is, they were battles between two parties where "bench" and judge gave the verdicts. In Sweden the courts evolved toward a more inquisitory form later on; that is, they themselves took the initiative to investigate states of affairs.

This situation is more noticeable in the court records at the end of the seventeenth century. These records sometimes were actually in the form of questions and answers, after which the judge and bench made their decision. This occurred, no doubt, because the professional judges had an academic education and were influenced by continental doctrines. The annulling of "twelve men's oaths," which allowed one to swear oneself free with the help of eleven friends, is a link in the same chain. The legal theory of proof—that is, the demand that two witnesses and a confession were required as a conclusive demonstration of proof—became more and more accepted. This theory of proof has been regarded as one reason that torture was used on the continent to gain conclusive demonstration of proof in serious criminal cases.[5] In Sweden, torture was used only in extreme cases, such as in witch trials and when the safety of the king or the state was regarded as being in jeopardy. When the evidence was very encumbering but not decisive, then the court could, in individual cases, sentence someone to prison pending a confession.

During the course of the seventeenth century local constables and sheriffs came to be used more frequently to look out for government interests at court proceedings. New offices were also created for similar duties, for example, to combat poaching and the illegal felling of forests. This was of importance, as the statutes that protected the interests of the church and state were not always popular with the common people. Cases of not discharging obligations were self-evident, but neighbors were also unwilling to report one another for illicitly distilling alcohol or felling oaks. Nor was it easy to find willing witnesses. These public officials originally appeared in court primarily when the interests of the church or state were directly threatened, but they gradually came to act as prosecutors, alongside civil plaintiffs, even regarding thefts, crimes of violence, and similar disputes of a more personal nature. The embryo of a modern police force and prosecutor's office had come into being.

While the latter part of the seventeenth century and the eighteenth century were mainly characterized by the infiltration of local justice by central government (and the church), a new trend emerged in towns during the beginning of the nineteenth century. In Linköping, primarily, the number of people sentenced for crimes against local statutes and bylaws increased substantially, while government interests tended to fade into the background. We are on the road to "the organized community," where one of the consequences is increased regulation, not least locally. Furthermore, civil disputes had increased compared with the number in the seventeenth century. Yet, some criminal cases were still settled as disputes between private citizens. In spite of the fact that one can speak of a centralization of justice in many respects, many parties were involved. This leads to the question of how the courts could achieve a balance between these interests.

During the seventeenth century, when the nobility enjoyed its golden age, the district court in Gullberg occasionally took a stand on the side of the common people against the nobility. Repression by the central powers of authority is most apparent during the Carolingian autocracy (1680–1718) and as a result of the alcohol policy of Gustavus III during the last decades of the eighteenth century. However, even then the farmers and merchants were not completely powerless. State statutes could be obstructed by passive resistance and by people's unwillingness to witness against neighbors. The high demands on evidence saved many illicit distillers, innkeepers, and woodcutters from punishment. The farmers and merchants were not politically powerless either. In the period from 1720 to 1772, in particular, they were sometimes able to influence the laws to their own benefit. The court sessions became in a double sense a negotiation between different parties in a social game, where the parties certainly could place different weights on the scales of justice.

Furthermore, the state, the church, and the public agreed on many questions. Even before government and the local elite became seriously involved in mediating fights and quarrels, ordinary people had become used to settling disputes in court. In many cases when local elites and central authorities disagreed about a particular sentence, it was probably a matter of degree. Most people thought that legal measures should be taken against serious crimes of violence and it was usually not difficult to find witnesses willing to testify against thieves. Justice was not conceived as purely negative, nor, for that matter, as completely positive. It was an instrument that could be restructured over and over to suit different purposes.

International literature often portrays the judicial revolution as a process where the central government, by hook or more often by crook, replaced the old feudal courts with modern instruments to fulfill its own aims. In Sweden it was more a question of gradual infiltration by church and state, sometimes with and sometimes without the approval of the farmers and merchants. The term "revolution" is misleading, but to substitute it with "evolution" could suggest an altogether too harmonious development. The courts had the task of acting both for state and church as well as for the common people. It is this difficult role that makes the study of their records so fruitful, if one wishes to increase one's knowledge of older society.

Why did people submit to the centralization of justice without more open protests? Was it because the state and the church, together with the professional officers of the legal system, were so strong that all opposition was fruitless? When the interests of the state were sufficiently threatened then it seemed that it was capable of forcing its aims through, at least without open revolt. However, another important factor must be mentioned, namely the growth of the marginal, poor, and geographically mobile population. This was not particularly evident in Sweden during the seventeenth century, as the country suffered then from a lack of population rather than from overpopulation. However, even before the middle of that century, it can be seen how, in the district of Gullberg, people complained of and tried to regulate the settling of paupers on the parish commons. Without support from the central government it was difficult for the local community to handle a geographically mobile population, which was less sensitive to established concepts of "honor" and to informal social control. In the southern part of the country, above all, this problem grew during the latter part of the eighteenth century and culminated during the nineteenth century. It was especially evident in towns, where it left traces in the registering of fines over drunkenness, street fighting, and thefts. The number of ragamuffins and vagrants grew and the question of welfare and vagrancy became burning issues in every parish and town. These questions could not be solved by local administration alone. In comparison with England this development took the same direction, but the chronological order of events took place later in Sweden.[6]

◆ Punishment as Reconciliation and Warning

It is difficult to write of the system of punishment and changes to that system in preindustrial society without referring to the influence Michel Foucault has had on researchers of the last decades.[7] Foucault's ideas have been interpreted in several different ways and it is no easy task to describe them briefly. However, here I would focus on the role of punishment as a social instrument of control. Foucault states that, previously, punishment was directed against the individual's body, but that during the Age of Enlightenment, it increasingly came to be concentrated on the soul. The death penalty lost its importance and other forms of corporal punishment gradually disappeared. Prisons became the main instrument of the new forms of control. Foucault rejects the idea that it was primarily humanitarian motives that lay behind this change.

Criticism against Foucault has been especially harsh from those historians who have tried empirically to follow the changes in the penal system. Pieter Spierenburg has, among other things, pointed out that the prison system had evolved long before ideas on enlightenment had gained ground at the end of the eighteenth century. Spierenburg refers to a mentality-historical tradition and emphasizes the gradual emergence of a disassociation from physical suffering, followed during the nineteenth century by the bureaucratization of government, including institutions of punishment.[8]

In the wake of the Age of Enlightenment and bureaucratization there followed undoubtedly an increased belief in "reasonable" solutions. This pertained also to the function of punishment. This aspect has been emphasized by David Garland, who refers to Max Weber's theory about the role of rationality in a modern, bureaucratic society.[9] Garland places the emphasis on a change in punishment from serving an "emotional" and moralizing purpose to becoming a "penitentiary science" administered by a select group of bureaucrats. He says, however, that emotional, moralizing, and "irrational" elements are still to be found in court proceedings today.

Jukka Kekkonen, from Finland, has recently given his, and Heikki Ylikangas's, proposals for another interpretation, one that emphasizes the connection between the form of governmental rule—above all the degree of democratic participation—and social control.[10] According to these researchers, a more even distribution of the resources of a community (manifested in political power) leads to moderation of the control over individuals, while a concentration of resources leads, among other things, to the exact opposite. For example, the growth of absolute sovereignty was followed by a tightening of the penal system and other forms of social control, while the process of democratization entailed the opposite.

I do not intend to give a comprehensive summary of the debate on the causes of the changes in the penal system in Western Europe in general, and in Sweden in particular. I wish only to sketch the background to the picture I myself have gained from events that took place in the areas I investigated and in Sweden in general before the middle of the nineteenth century. It appears to me that my Finnish colleagues' emphasis on the social and political realities is a fruitful point of departure, one that has not received sufficient attention. Foucault makes it hard to affix power to individuals or groups of individuals, while Kekkonen and Ylikangas primarily place it with the state apparatus as a reflection of social relations. This makes it easier to search for the causal connections. Spierenburg has not primarily analyzed the importance of the social transformation for the legal system and the development of punishment. Garland's description of the rationalization-biased bureaucracy could, in itself, be correct, but I find it difficult to accept his one-sided image of an earlier penal system that, as its main feature, was bent upon satisfying emotional and moralizing requirements. I would like to assert the opposite, that justice even then in most cases acted from "rational" motives.

The Swedish penal system in the early part of the seventeenth century was based on the idea of compensation to the injured party and required a socially and economically homogeneous society. The primary punishment was, except for the most grave crimes, a fine and this could be paid only by those who owned some property. During the latter part of the seventeenth century the weakness of the system became obvious when more and more of those sentenced, for example, unmarried mothers, did not have the material resources necessary to satisfy their adversaries. Previously the sentence could have been amended to fit with the delinquent's ability to pay, a method that was used even in other countries, such as England. Individuals could also work off their fines to the injured party if this was necessary.

This state of affairs became more complex when the government, via the courts of appeal, forced the district courts to apply the letter of the law, without exception. It was while discussing the poor that officials devised the punishment of flogging for men and birching for women, if fines were not paid. Running the gauntlet, which was applied toward the end of the seventeenth century, is a military innovation in Swedish law. The military influence during the seventeenth century should, on the whole, have lessened resistance to the use of corporal punishment and contributed to the extensive role that such punishment was to play in civil justice. It is interesting to note that, at the same time, the mutilation of ears, noses, and other parts of the body disappeared. Nor did torture come to play a prominent role in the Swedish legal system. At the end of the seventeenth century, however, there was an increase in the number of unmarried mothers and others who were dealt with by birching, flogging, and cudgeling. The means of control became more heavy-handed during the period of absolute sovereignty, but it should be noted that this was a development that had to some extent been suggested and supported even by the local elite, who could not find methods within the old system to control the marginal population. The increased use of corporal punishment can thus be explained by the widening of the social gap between the administrators of justice and certain of the delinquents. As one byproduct, executions also became emotional symbols in the theater of power.

Governmental legal requirements were often accompanied by large fines for violations, among other reasons because the risk for discovery was so low. This frequently led to even prosperous farmers' being forced to submit to corporal punishment, for example, when they had been caught felling high-grade timber. While it is plausible that people would accept thieves' being subjected to this ignominy, it could hardly have been popular treatment of otherwise honorable citizens. Furthermore, attitudes toward violence, even as punishment, were more negative during the course of the eighteenth century than during the warlike seventeenth century. At the end of the seventeenth century it was already difficult to recruit people who were willing to supervise the running of the gauntlet outside the court doors. In reality, punishment by birching or flogging, except in cases of theft and other particularly serious crimes, was abolished during the eighteenth century and replaced by terms in prison on bread and water. Prison combined with hard labor in fortresses began to be implemented as a complement to fines and as a replacement for the death penalty.

The death penalty and physically cruel punishments were reserved for very serious cases as deterrent instruments in a society with an ineffectual apparatus for tracking down criminals. It should be noted that the death penalty, in Sweden as well as in countries such as England, very frequently was changed to a fine, corporal punishment, prison with hard labor, or similar treatment. One way to save thieves from the gallows was to assess the value of the stolen goods at a figure that was lower than that which the law stipulated for the death penalty.

At the end of the eighteenth century more and more voices were raised against the barbarism of the death penalty.[11] One of the best-known debaters, even in Sweden, was the Italian Beccaria, who advocated the deterrent effect of prisons on the populace. It is quite clear that Beccaria acted more from an overestimation of the deterrent effect of a prison sentence than from humanitarian motives, but even "philanthropical" arguments often entered the debate. One cannot disregard the fact that both points of view contributed to the reforms. Only later did the belief that prisons could improve the inmates, so that they would leave as reformed human beings and better members of society, grow in strength. The ideas on reformation should naturally be regarded in connection with a generally growing belief that it was possible to find methods to solve the problems of society in the spirit of the Age of Enlightenment. On the continent the concept of the reeducation of degenerate citizens can be traced back to the end of the sixteenth century and in Sweden to the seventeenth century.

As long as state resources were used for other purposes and most prisons were so-called public prisons with many inmates, sometimes of both sexes and held in the same room, it was difficult to believe that these institutions could contribute to the individual improvement of the prisoners. Prisons with cells were first introduced in Sweden during the 1840s, when the government could afford to build them. One of the arguments for them was that they would contribute to reforming the prisoners and in the long run make social control more effective and less expensive. Many of the advocates, for example, Crown Prince Oscar, emphasized the humanitarian aspects at length. Prisons came to be a social experiment for individual prevention, although to begin with they were, both in Sweden and in other countries, primarily a place where those convicted of crimes were simply kept in custody due to lack of other facilities.

The history of punishment shows the dilemma that a geographically mobile, unpropertied class created. Banishment occurred during the Middle Ages and the sixteenth century, but this was not a feasible alternative in Sweden, which was on the road to becoming a national state. The small country town and the small county district found it difficult to find suitable sanctions and maintain their authority when monetary fines were not sufficient as compensation or deterrent. The function that prisons attained in time had relatively little to do with their historical background. A constellation of factors contributed to this development and different ideologies gave theoretical justifications for the few instruments that were available to maintain a working system of sanctions. While the institutions were roughly the same, the motives for their existence changed.

◆ From Violence to Theft?

One model that is often discussed states that society in Europe in the Middle Ages was characterized by widespread everyday violence, which successively decreased during later times and was replaced in the courts by an increase in crimes against property. This statement was put forward partly as a result of a number of French investigations where the transition *de la violence au vol* appears to be confirmed empirically. Later this model was criticized by French researchers as well as by colleagues in other countries.[12] In the present study it can be seen that there is no support for this model in its original form. Crimes with elements of physical violence did vary in total over time, but no linear decrease can be traced in this area of investigation. Nor is it possible to discern any unequivocal rise in the number of crimes against property. Instead it seems that the latter have fluctuated in pace with the economic situation in preindustrial Sweden.

The model does seem to be confirmed in one instance, by our figures as well as by those of others, namely concerning the most serious acts of violence resulting in death.[13] Everything points to the fact that the number of murder and manslaughter cases, especially those that were unpremeditated, decreased in relation to the population from the first half of the seventeenth century to the middle of the nineteenth century. The relationship between the two periods is difficult to determine, but the major decrease appears to have taken place at least before the middle of the eighteenth century. It is, however, difficult to find any similar decrease in less violent acts in the court records. Where Linköping is concerned it can be seen that the number of recorded thefts increased at the beginning of the nineteenth century, although not to such levels that the relationship between violence and theft in any decisive way was altered. Rather, the number of recorded crimes against property decreased at the end of the nineteenth century. A significant increase did not occur until after the Second World War.

The elementary theory must, at least on Sweden's part, be rejected but that does not mean that important events did not take place. In order to understand this it is necessary first and foremost to stop regarding violence and theft as chronological covariances, even if one can find certain factors common to their existence. Let us first discuss acts of violence and dispute, as they appeared in this investigation, and as a starting point consider the decrease in violent crimes resulting in death. Norbert Elias's theory that a disciplining of people took place by means of a state monopoly of violence is then not very illuminating.[14]

The state did not always have a dampening effect on violence. It exercised forms of not insignificant violence itself in connection with war operations during the seventeenth century, among other instances, manifested in the wars in the border counties between Denmark and Sweden. Nor did the "pacifying" of the previous border counties, at the end of the seventeenth century, pass by without any spectacular use of repression by the central powers. These events contributed instead to an increase in violence, including that which was exercised by others than the state's own representatives. Nor is there any clear proof that the government would have been capable of bringing violence to a lower level in its inner domains than on its perimeters.[15]

There are, therefore, no unequivocal connections between the increased influence of the central government and the level of violence. Everything depended on circumstances, for example, the presence of undisciplined soldiers. What is also striking in the verdict books from the seventeenth century is how often weapons were used in disputes in inns, at weddings, and on other occasions, when intoxication had heightened feelings. The fact that people were so often armed was in certain areas—the district of Göinge, for example—partly a result of the turbulent conditions created by the presence of two central powers, Sweden and Denmark. During the eighteenth century, when weapons became less usual everyday objects, the number of fights resulting in death decreased. It is self-evident that over a period of time these factors contributed to influencing attitudes against the use of violence. The more often a dispute ended with bloodshed, the more natural violence appeared, and vice versa.[16]

Two hundred years later the social makeup of the perpetrators of violence had changed, in comparison with the situation at the beginning of the seventeenth century. It was not surprising that the mayor himself was involved in disputes of a physical nature in Linköping in the 1600s. In Uppsala, the University Council had great difficulty in curtailing the students' rampages with rapiers and other weapons in the streets of the town. Violence was part of Sweden's era as a great power, both on the battlefield and in everyday life. A large number of merchants, master craftspeople, farmers, and other relatively propertied persons were among those sentenced to fines. In the nineteenth century the lists of fines from Härnösand and Linköping show that unpropertied individuals are overrepresented even in relation to their growing share of the population. This would confirm Norbert Elias's theory that self-control of one's actions occurs first among the more established in society and later on spreads to those who are lower on the social ladder.

The lists of fines from the north of Sweden show that even lay members of the jury and other established farmers were involved in violent battles during the latter part of the sixteenth century, an occurrence that appears to be less usual during the seventeenth century. A greater measure of respectability seems to have spread among the elite in the local community. Violence was becoming less accepted as a means of solving disputes. A form of disciplinary process probably took place, of which certain traces are visible in peaceful areas during the seventeenth century and which had even more tangible effects during the eighteenth and nineteenth centuries. The question is then, What type of factors brought about this change? One has been mentioned previously: access to weapons. But people did not bear weapons unless they assumed it would be necessary to use them. A high level of violence was self-perpetuating. There existed a reciprocal connection between conflicts in general, access to weapons, and the level of violence.

The Swedish historian Johan Söderberg discusses a development that may have been of importance, even if it is difficult to define the respective determining factors.[17] He points out that during the seventeenth century the courts were used increasingly to solve civil disputes. This can be interpreted as a signal that nonviolent, legal disputes had, to a certain extent, replaced disputes of a physical nature. When it comes to the worst acts of violence then this is compatible with empirical results. Written agreements could neutralize many conflicts where previously fists had been used to defend rights. Honor and renown were more important for the survival of the individual in an illiterate society, compared to later years. This can also explain why the number of cases of defamation decreased in time.

The more propertied farmers and merchants, who often were involved in disputes concerning economic resources, in time came to find nonviolent solutions to their problems. It is not necessary to embrace Norbert Elias's theory on state monopoly in order to explain why the common people became more disciplined. Peaceful solutions to disputes were in their own best interests. This interpretation presupposes that society at large became more peaceful, which was undoubtedly the case after the warlike seventeenth century. In other parts of Europe it is evident that, for the English, Germans, and French, for example, the seventeenth century was considerably more unsettled than the following century, before the French Revolution. This does not exclude the idea that the transition to a certain extent was promoted by the "reeducating" activities that were being carried out from above, not least by the church at a local level. Church discipline, as it was exercised in the parishes during this period, was a means to combat all kinds of bad habits. It is an exaggeration to state that church discipline in its entirety was met with the understanding and support of the parishioners, but there is no reason to suppose that it always had been opposed. On the contrary, the efforts of the priests and the established farmers could sometimes go hand in hand, when it was a case of dampening conflicts and educating unruly neighbors.[18] Such morality-governing tendencies with the permission of the local establishment have been found in seventeenth-century England, too.[19]

The battle for law and order was not a purely repressive instrument reserved for the central government, if considered externally, from the point of view of the local, established community. In time the legal system and the activities of the church increasingly came to concentrate on the socially and economically marginal part of the population. The local elite, especially in areas with a growing unpropertied population—and this already was the case in towns the size of Linköping at the end of the eighteenth century—saw a need to sharpen its control. Crimes against property grew in number, which was interpreted as proof that those without property were in the process of creating "a dangerous class."[20] The French Revolution had shown what could happen if one wasn't on guard.

While the town courts in the seventeenth century primarily were occupied with the settling of disputes between equals, there was a rapid growth in the number of directives regarding fines against propertyless persons, apprentices, and servants. Sometimes even groups of craftspersons who were dissatisfied with the direction the economic transition had taken appeared in the lists of fines. A large number of crimes of dispute and order, to which the court records bear witness, were partly of a different kind than those of the seventeenth century, even if a certain percentage of the cases still were concerned with the settling of disputes between individuals. Justice had, to a greater extent than previously, become an instrument for repression against the unpropertied. It is difficult to determine how much of the intensified control was caused by an increase in social discontent and drunkenness. It probably resulted from an interplay of different factors. That socioeconomic conditions influenced the number of disputes and thefts was obvious even toward the end of the nineteenth century, when these crimes decreased in step with the lower classes' gaining better material standards. The need for repressive measures lessened then, at the same time as the working classes channeled their demands and feelings into more organized forms.[21]

The model that describes a linear transition from violence to theft in tandem with the emergence of a capitalist society does not correspond with the Swedish example. However, the use of physical violence in everyday life did decrease in the long run, first in the form of fewer murders and cases of manslaughter and even later in the form of fewer fights between "ordinary" citizens. This development undoubtedly was the product of several factors. It came partly from the fact that weapons were less easily available after Sweden's period as a great power, which reduced the danger to life and limb in disputes, and partly because times were less trying, which in its turn caused the functional need for violence to decrease. Justice came more and more to be used in peaceful civil disputes. Periods of social tension left traces in the lists of fines because of increased uneasiness on the town streets and an intensified campaign of repression by the local authorities. Because of this the development is not linear, even if the curve of recorded violent acts finally does point downward. The number of thefts was primarily influenced by economic factors. It is not until present times that the number of thefts and pilfering has been doubled many times over, but the data in the present investigation does not extend to this.

◆ Town and Country

It was easier to bring a complaint to the town magistrates than to the rural court. The magistrates' court convened more often, sometimes several times in one week. The district court normally had only three sessions, one in the autumn, one in the winter, and one in the spring. In Säbrå there were only two sessions, one in the autumn and one in the winter. The district courts were usually geographically further away from the parties involved than were the magistrates from their subjects. The cases brought before the district court had often mellowed for a while, and many settlements were agreed upon before the sessions started. The village community council, parish general meetings, and church councils of elders also came to be alternate, more informal instruments for settling disputes in rural areas. It is, therefore, not particularly surprising that a greater number of the cases led to a conviction in Gullberg's rural district than in the town of Linköping during the seventeenth century, nor that the percentage convicted for failure to attend hearings often was greater in the sparsely populated, but geographically larger, Säbrå district court.

The supervision of undesirable conduct was more intensive in towns. Town watchmen patrolled the streets with the task of seeing that the fire regulations were kept, that young people went home before their curfew, that no one stayed in an inn too long, and that no one was too drunk or made more noise than was tolerable. During market days these watchmen received reinforcement that, especially during the nineteenth century, resulted in a number of notations in the lists of fines. Some acts, such as drunkenness, were regarded as criminal only when they took place in public places, and there were more of these in the towns. In the country it was primarily the church, the church lane, and the meetingplace of the court that could be called public places. It is important to remember these facts when comparing the number of fines in towns to those in rural areas. If we are interested in the behavior of the individual then we must count on the dark figure's being much higher in rural areas than in towns. If it is the conduct of the controlling apparatus that concerns us then we must remember that there were several institutions, which we cannot reconstruct via verdict books and lists of fines. It is true that the town guilds exercised a controlling function, but quantitatively they were probably of less importance than the village council of elders and parish councils in rural areas.

In all the courts the majority of plaintiffs and defendants were residents of the area of jurisdiction, but in the towns, strangers were more frequently cited. This was true especially in certain types of crimes of order and unlawful trading. In the case of lesser fights, drunkenness, verbal disturbance, and similar infractions, the towns' higher figures are created partially by those passing through and by country dwellers coming into towns to buy and sell. All in all, as could be expected, more people were fined in the towns than in the rural areas in relation to population. Regarding crimes of dispute and order the figures were most often around ten times higher in Linköping and Härnösand than in Gullberg and Säbrå. This concerns the lesser crimes of order in particular, but there were also more disputes involving physical violence. In Linköping these figures increased from being four times higher than those of the district of Gullberg during the first half of the seventeenth century, to becoming six times higher at the beginning of the nineteenth century. The number of persons convicted of murder and manslaughter was two to four times higher in the towns. The comparative figures for Härnösand versus Säbrå for all crimes involving some form of physical violence were ten times as high during the period 1680–1729, five times as high during the years 1730–89, and again ten times as high between 1790–1839.

We have established that this does not necessarily mean that the inhabitants of a town were more inclined to disputes and unruly behavior, but rather that these were caused by the town's character as a meetingplace for public activities. It should also be pointed out that extra emphasis was placed on the supervision of the young and the unpropertied, primarily in Linköping, at the end of the eighteenth century and beginning of the nineteenth. In some towns the social effects of the increase in population and proletarianization came to be more noticeable in the courts. That traces of these factors were so few in the rural courts is probably due in part to the problem's being experienced as less significant, but even there it was handled mainly at the parish and village levels. Serious violence was very rare all the time and none of our investigated areas seems to have been a place where anyone need fear for life or limb on account of physical violence, not even when the figures were higher at the beginning of the seventeenth century. Yet it did happen that people were involved in smaller fights.

In the towns, even the number of prosecuted thefts was larger than in the rural areas, in relation to the size of the population, but nowhere were the figures excessive. In one year and per 1,000 inhabitants on average there were approximately two convictions in Härnösand during the greater part of the period, with a slight increase at the beginning of the nineteenth century. These figures can be compared with those in Säbrå, where to begin with they were approximately 0.5 and at the end of the period 0.25. Linköping's figure was approximately 2 before the middle of the eighteenth century and increased to around 5 after 1770, while in Gullberg the figures fluctuated around 0.5 per year per 1,000 inhabitants. The dark figures are impossible to estimate, but it is probable that the large supply of goods that were attractive to thieves caused more thefts and pilfering to take place in the towns than in the rural areas. The increase in Linköping at the end of the period can also be seen in connection with the migration to towns and the increase in the number of propertyless persons. A criminal class did not exist, but a small group of relapsed criminals can, at this time, be traced in the court sources.

During the eighteenth century, violations of laws governing sexual acts became more frequent in the towns than in the rural areas, as a result of the increasing number of illegitimate children born in towns. At first this fact left tangible traces in the lists of fines, but in time, first men and later women were punished less and less. This decrease in punishment began in the towns, so that the courts in rural districts had a larger share in relation to the total number of crimes. This trend was reinforced by the fact that other types of crime, above all crimes of order and dispute, seldom had any measures taken against them in rural areas. The traces left in the source material concerning laws governing sexual acts and the large number of illegitimate children reveal that the towns were becoming less strictly controlled in some aspects, while in other ways great efforts were exerted toward upholding law and order.[22] Compared to the seventeenth century, the town culture in the eighteenth century became more heterogeneous, both socially and culturally, and the court records bear witness to this. The informal control worked less well and in return the formal control was intensified in certain respects, while the battle was lost regarding other aspects of morality.

The state's increased use of the local courts for control purposes was first apparent in the towns. The Swedish historians Eva Österberg and Dag Lindström have already traced this trend within the sixteenth century.[23] There are also a number of court cases in the records from Linköping's municipal court during the decade starting in 1640. They concerned primarily customs duties, trade, and the illicit sale of ale and alcohol, where the state had a fiscal interest to guard. The forms for trade and craft were otherwise not primarily regulated by the municipal courts in Linköping and Härnösand. These cases usually were only a small part of the agenda. Under the final stages of the guild system and the older forms of trade regulations it was possible to discern a mobilization of the legal system. The number of fines for illegal markets and marketplace trading increased around the year 1800, as did the number of people fined for street hawking and illegal handicraft. There were also more cases involving goods of inferior quality, weights not stamped with a crown, and similar offenses. By then the guild associations seem to have found it difficult to maintain their system without the help of the legal system.

At the end of the seventeenth century it is the state's fiscal interests that are most noticeable in the district courts' judgment books. The felling of timber and distillation of alcohol were rural occupations, and when the government made higher demands in both these areas the number of those convicted rose. Considering the difficulties in gaining conclusive evidence against the lawbreakers, the dark figure should also have been very large. It was also the rural population that primarily suffered from government claims on transportation by horse and carriage and on road maintenance. The latter led to many instances of directives concerning fines. The towns were relatively free from such cases, even if bootlegging in time became a cause for fines. The illicit sale of alcohol became more a local question than a governmental concern.

When an increase in the category of "crimes against statutes and special regulations" is found in towns, then the infringements are primarily directed against local decisions. The flouting of fire regulations was, to a certain extent in Härnösand but to a greater degree in Linköping, the most often cited cause of fines in the records from the beginning of the nineteenth century (with the exception of fines for not appearing as parties or witnesses at court proceedings). A local elite started to deal with the internal problems of the town. Bylaws were written and revised and a control system was initiated to supervise them. The intensity of the control was greatest in the towns, as problems with fire and sanitary conditions were greater there. Yet this form of control existed even in rural areas, which is evident in records that survived from village and parish meetings.

In spite of the differences found between town and rural areas, which were determined primarily by social, economic, and commercial structures and secondarily by subsequent regulations for social control, most things were very similar in all the courts. The tasks of the courts were, during the first part of the seventeenth century, first and foremost the settling of disputes between private citizens, whether it was in civil disputes or criminal cases. Even verbal disputes and fights were, finally, often reduced to a battle of resources either material or immaterial, in the form of honor and honesty. In time other regulatory interests came to take up more room, initially because of the increasing demands made by the government, and later because of the ambitions of the local elite to maintain order.

◆ Men and Women

Crimes committed by women can be linked for the most part with their roles in society. This can be seen, for example, when the content of the different main categories of crime is studied in more detail. Among crimes concerning disputes, women's share is greatest regarding defamation and quarrels, while few women committed grave acts of violence. Few women undertook thefts of a serious nature, while more had pilfered or bought and hidden stolen goods. When women offended against different bylaws or regulations, it was primarily a question of areas where women had specific responsibilities, for example, the care of fire in the household, or the serving of ale and alcohol. If it was a question of a crime connected with the management of property, then it was primarily widows who were to be found among the women fined.

There were few women found at all in the lists of fines for the second half of the sixteenth century. Women did, however, increase their percentage of convictions from this period until the eighteenth century (see fig. 8–7). The position of women as capable of representing themselves and being responsible for their actions was strengthened. Here the church played an important role. The fact that unmarried mothers were criminalized in cases of fornication during the seventeenth century can be seen as an important symbol of this involvement. At the beginning of the seventeenth century women were still a minority of those prosecuted and fined for violations of the laws governing sexual conduct. During the eighteenth century they came to be in the majority, not least after men started to escape from responsibility. Even if the fines in these cases were less for men, in reality it meant that women were punished more harshly than men, in spite of the fact that to outward appearance the laws seemed equal. Women were often overrepresented among those who had their sentences changed to being beaten (flogging for men and birching for women) or, later, being confined to prison on bread and water.[24]

The demographic consequences of Sweden's period as a great power can have played an important part in this context. Many men went off to war and never returned, as in most wars, and this placed greater responsibility on the shoulders of the women who remained at home. The administrators of jus-

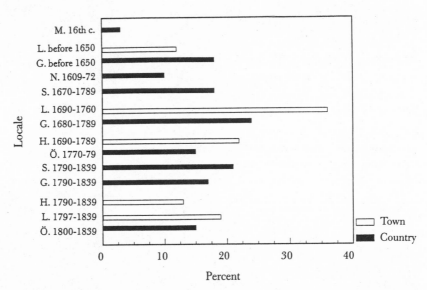

Figure 8-7. Percentage of women convicted of all types of offenses during different periods.

Key: M = Medelpad, countryside; L = city of Linköping; H = city of Härnösand; G = Gullberg; N = Njurunda, countryside; S = Säbrå; Ö = Östra Göinge, countryside

Sources: Court protocols and lists of fines in the Provincial Archives of Vadstena, Härnösand, and Lund.

tice were forced to take this fact into consideration. During the first half of the seventeenth century the number of women who were parties or witnesses in cases, or even oath-takers when a women was the accused, was greater than it appears to have been during the sixteenth century. Later on these figures rose even more. It is primarily because witch trials were held in special courts that those cases have not been paid much attention in this study. It is clear, however, that among the number of women who were sentenced and burned at the stake there were those who had challenged male hegemony by acting in a manner that was contrary to the traditional view of women's roles. Witch trials and the control of extramarital relations contributed to defining the limits of the female role.[25]

That the total number of women with convictions was greater in Linköping than in Gullberg, at the beginning of the seventeenth century, was above all a product of the fact that the categories of crime were determined differently in towns than in rural areas. There still seemed to be no decisive difference between town and country concerning the role of women, except for cases of pure theft, where more women were accused in towns. The latter result has also been found to be true of England in the same time period. In the eighteenth century a clear difference arose even regarding the total number of crimes, inasmuch as the percentage for women was greater in Linköping and Härnösand than in Gullberg and Säbrå. This was partially because the number of illegitimate births grew more rapidly in the towns, but even other categories of crimes were involved. It was especially apparent concerning crimes against property, where women now were nearly equally represented in towns, but in rural areas they constituted only a fifth of all those fined.

The number of cases concerned with fornication increased in town and country. There was also a rise in the number of women accused of pilfering, due partly to women's legal responsibility having increased and partly to there having been a steadily growing number of unmarried women who had come from rural areas to work as housemaids. Research in England has brought attention to the insecure situation of this group. In countries that were industrialized relatively early, there arose a new group of working women who were sensitive to changes in trade cycles. In Sweden at this time it was more telling that those moving to towns had left the social control and safety net of their native district behind them. The temptations for a young maid in a middle-class household could be far too strong to resist. One can assume that in a patriarchal society, thieving by servants was often regulated without the intervention of the courts; but when patriarchy began to disintegrate, as a result of migration and proletarianization, it is likely that the masters and mistresses more often turned to the formal instrument of control. The punishment for theft within a household had been made more severe during the eighteenth century, a sure sign of this trend. The percentage of women among the total number of those individuals who were fined did decrease in towns at the end of the eighteenth century. This was above all because fewer women were convicted of fornication, even though the law was still formally being enforced.

If we return to crimes against property then it can be ascertained that the lessening ratio of women involved, in towns, is attributable to an increase in the number of male criminals. In Linköping, for example, thefts by females did not increase to the same extent as did those carried out by men. This development has also been linked with the increase of proletarianization in the towns. During the first half of the nineteenth century Linköping accommodated a growing number of unpropertied inhabitants, both men and women. The question is then why this development did not leave just as many traces among the women. One important explanation is that a larger percentage of women were members of households, working as servants. Those men who were convicted had often committed more serious forms of theft, with or without burglary, and many of them were marginals, outside the patriarchal society.

When it comes to economically weak women, theft does not seem to have been the first way out for them. Instead we find them, among other things, as street hawkers, with or without permits, or as owners of small legitimate or illegal inns. At the beginning of the nineteenth century 40 percent to 50 percent of people convicted of the illicit sale of alcohol and of allowing people to stay too long in an inn were women. Another possible source of income for women was, of course, prostitution. On isolated occasions it can be seen from the records that prostitution existed, but it is not possible to calculate its proportions.

The lowering of the female crime ratio is not explained primarily by the fact that women less frequently dedicated themselves to pilfering or other illegal activities. Instead it is explained by the fact that certain sexual behaviors were slowly decriminalized and that the number of convicted men rose strongly in several categories, such as drunkenness or other disorderly conduct. But even women, from time to time, appeared in the lists of those fined and inhabited the workhouses.

◆ The Unique and the Common

What took place in Linköping, Gullberg, Härnösand, Säbrå, and other places in preindustrial Sweden was a product, on the one hand, of specific circumstances and, on the other hand, of common trends. We have been able to see that courts' agendas and the composition of the parties involved underwent great changes, often reflecting what was happening in the rest of Sweden and in other European countries at the same time. There was a transition everywhere, from justice dominated by local interests to justice with greater influence from central government and the experts.[26] In Sweden this happened more through infiltration in old, existing institutions rather than by means of revolutionary innovations, and this should explain why local interests, in spite of everything, could assert themselves to a certain extent.

The events that took place in Linköping at the beginning of the nineteenth century occurred against the backdrop of a similar development in the whole of Western Europe, but it was the local elite who primarily acted toward keeping the unpropertied in order and creating a cleaner and more well-administered town. Religious powers everywhere made their own moves, within the framework of secular law, under the flag of the Reformation and Counter-Reformation. The forms and degrees of these activities could vary but the trends were similar. Where the exacting of local justice was concerned, there seems to have existed everywhere a difference between those who belonged to a class of respected and accepted citizens and those who were regarded as unacceptable or marginal.

If we compare society today with that of earlier times, we find there was considerably more physical violence between people in the past. The reasons this changed can vary somewhat between different environments, but certain phenomena should be common to all. Among other things, middle-class citizens and farmers stopped carrying weapons in everyday life, which helped lessen the most serious acts of violence. Times gradually became calmer, when great wars were no longer fought in the midst of the civilian population by more or less undisciplined troops. Attitudes toward physical violence, whether at the hands of an individual or the state, became more disapproving. The belief that a person could solve problems with the help of rationality grew, which is also one explanation as to why laws and ordinances increased in number to regulate more and more details of everyday life.

The conception that the growth of capitalism automatically leads to more crimes against property has been difficult to substantiate. Until the latter part of the nineteenth century, theft and pilfering appear to have fluctuated in pace with trade cycles, without any long-term tendency to increase. Certain environments attracted a Lumpenproletariat, and there the number of crimes was greater, but when economic and social factors became more favorable, then criminality decreased. The connection between urbanization and criminality was subtle. During certain periods the towns, including the small Swedish town of Linköping around the year 1800, offered a more anonymous environment; there, patriarchal control certainly existed although it worked less well. Traditional concepts came to be questioned and sometimes had to be buried, as was the case concerning the criminalization of premarital intercourse.

On some occasions it is possible to pinpoint decisive moments in time, as, for example, when the courts were affected by the 1778 reforms of Gustavus III, which were aimed at relieving the situation of unmarried mothers.[27] Developments were frequently more evolutionary than revolutionary, which makes it more difficult to give a decisive chronology. The penal laws often belatedly codified a previously changed practice. By observing long periods of time, it is relatively easy to see that things had changed, but for briefer periods we have to be satisfied with tracing trends. The chronology is also different in different countries; sometimes it differs even from area to area within a single country. In Sweden, for example, some types of events occurred in the towns before they took place in the rural areas; some happened earlier in more densely populated and proletarianized areas on the flat plains of the south than in the forest districts of the north.

In order to point out some important factors that have played a crucial role in developments, then, economic and social factors should be considered at the outset. When a local community became more heterogeneous, it also found it more difficult to maintain justice in the same form as in the past. Many patterns can be traced back to a particular social transition. The centralization and increased importance of government are partially a result of this change, yet they are also more complicated phenomena. Even so, this development left traces everywhere in the work of the courts. Society became more professionalized and more thoroughly bureaucratized, which influenced the balance of power within the courts. The hope grew that it would be possible—with the aid of what in modern Sweden is referred to by the much worn concept of "social engineering"—to be able to use new laws to help solve this problem. During one period, religion came to be an important guide for the administration of justice, while later on, secularized "rational reasoning" was in control.

. . . .

To take a strong stand on the question as to whether the legal system has been an instrument of conflict or consensus would, to my way of thinking, be to distort reality. We often use concepts such as "central government" or "the state" to denote opposites to the local community. This "state" is in fact not an organism with an unequivocal will that dominates particular interests, even if it has been described as though that were the case. As is the situation with the courts, the state can also be described as an arena or an instrument at a high level for different parties who attempt to put forward their own interests. This does not deny that the abstract concept of the state, by virtue of its existence in the ideological world, has influenced political reality.

The courts' work was always concerned with settling disputes, to a certain extent. Sometimes these disputes were solved by mutual agreement, including that of the defendant, and sometimes by pure repression. Justice is an instrument that serves many purposes. Perhaps one of the most important changes took place during the nineteenth century when justice began to be used to a greater extent to reform recalcitrant individuals. One of the law's greatest contradictions today lies between its role in conflict solving and its function as individual therapy. While the local community in the seventeenth century primarily emphasized the solving of conflicts and, occasionally, the deterrent effect, we now discuss whether one can sentence somebody to social or mental improvement—if punishment is a social remedy. History shows the roots of this discussion and how earlier communities tried to solve their problems.

Notes

1. Jan Sundin, *För Gud, Staten och Folket: Brott och rättskipning i Sverige, 1600–1840* (Lund, 1992). Unless indicated otherwise, I am referring to results in this book, where there are also more references to my colleagues.

2. On Swedish church discipline, see Jan Sundin, "Control, Punishment and Reconciliation: A Case Study of Parish Justice in Sweden before 1850," in *Tradition and Transition: The Demographic Data Base,* ed. Anders Brändström and Jan Sundin (Umeå, Sweden, 1981), 9–65. On sexual offenses, see Jan Sundin, "Keeping Sex within Marriage: Legal Prosecution of Extra-Marital Sex in Pre-Industrial Sweden," *Social Science History* 16, no. 1 (1992): 99–128.

3. Bruce Lenman and Geoffrey Parker, "The State, the Community and the Criminal Law in Early Modern Europe," in *Crime and the Law: The Social History of Crime in Western Europe since 1500,* ed. V. A. C. Gatrell, Bruce Lenman, and Geoffrey Parker (London, 1980), 11–48.

4. See Sundin, "Control, Punishment and Reconciliation."

5. See also John Langbein, *Torture and the Law of Proof: Europe and England in the Ancien Régime* (Chicago, 1977).

6. James A. Sharpe, *Crime in Seventeenth-Century England: A County Study* (Cambridge, 1983); idem, *Crime in Early Modern England, 1550–1750* (London, 1984).

7. Michel Foucault, *Discipline and Punish: The Birth of the Prison,* trans. Alan Sheridan (Harmondsworth, 1986).

8. Pieter Spierenburg, *The Spectacle of Suffering: Executions and the Evolution of Repression: From a Preindustrial Metropolis to the European Experience* (Cambridge, 1984).

9. David Garland, *Punishment and Modern Society: A Study in Social Theory* (Oxford, 1990).

10. Jukka Kekkonen, "Explaining Historical Change in Social Control," in *Theaters of Power: Social Control and Criminality in Historical Perspective,* ed. Heikki Pihlajamäki (Jyväskylä, Finland, 1991), 143–57.

11. Jan Sundin, "Prisons préventives et reformatrices: Ambitions et réalités dans la Suède du XIX siècle," in *La Prison, le Bagne et l'Histoire: Deviance et Société,* ed. Jacques G. Petit (Geneva, 1984), 201–11.

12. See articles in *Annales de Normandie* between 1962 and 1972. Criticism has been heard from Arlette Farge and André Zysberg, "Les théâtres de la violence à Paris au 18ième siècle," *Annales* 34 (1979): 984–1015, and Steven G. Reinhardt, "Crime and Royal Justice in Ancien Régime France: Modes of Analysis," *Journal of Interdisciplinary History* 13 (1983): 437–60, among others. For the English debate, see, for instance, contributions by Lawrence Stone, "Interpersonal Violence in English Society, 1300–1980," *Past and Present* 102 (1983): 22–33; James A. Sharpe, "The History of Violence in England: Some Observations," *Past and Present* 108 (1985): 206–15; Lawrence Stone, "A Rejoinder," *Past and Present* 108 (1985): 216–24; and J. S. Cockburn, "Patterns of Violence in English Society: Homicide in Kent, 1560–1985," *Past and Present* 130 (1991): 70–106. For Sweden, see Eva Österberg, "Criminality, Social Control, and the Early Modern State: Evidence and Interpretations in Scandinavian Historiography," *Social Science History* 16, no. 1 (1992): 67–98.

13. See Österberg, "Criminality, Social Control."

14. See Norbert Elias, *Über den Prozeß der Zivilisation: Soziogenetische und psychogenetische Untersuchungen* (Frankfurt, 1977).

15. Jan Sundin, "Bandits and Guerilla Soldiers: Armed Bands on the Border between Sweden and Denmark in Early Modern Times," in *Bande armate banditi: Banditismo e repressione di giustizia negli stati europei di antico regime,* ed. Gherardo Ortalli (Venice, 1986), 141–66.

16. This is also underlined by Cockburn, "Patterns of Violence."

17. See Johan Söderberg, "En fråga om civilisering: Brottmål och tvister i svenska häradsrätter, 1540–1660," *Historisk Tidskrift* 2 (1990): 229–58.

18. See Sundin, "Control, Punishment and Reconciliation."

19. See, for instance, John Brewer and John Styles, eds., *An Ungovernable People: The English and Their Law in the Seventeenth and Eighteenth Centuries* (London, 1980); David Flaherty, "Law and the Enforcement of Morals in Early America," *Perspectives in American History* 5 (1971): 203–53.

20. See the classic study of Louis Chevalier, *Classes laborieuses et classes dangereuses à Paris pendant la première moitié du XIX Siècle* (Paris, 1958).

21. See Jan Sundin, "Theft and Penury in Sweden, 1830–1920: A Comparative Study at the County Level," *Scandinavian Journal of History* 1 (1976): 265–92. For England, see V. A. C. Gatrell and T. B. Hadden, "Nineteenth-Century Criminal Statistics and Their Interpretation," in *Nineteenth-Century Society: Essays in the Use of Quantitative Methods for the Study of Social Data,* ed. E. A. Wrigley (London, 1972), 336–96; and V. A. C. Gatrell, "The Decline of Theft and Violence in Victorian and Edwardian England," in *Crime and the Law,* ed. Gatrell, Lenman, and Parker, 238–338.

22. On sexual offenses, see Sundin, "Keeping Sex within Marriage."

23. Eva Österberg and Dag Lindström, *Crime and Social Control in Medieval and Early Modern Swedish Towns* (Uppsala, 1988).

24. Sundin, "Keeping Sex within Marriage."

25. On witch trials in Sweden, see Bengt Ankarloo, *Trolldompsprocesserna i Sverige* (Stockholm, 1984); Bengt Ankarloo and Gustav Henningsen, eds., *Häxornas Europa, 1400–1700* (Lund, 1987).

26. See Lenman and Parker, "The State, the Community, and the Criminal Law."

27. See Sundin, "Keeping Sex within Marriage."

9

Urban and Rural Crime Rates and Their Genesis in Late Nineteenth- and Early Twentieth-Century Britain

Barbara Weinberger

Are analyses of recorded crime rates in urban and rural areas able to uncover anything relating to essential differences between such areas? If the analyses were to reveal consistent differences between the two rates, what is it that they are in fact describing? Do they reveal differences between urban and rural forms of criminality, ones that depend for their variation on the different forms of production and social relations in these environments? Or do variations in the perception, priorities, and bureaucratic and judicial procedures of the law-enforcing authorities account for the differences? Where does variation in the propensity of the private prosecutor to bring a case to court fit into the picture? In the account that follows, attention will be paid to all these questions, since all contribute to the statistical end product. What we are not, however, entitled to do is to draw conclusions therefrom about any essential differences between "real" urban or rural rates of crime. These are quite simply unknowable.

The debate about the meaning and usefulness of criminal statistics is a hard fought and ongoing one among historians of crime. In that discussion, early joy over long statistical runs—either published or deducible from the court records—as a new source that could yield important insights and answers to old questions, above all on the relationship of crime to economic change or variations in the trade cycle, has faded as doubts about what is being measured have grown. However, while it is generally acknowledged that crime statistics are not a measure of the actual extent of criminal behavior in society, historians have nevertheless been loath to relinquish them as a source for statements about trends in crime.

But this has also attracted criticism. In a critique of such "double-dealing," Sindall has recently condemned the practice of using such material to produce a picture of trends in crime while at the same time warning of the need for care and judgment in the use of the statistics, thus allowing the fact that the numbers are almost irrelevant to the true state of crime to fade into the background.[1] Another recent publication has exposed the frailty of the meaning of recorded crime as it enters the system through the action of the police. There are immense ambiguities involved in a single such entry, where the range can vary greatly: one incident can be noted as one crime at a given date, or it can be held over for later entry in the books in order to boost the figures if these had reached a statistical norm in the current period; a single event can be entered as a number of different crimes by splitting it into its component parts; a crime might be entered in the returns even if the defendant was subsequently acquitted; a myriad of figures might be entered on the basis of one arrest through the "numbers taken into consideration"; "rubbish" crimes might even disappear, if they would involve the police in too much paperwork for too little return. These ambiguities provide crushing evidence against a simplistic view that even known crime is something that can be straightforwardly counted.[2]

Further difficulties arise over definitional changes in the categorization of offenses, or in the creation of new ones. The police then have to decide to which category they should assign an event, whether it is to be regarded as a crime or an offense, whether it is to be known as an assault or an obstruction, as burglary or malicious damage, such alterations being both contingent and arbitrary. Moreover, systems of classification change not only over time but also among police districts, whereby—in the words of the Recorder of Birmingham, the city with which this account is largely concerned—"Manchester and Liverpool persistently return under the heading 'crime' something no other English borough returns."[3] The unavoidable conclusion must be that the criminal returns, which were collected and put forward by the police, district by district, and then merged to form the national crime rate, reflect little that is reliable about the state of crime but much on the purposes and priorities of the police. Unfortunately, given the absence of earlier participant observers, our knowledge of what those purposes and priorities were in previous periods must remain sketchy and conjectural. We can only take as axiomatic that a major objective of the recorded statistics, whatever their official purpose, was to present as favorable a view of police activities to the various authorities up the hierarchy as possible. In other words, their chief value to the police was as recommendation or self-justification to others within the system; and the discussion of trends in the various categories of offense that follow should be read in that light.

In the meantime, there is of course another aspect that must be considered in any discussion of crime statistics. This cannot fully be entered into here, but it relates to the factors encouraging or discouraging private prosecutors from bringing cases to court, or to the notice of the authorities. Their significance is, however, made clear by the authors of essays on private prosecutions in Britain in the late eighteenth and nineteenth centuries, where they graphically demonstrate the complexity of the motives and expectations of those initiating court procedures and the extent to which the crimes involved might be fictitious, maliciously labeled as such, or dealt with by alternative, informal, means.[4] Discussions of this nature must throw doubt on how much weight we can attach to a straightforward acceptance of theories of a long-term trend *de la violence au vol,* which have been stimulated by Norbert Elias's influential work.[5]

In short, the use of criminal statistics is hedged about with qualifications. However, this does not mean that they do not have something historically meaningful to tell us about changing perceptions of what constituted crime and how it should be dealt with, and in particular about the way in which the police functioned in response. What follows illustrates these points, in the context of an urban-rural comparison in late nineteenth-century Britain.

◆ The Urban versus Rural Setting

Given the importance of the topic of public order and the security of persons and property to British nineteenth-century policymakers, and early concerns over the morally deleterious effects of rapid urbanization, it is perhaps surprising to find that few direct comparisons were made at the time concerning the state of security in town and country. Instead, the debate advanced in seesaw manner, with a concentration on the iniquitous state of the large towns in the 1820s giving way to a focus on the disturbed state of the countryside in the late 1830s. These debates resulted in parliamentary legislation, leading first to the formation of a professional police force in the metropolis, under the Metropolitan Police Act of 1829; then to the setting up of Watch Committees in the towns, drawn from elected members of town councils, who were required to appoint "a sufficient number of fit men" to police them (under the Municipal Corporations Act of 1839); and then to the policing of rural areas, under the County Police Act of 1839.

But since the 1839 act was permissive, and as the remit to the boroughs was totally imprecise as to numbers, mode of operation, and conditions of service, police forces to cover the whole country were not secured in Britain until the Police Act of 1856. This act made the establishment of police forces obligatory if the boroughs and counties wished to avail themselves of the central government grant to cover a quarter of the cost of the police. In addition, all forces needed to satisfy a government inspector annually of the state of efficiency of their force, amounting in practice to little more than an agreed ratio of roughly one policeman per 1,000 population in the counties and 1:500 population in the larger towns.

By 1860, 257 separate police forces were in place in all the counties and boroughs of the country, and Britain became a policed society. At the same time it was only then that the Home Office was able to publish comprehensive annual Judicial Statistics, compiled from the returns sent in by the police, and on which all official assessments of the state of crime were to be made.

The comparison undertaken in this essay thus starts in 1860 and covers a fifty-year period, designed to discover what meaningful differences, if any, existed between the policing policies and strategies in rural and urban areas, in what was already a highly urbanized society with over 60 percent of the population living in towns (see fig. 9-1). The main units of comparison, to which the graphs in this chapter refer, are the county of Warwickshire, situated in the heart of England, and the city of Birmingham, located within that county. At the start of the period the population of the county was 191,963 and Birmingham's was 288,943, while by 1911 the county's population stood

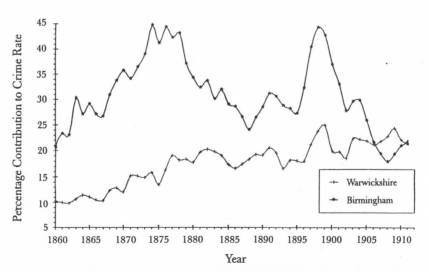

Figure 9-1. Crime rate per 1,000 population, Warwickshire and Birmingham.

at 277,020 and that of Birmingham at 810,202. Whereas the population of the city continued to grow at an accelerating rate throughout the period, Warwickshire's increased only slowly up to 1901, after which it began to decline.

These demographic facts are likely to have had an important bearing on the nature of policing in the two areas. And because each separate police force was under the control of a local body, differences in each authority's outlook, priorities, and purposes should, in theory, be more clearly discernible than might have been the case in a more centralized system. Fluctuations in the offense rates here may be able to tell us something meaningful about policing in urban and rural areas in response to pressure from the public, local authority, or the chief constable (or the absence of such pressure), and about public recourse to the machinery of justice. One of the major social structural differences between town and country was the absence of a bourgeoisie in the countryside, precisely the group—before the rise of labor—who had firm control of town councils in urban areas, while the people of influence in the countryside were the landed gentry who held office as justices of the peace on the basis of their social standing in the community, rather than as elected members, as in the towns.

This changed to some extent under the Local Government Act of 1888 when control of the county police by the justices came to be shared with elected county councillors, in what were designated as Standing Joint Committees. The SJCs met on a monthly basis and left the management of police matters largely in the hands of the chief constable. These functioned in a manner dissimilar to the Watch Committees in the boroughs, who met weekly to discuss policing matters and kept a tight rein on the operations of their chief constable. The result was that the chief constable of a county was a far more powerful figure, drawn from a higher social class, than was his urban counterpart, who tended to be regarded by his Watch Committee as its servant.

How far did these differences in police management manifest themselves in different policing methods and outcomes? To answer this question, evidence will be drawn from a comparison of the criminal statistics for a range of the main offenses dealt with by summary jurisdiction in the period.

◆ The Offenses

Poaching

We will look first at poaching, in what was unequivocally a rural offense, although already closely related to demand in the towns. While the struggle between gamekeepers and poachers was an ancient one, the licensed and unlicensed acquisition of game was becoming an increasingly commercial proposition in the Victorian era, and one that could bring large monetary rewards. Poaching was no longer primarily a contest between those defending common-law rights to the produce of the wild and landowners seeking to deny those rights; it had become largely an illegal market activity, which it was the police's task to curtail.

The attempt by local landowners in Warwickshire to employ the newly established county police for their private purposes and to ask them to watch their game reserves and act as beaters on their estates was deemed inappropriate, and the chief constable soon put a stop to this practice.[6] The new police were there not in order to side so overtly with the propertied against the propertyless, but to apply the law. Here, the Night Poaching Act of 1844, and above all the Poaching Prevention Act of 1862, which gave the police extended powers of search and confiscation, were the means by which poaching was to be put down. The effect of the 1862 legislation giving greater police powers against poachers shows up clearly in the offense rate for Warwickshire, which peaked at that time, declining thereafter almost steadily to the end of the century and beyond (see fig. 9–2).

How are we to account for this decline in police action? While the 1862 legislation gave incentive to the police to act with vigilance against poachers, it is hardly likely that the subsequent statistical decline was due to growing

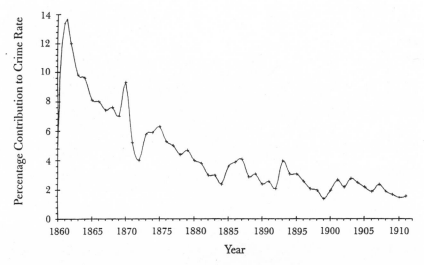

Figure 9-2. Percentage of poaching offenses, Warwickshire.

indifference on the part of authority or to less-efficient policing.[7] Maybe the greater risk of being caught made poaching no longer seem worthwhile; but increasing mobility and wider economic prospects, which pushed poorer laborers off the land into the towns (and away from a more static relationship between poaching and economic hardship), probably played a larger part. Nevertheless, the deterrent effect of stricter policing should not be discounted, as witnessed by Joseph Arch, who claimed that the 1862 act placed innocent working people under constant surveillance, and by Flora Thompson at the end of the century, who observed of her native Oxfordshire village that "the hamlet men are not habitual poachers. They call it a mug's game, with one month in quod [prison] and one month out."[8]

But if this was the case, the decrease took place in conjunction with other factors, ones of an economic nature. Poaching was not just something countrymen turned to in order to help feed their families or to bring in some cash in the local market; it was an organized and large-scale trade. By midcentury it had developed into a major economic undertaking involving an extensive network of suppliers and retailers, with the countryside responding to the spiraling demand for cheap meat from the urban working class. How far this demand was met by the legal—as opposed to the illegal—trade in game is difficult to establish, but the size of the trade was remarkable. In the early 1870s, half a million rabbits were being sold by tradespeople in Birmingham during the winter months, with poaching gangs sending their catch to the city by train.[9] But the decline in the poaching statistics from the 1870s onward, despite the economic depression in the middle of that decade, bears witness to changing attitudes and opportunities. Migration to the towns, as well as the introduction of cheaper food for the mass market with the coming of refrigeration and the importing of frozen meat from the colonies, brought competition and alternatives to the hazardous illegal activities of the poacher. (The variety and complexity of the poachers' situation throughout the country has been well described by David Jones.) The shift in the balance underlying the interdependence of town and country in the supply and demand for illegal game as well as the continuous police surveillance remain as important factors affecting the poaching offense statistics for this most rural of crimes.

Drunkenness

The offense rate for drunkenness in rural areas in the first half of the period was higher than that for the city, and it accounted for between 25 and 30 percent of all summary offenses in the countryside in the 1870s (see fig. 9–3). One explanation is that this offense was one of the most easily detectable by what was a chronically understaffed force. Throughout the first twenty years of the establishment of the Warwickshire county force, the chief constable complained of the shortage of recruits and of the difficulty in getting efficient men to remain in the service. Low rates of pay put many men off, but the primary difficulty, according to the chief constable, was the proximity of the towns and above all of Birmingham, with their better employment prospects. Many men joined the force only long enough to get a certificate of good character and then left for more lucrative and less unpopular work.[10]

In these circumstances, one easy way to have the records show that the police were doing something about law and order—a method that would not tax their skill and intelligence too greatly—was simply to direct them past the beer houses and pubs around closing time, when drunken brawls would spill out into the streets and arrests would be a straightforward matter. After the new licensing laws were introduced in 1869 and 1872, more stringent measures were taken against public drunkenness. Here the chief constable of Warwickshire was in the forefront of the campaign against drink, recommending the withholding of licenses to new beer houses until the ratio of pubs and beer houses per population had been reduced from 1:159 to 1:250. The high rate of drunkenness arrests in the mid-1870s he put down not to an increase

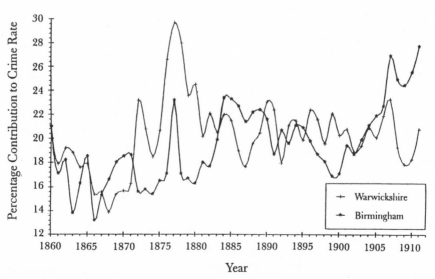

Figure 9-3. Percentage of drunkenness offenses, Warwickshire and Birmingham.

in drunkenness, but to the greater attention being paid by the police to this class of offender.[11] There was a similar drive against drink in the same period by the police in Birmingham, with the appointment in the 1870s of special police to act as public-house inspectors (although the scheme raised such a public outcry that magistrates refused to convict and the scheme was soon dropped).[12]

The unruly behavior associated with drunkenness was coming under attack by the authorities in both town and country, fueled by the parliamentary successes of the temperance movement in getting antidrink legislation onto the statute book and by the growing desire for regular work habits and orderly behavior from employers in a wide range of enterprises. High rates of drunkenness arrests therefore stemmed not only from the ease with which such arrests could help to swell the "offenses detected" rate, but from continuing official concern about the seriousness of the drink problem in Victorian society—which, however, proved an intractable one, little capable of being solved by legislation or police action.

As Brian Harrison has pointed out, although arrest statistics strikingly reveal the extent of the Victorian drink problem, it is doubtful whether they indicate changing levels of drunkenness. Sharp variations in the number of proceedings in different parts of the country reflect differences in enforcement policies rather than in drinking habits, as in 1870, when there were 21,113 drunk and disorderly offenses determined summarily in Liverpool but only 2,244 in Birmingham.[13]

Some true decline in the incidence of drunkenness may have set in toward the end of the nineteenth century with the growth of counterattractions to the pub, higher standards of comfort and privacy in the home, and a growing endorsement of the values of respectability within the working class; but the upward city trend after 1900 points to the temporary nature of any perceived decline. As far as the high rates of drunkenness arrests were concerned, statistics indicate that both urban and rural authorities were equally committed to showing that they were serious in their efforts to stamp out public drunkenness.

Common Assault

The recorded rate for common assault was one that relied almost entirely in its incidence on initiatives from private prosecutors, so that fluctuations in the official rate can best be seen as changes in the prosecutor's propensity to bring such cases to court.[14] The downward trend in the rate in both town and country was mirrored in a national secular decline from the mid-1860s to the end of the period (see fig. 9-4), raising interesting problems of interpretation. Here was a "national," or aggregated, rate that relied to a large extent on the direct actions of private prosecutors more than on the mediated response of the police.

How should we account for this? Previous work on the question shows that interpersonal violence was a prominent feature of working-class life in the nineteenth century.[15] Although it was the threat of violence that the bourgeoisie feared most about the working class, this violence was in fact almost exclusively directed against other members of the same class. The peaceful nature of midcentury interclass relations, which has been so often commented on by contemporaries and historians, was not mirrored in the behavior of certain social-class equals; and where relationships were not constrained by social distance, deference, or fear, violence—among a section of the working class—was a common method for settling disputes.

Although there were few new legal initiatives to deal with physical violence in the latter half of the nineteenth century, the rate for violent offenses brought to court began to decline steadily. This is the more striking in that access had been made easier and cheaper for private prosecutors from midcentury onward. Since it seems unreasonable to suppose that perceptions of violence had altered so as to make petty assaults seem unimportant, in a so-

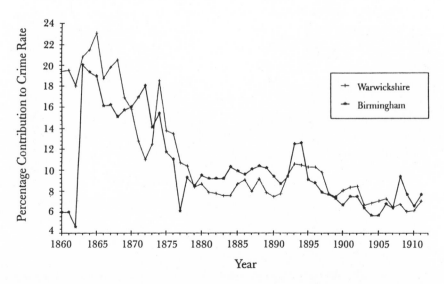

Figure 9-4. Percentage of common assault offenses, Warwickshire and Birmingham.

ciety where contemporaries repeatedly commented on its growing peaceful-
ness and orderliness, the conclusion must be that there was indeed a real
change in public attitudes toward assault and a move away from the earlier
widespread casual violence. This shift in working-class values and standards
of behavior points to the spread of the well-attested cult of respectability
within the working-class, and not simply to its imposition from outside the
community. Abstention from violence as a means of settling disputes should,
it seems, be added to the factors that formed part of the "remaking" of working-class culture in both town and country in the period 1870–1900,[16] in
which conflict and confrontation were exchanged for respect, respectability,
and acceptance of the status quo.

Vagrancy

Vagrancy was one of the great social problems of the nineteenth century at a
time when the concept of unemployment as a consequence of the workings
of the economic system rather than of individual failing was not generally
accepted. But what to do with the homeless and rootless—how to encourage them to get back to work, to discourage them from begging, and to provide a place of last resort to prevent the destitute from starving—was of major concern to all authorities. It was one of the few instances where they were
encouraged to act according to the directives of central government.

The Poor Law Commissioners, appointed under the Poor Law Act of
1834, evolved a policy to deal with vagrants that differed from the establishment of workhouses offered to the settled poor. Vagrant, or tramp, wards
attached to workhouses were opened, where vagrants were given bed and
board for the night in return for the performance of a task of work, while
constant efforts were made throughout the century to find means to distinguish the deserving traveler in search of work from the worthless loafer.

From the 1860s the police became more closely involved in this effort.
While arrests had all along been made under the Vagrancy Act of 1824, whereby it was an offense to be found sleeping out of doors or begging, the rising
tide of vagrants in the 1860s led the Poor Law Board in 1868 to recommend
the appointment of the police as relieving officers in the tramp wards, to
ensure more precise discrimination between the deserving and the scrounger.
The police undertook this task in Birmingham from 1869 onward, while the
Warwickshire police adopted much more stringent action against vagrants
from the same date (see fig. 9–5). Local experience of vagrancy and encour-
agement from the central Poor Law Board for stricter measures led both

authorities to take firmer action. But where the Birmingham authorities realized that the city acted as a permanent magnet for the indigent, in Warwickshire there was the hope that vagrants could be driven out of the county. It was clear that in Birmingham the problem could not be solved in this manner, and police action there was concentrated on arrests for sleeping in the open, with the idea of driving the homeless into the tramp wards of the workhouse where they could be subjected to some sort of discipline and police surveillance.[17]

In Warwickshire, by contrast, most arrests from 1869 onward were for begging, after the chief constable had issued printed warnings to beggars to be displayed in all the lodging houses and public buildings in the county. This practice, he claimed, had had the effect of driving a great number of mendicants from the county.[18] From this time onward, action against vagrants remained at a high level in the county, with a special Vagrancy Committee later set up among the justices to keep an eye on the problem, and with each police district required to submit quarterly reports on the state of vagrancy. Levels of arrest remained high, to the extent that lodging-house keepers in a number of police districts were led to complain that police action was depriving them of their customers,[19] and continued to the end of our period of investigation, amid claims that this pressure had brought success in clearing the county of vagrants.

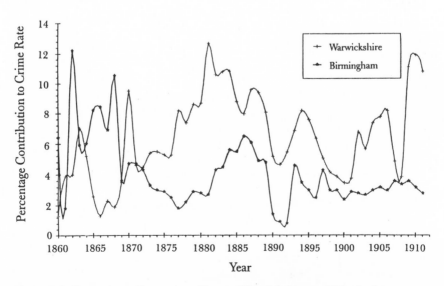

Figure 9-5. Percentage of vagrancy offenses, Warwickshire and Birmingham.

In Birmingham, on the other hand, the firm action taken against vagrants in the 1860s and the lack of police interest in subsequent years bear all the hallmarks of a response to a moral panic, well attested to in the strong press interest in the problem at the end of that decade. Once this died down, and given the fact that there were well-established Poor Law institutions to cater to the vagrants, the local authority seems to have been content to leave well enough alone, and the high level of arrests in that decade was not repeated during the rest of the period. Higher arrest rates in rural areas reveal the greater concern and self-interest of the ruling local gentry in this question, for whom vagrants roaming the countryside brought a direct sense of threat to the security of their property. The high rates may also be regarded as a measure of the different way in which it was thought the vagrancy problem could be solved. When the chief constable of Essex was told that his antivagrancy measures had driven thousands of vagrants into neighboring Kent, he cheerfully replied, "that is what I intended them to do."[20]

Thus the varied pattern of local control and police activity did little more than push the vagrancy problem around the country, with the counties in particular concerned only to protect themselves from the trouble and expense of having to deal directly with the issue. These contrasting methods illustrate the way in which the decentralized nature of the British governmental and administrative system served to accentuate a spurious rural/urban divide in the incidence of these offenses.

Simple Larceny

In considering simple larceny, an indictable offense that was tried summarily, it is interesting to note the almost consistently higher recorded rural rate for this offense down to 1892 (after which the statistics were entered into a differently aggregated table, and have therefore been excluded). The higher rate in both areas after 1879 was a consequence of the Criminal Justice Act of that year, which made larceny charges easier and cheaper for the private prosecutor (see fig. 9-6).

However, it is not only the difference between town and country that is noteworthy; the relatively low rate for larceny offenses in both areas is also remarkable. This is a reflection partly of the fact that the vast majority of police work related to victimless offenses where a summons or arrest was initiated by the police, and partly of the fact that there was a very low success rate in the detection of culprits in larceny cases. Without the greater cooperation of private prosecutors, as occurred from 1880 onward after the

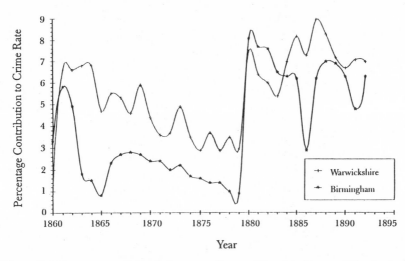

Figure 9-6. Percentage of simple larceny offenses, Warwickshire and Birmingham.

passing of the Criminal Justice Act, or indeed without their wish to bring such prosecutions, it was difficult for the police to substantiate charges of theft. Nearly 80 percent of all police charges related to noncriminal offenses, with an average of only 4.3 percent in the country and 2.3 percent in the city concerned with simple larceny before 1880. The higher rural rate may be due to the fact that few larceny charges could be proved without evidence from the victim, and in small rural communities the victim was more likely to know the identity of the thief than in the towns. But the low proportion of such charges in either area reveals the extent to which the "crime rates" chiefly charted events that had little real connection with crime.

The overriding influence of private prosecutors' decisions on the crime rates is especially important in cases of larceny; here Jennifer Davis reminds us of the need to recognize that prosecuted law-breaking represents only a tiny proportion of similar behavior that for various reasons never reaches the courts; and that this calls into question the widely held assumption that declining official crime rates in the second half of the nineteenth century were necessarily a reflection of a real decrease in law-breaking behavior.[21]

Bylaws

The enormous bias in the Judicial Statistics toward bureaucratic, victimless, and noncriminal offenses is well illustrated in the offense rates against the bylaws and the education acts, which together accounted in some years for at least half of all offenses tried summarily. Universal education for children between the ages of five and ten was first introduced in the 1870 Education Act, although it took several years to be fully implemented (not being made compulsory until 1876). Authorities in Birmingham were in the forefront of those who had been pressing for this measure.

The provisions of the act were swiftly taken up in a city that was bringing in many changes under the reforming zeal of Joseph Chamberlain's mayoralty in the 1870s.[22] A governing elite of Liberal magistrates and councillors saw education as a panacea and as an imperative for the rational and well-ordered environment and workforce that they were seeking to establish, and that their large-scale businesses required. Universal education, they firmly believed, would offer the necessary correctives to antisocial behavior. To this end, truancy officers, appointed by the Birmingham School Board, were enrolled to work closely with the police in this field, and the high rate of charges under the Education Act against parents for failing to send their children to school speaks for itself in this respect (see fig. 9-7).

The high Birmingham rate for transgressions against the bylaws is part of a similar bias in police work toward victimless offenses (see fig. 9-8). These were not statutory offenses but transgressions of town council rules covering a huge range of behavior that might annoy or endanger the citizens of the

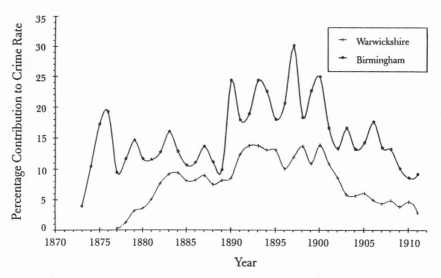

Figure 9-7. Percentage of educational offenses, Warwickshire and Birmingham.

town, from dropping litter, to playing games in the streets, to uttering street cries or obstructing the footpath. These bylaws cover several pages of tightly packed print, in contrast to a much more meager list of Warwickshire county bylaws. Not only were far fewer bylaws passed in the county, but much less use was made of them before the end of the nineteenth century; similarly, less effort was made in the county to enforce the provisions of the Education Act, and less expense was incurred in the employment of enforcement officers.

It is here that we can see the effect of the main difference between policing in the towns and in the countryside during the period. The bylaws were basically instruments for the regulation of life in urban environments for the benefit of businesses and of the general public, whereby the control of traffic and of behavior that might materially discomfort or endanger others was a primary responsibility of the local authority. There was far less need for such regulations in low-density rural areas; and in the counties, where the personal authority and rule of the justices still held sway, the administration of justice took longer to become fully bureaucratized. Nevertheless, the trend toward more representative forms of local government and a more bureaucratic system of administration proved irresistible, so that by the end of the period the rates for bylaw and educational transgressions were coming closer together, as indeed were the overall offense rates for the two areas. How far this was imitation, how far the county outside Birmingham was becoming suburban-

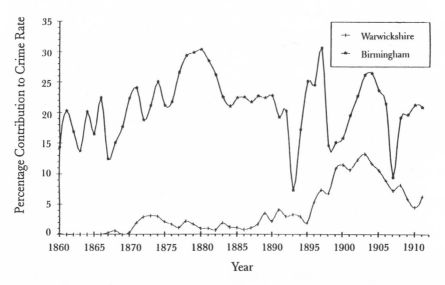

Figure 9-8. Percentage of bylaws offenses, Warwickshire and Birmingham.

ized, or how far the police service was being subjected to similar public or organizational pressures and demands is difficult to judge. Nevertheless, the result was that where Birmingham led, the rest of the county soon followed.

◆ Conclusion

What can these contrasting statistics tell us about differences in urban and rural policing in Britain? It is clear that if we had chosen a more rural area that had no large city in the vicinity, the figures might have looked different. Indeed, in the first official discussion of urban/rural differences (in a committee report in the Judicial Statistics for 1893) it was noted that rural Cornwall and Wales had the lowest crime rate against property and persons, respectively, in the period 1889–93.[23] Paradoxically, however, two of the more urbanized Welsh counties (Monmouthshire and Glamorgan) had the highest property crime rates in the same period, while the rate for drunkenness in rural Cumberland exceeded that for Liverpool. Thus, any hard and fast statements about a positive association between low crime rates and low levels of urbanization cannot be maintained even at face value. Indeed, this was acknowledged by the Criminal Registrar when he stated in 1899 that "to say that pauperism is a characteristic of rural communities, and crime that of the great towns, is misleading."[24]

What the Warwickshire statistics do seem to show, when we look at the overall rates, is that the higher and much more volatile offense rate in the city is evidence of a higher degree of police activity, with concerted police drives in the mid-1870s and 1890s against undesirable forms of social behavior—such drives being initiated by decisions of the Watch Committee, often in response to public pressure. The much steadier graph for the county reflects a different style of police management, with less direct intervention by the justices or the Standing Joint Committee, where the chief constable could satisfy his committee with an expected norm of police action, and where there was less of a vocal middle class prodding the police to respond to their public-order concerns. In addition, the lower county rate is also the consequence of a lower police/population ratio, and of the difficulties of gaining sufficient recruits to make up this lower ratio. But whatever the differences in style of police management, the impact of the large cities and towns on the countryside and the consequent interdependence of rural and urban economies by the end of the nineteenth century was such that there was really no substantive difference between the two in Britain (as the merging of the summary offense rates indicates)—and this included the role, function, and purposes of the police.

Notes

1. See Rob Sindall, *Street Violence in the Nineteenth Century* (Leicester, 1991), chap. 2, for a discussion on "a new approach to criminal statistics."

2. See Malcolm Young, *An Inside Job: Policing the Police Culture in Britain* (Oxford, 1991), chap. 5. See also D. H. Bayley, "Knowledge of the Police," in *Control in the Police Organization,* ed. M. Punch (Cambridge, Mass., 1983). Bayley lists nineteen factors affecting the correspondence between reported and actual crimes (pp. 24–25) and concludes that reported crime figures should not be used when evaluating police performance.

3. Birmingham Recorder's address to the jury at Quarter Sessions, 24 October 1871. Reported on that date in the *Birmingham Gazette* (hereafter *BG*).

4. See the contributions of Ruth Paley, Douglas Hay, and Jennifer Davis in *Policing and Prosecution in Britain, 1750–1850,* ed. Douglas Hay and Francis Snyder (Oxford, 1989).

5. See Norbert Elias, *The Civilising Process* (Oxford, 1982).

6. Police Orders, issued by Warwickshire's Chief Constable, 1841–76, Warwick County Record Office (hereafter WCRO).

7. David Jones, *Crime, Protest, Community and Police in Nineteenth-Century Britain* (London, 1982), 66.

8. Flora Thompson, "Larkrise to Candleford," quoted in Jones, *Crime, Protest, Community and Police,* 84.

9. Jones, *Crime, Protest, Community and Police,* 67.

10. Chief Constable of Warwickshire's Reports to Quarter Sessions, October 1870, WCRO.

11. Ibid., October 1876.

12. Birmingham Watch Committee Minutes, January 1872, City of Birmingham Reference Library.

13. Brian Harrison, *Drink and the Victorians* (London, 1971), 315, 276.

14. Nevertheless, even here the police response to requests for assistance in laying a charge by the would-be prosecutor are variable and contingent, so that Chatterton has concluded that "assault statistics are more accurately interpreted as the product of [police] organizational processes and not as the indices of violent behavior that they have often been assumed to be." See M. Chatterton, "Police Work and Assault Charges," in *Control in the Police Organization,* ed. Punch, 220.

15. See Barbara Weinberger, "Law Breakers and Law Enforcers in the Late Victorian City," (Ph.D. diss., University of Warwick, 1981), chap. 5.

16. See Gareth Stedman Jones, *Languages of Class: Studies in English Working Class History, 1832–1982* (Cambridge, 1983).

17. *BG,* 14 April 1870.

18. Chief Constable of Warwickshire's Report to Quarter Sessions, October 1869, WCRO.

19. Ibid., January 1870.

20. Parliamentary Papers, 1852–53, vol. 36, qu. 712; quoted in Jones, *Crime, Protest, Community and Police,* 191.

21. Jennifer Davis, "Prosecutions and Their Context," in *Policing and Prosecution in Britain,* ed. Hay and Snyder, 399–400.

22. The effect of a zealous and reforming council on the crime rate shows up in the peaks recorded in Birmingham for the years of Chamberlain's mayoralty in the 1870s.

23. Report of the committee appointed to revise the criminal portion of the Judicial Statistics, Parliamentary Papers, 1893, vol. 108.

24. Criminal Statistics for the Year 1899: Report by John Macdonell, Parliamentary Papers, 1901, vol. 89.

10

Urban and Rural Crime in Germany, 1871–1914

Eric A. Johnson

Criminologists, clergy, popular writers, social philosophers, historians, social scientists, and politicians in virtually every country have long debated the influence of environmental factors such as urbanization, ethnicity, and poverty on criminal activity. Their arguments have been and remain of considerable import to policymakers and citizens alike who view criminality as a societal evil for which political measures might be taken in order to make the social and economic environment less crime inducing. For far too long, too many societies have taken the basically conservative view that crime is not caused by economic hardship and by discrimination, against which society could act. In this view, crime is a product of irrational impulses and moral weaknesses engendered by certain ethnic and religious groups and by big-city living, which no social engineering can hope to influence.

Worse yet, the conservatives' arguments have often been propped up by scholarly studies and theories that seem to lend credence to their antiurban, antiethnic, and moralistic political policies. This has worked to the detriment of not only certain groups but whole societies, as witness the sorry urban wastelands and soaring crime rates in much of present-day Britain and America, to name only two glaring examples. The scholars are usually not to be faulted for consciously doing the conservatives' bidding. Rather, they have often developed their theories on the basis of inadequate and insufficient statistics, data that have no real historical or cross-cultural validity. Hence a sociologist in postwar America might easily find that large cities and black communities have higher crime rates than rural and white communities. But this does not mean that cities and blacks or any other ethnic population are prone to crime, in America or elsewhere. And it does not mean that citizens and politicians are making wise choices when they throw up their hands in dismay and vote for policies that ensure the further degeneration of cities and the continuing demoralization and stigmatization of certain ethnic groups. Indeed by looking at the past of America and other Western societies in a historical and sociological light, a number of scholars have begun recently to build an impressive body of evidence that challenges the assumptions of conservative policymakers and present-minded sociologists.[1]

The evidence in this essay was largely generated by employing modern quantitative techniques and a mass of census and justice data to test an array of sociological theories about the impact of urbanization, population growth, human hardship, and ethnicity on the incidence of criminal behavior in Imperial Germany. Based on such evidence, this essay will strengthen the emerging sociohistorical argument that cities are not necessarily dangerous or highly crime-prone environments. Furthermore, it will show that crime is not primarily irrational or the preserve of incorrigible ethnic groups who turn to crime because they are somehow biologically determined to do so; rather it is rooted in detrimental social and economic conditions and discrimination. Finally, the evidence presented will have a purely historical function as well. It will help to uncover how criminal behavior varied among different regions, ethnic groups, large cities, towns, and rural communities in Imperial Germany.

◆ Regions

One of the arguments often put forward to explain criminal behavior is that it is a kind of culturally determined and learned behavior passed on from one generation to the next and that it is often rooted in certain definable geographical regions, such as in the American south, where a culture of violence and lawlessness is alleged to reside.[2] The criminal justice authorities of the Bismarckian and Wilhelmian Reich were surely influenced by this viewpoint as is evident from the way in which they presented their statistics on criminal behavior. Each year from 1882 until the First World War the Royal Statistical Bureau published large volumes of criminal statistics. The bureau used the *Ort der Tat* (place of the crime) as the central organizing principle for ordering its statistical information. However, in most of the tables in these volumes the "place of the crime" that was listed and used to present other information about the criminal acts and criminal offenders was usually not the individual small community, or *Kreis,* where the deed transpired; rather the place given was the province or large administrative region (in Prussia and Bavaria, the *Regierungsbezirk*), which was comprised of many of these smaller communities. The authorities then did not generally use categories such as age, sex, occupational status, ethnic origin, or other characteristics of the criminals themselves for the presentation of their data (though they sometimes did). Instead they chose to focus on the characteristics of the large regions in which the crimes were committed. Operating in this way, if only partly consciously, the authorities were laying stress on the geographic and cultural environments in which criminal acts occurred.

Geographical and regional bases of criminal activity were stressed all the more by the use of maps that graphically contrasted the supposed lawless and law-abiding regions of the country. Two examples of these maps are presented here, one that charts the regional spread of crime in the late 1880s (fig. 10-1) and another that charts the regional spread of crime in the first decade of the twentieth century (fig. 10-2). In both cases the rates are for 100,000 population. Of course the broad brushstrokes used to darken in the high-crime areas in these maps obscure the great differences that often existed between individual communities even in the same general region. For example, in the administrative district of Gumbinnen, in the far northeast, which is darkly shaded in both maps, some communities had less than a third the "overall crime rate" of other communities in the district. In the five-year period between 1883 and 1887 the small, rural community of Heydekrug had an annual rate of 2,579, whereas the equally small, rural community of Darkehmen had a rate of only 801; in the period between 1903 and 1907 Heydekrug's rate was 2,647 and Darkehmen's rate was only 887.

But crude as these maps are, they are useful in helping us to observe where, broadly speaking, there was a relatively large or small amount of criminal activity in Germany (or at least where there were many or few criminal arrests and prosecutions). They also help us to see that, despite considerable continuity, a good amount of change transpired between the early and the later decades of the Reich. The information presented in table 10-1 brings these regional patterns into sharper relief. The shadings in the first map show that there was, in the 1880s, a tripartite geographical division of criminal patterns in Germany. The highest crime rates were to be found along the northeastern border regions of Prussia (regions that today all lie in either Poland, Lithuania, or Russia), specifically in the districts of Gumbinnen, Königsberg, Danzig, Marienwerder, Bromberg, Posen, Breslau, and Oppeln.

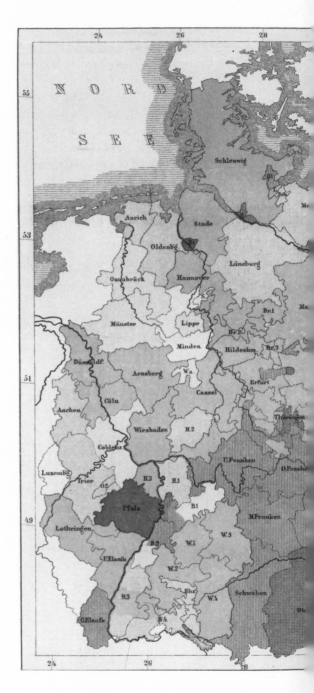

Figure 10-1. Criminal statistics for Imperial Germany, 1890.

30 32 34 36 38 40

55

53

51

49

32 34 36 38

OSTSEE

Strals.

verin

Stralsund

Strelitz

Potsdam

Berlin

Leipzig

Dresden

Zwickau

nderbayern

Stettin

Frankfurt

Bautzen

Cöslin

Bromberg

Posen

Liegnitz

Breslau

Oppeln

Danzig

Marienwerder

Königsberg

Gumbinnen

Zeichen-Erklärung.

Auf 100000 Personen der strafmündigen (über 12 Jahre alten) Zivilbevölkerung kommen
Verurtheilte überhaupt:

unter 500

500 bis unter 650

650 „ „ 800

800 „ „ 1000

1000 „ „ 1300

1300 „ „ 1700

1700 u. darüber.

*Der Reichs-Durchschnitt ist 1085, 9;
die kleinste Verhältnißzahl hat das
Fürstenthum Schaumburg-Lippe mit 428,5
die grösste der Kgl.preuß.Reg.Bezirk
Bromberg mit 2154, 8.*

Abkürzungen.

W.1 *Neckarkreis,*
W.2 *Schwarzwaldkreis,*
W.3 *Jagstkreis,*
W.4 *Donaukreis,*
B.1 *Landescommissariat Mannheim,*
B.2 „ „ „ *Karlsruhe,*
B.3 „ „ „ *Freiburg,*
B.4 „ „ „ *Konstanz,*
H.1 *Provinz Starkenburg,*
H.2 „ *Oberhessen,*
H.3 „ *Rheinhessen,*
Sch. *Landmehrkompagniebez.Schönberg,*
O.1 *Oldenburg-Fürstenthum.Lübeck,*
O.2 „ „ *Birkenfeld,*
Bel *Kreise Braunschweig,Wolfenbüttel,*
„ *Helmstedt,*
Br.2 „ *Holzminden,Gandersheim,*
Br.3 *Kreis Blankenburg,*
S. *Schaumburg-Lippe,*
H. *Hamburg,*
L. *Lübeck,*
Br. *Bremen.*

DEUTSCHES REICH.

Die Kriminalität
der Bevölkerung überhaupt.

Die Zahl der wegen Verbrechen und Vergehen gegen
Reichsgesetze **Verurtheilten** auf 100 000 über
12 Jahre alte Personen der Zivilbevölkerung im
Durchschnitt der 5 Jahre 1886/90

*nach preußischen und bayerischen Regierungsbezirken,
sächsischen Kreishauptmannschaften u.s.w. berechnet.*

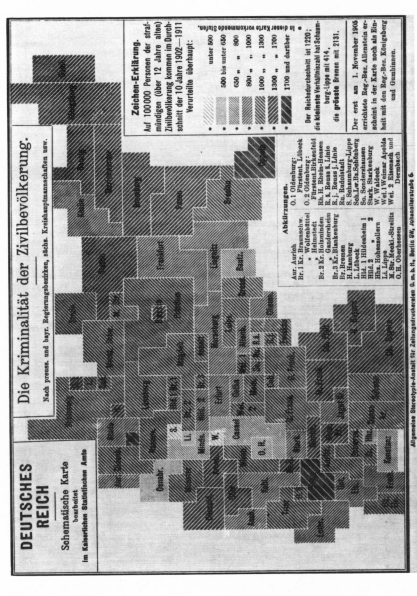

Figure 10-2. Criminal statistics for Imperial Germany, 1911.

Table 10-1. A Comparison of Crime Rates in Two Periods, 1882–91 and 1902–11 (by Gender, in Large Administrative Districts)[a]

District	1882–91			1902–11			Percent Change		
	T	M	W	T	M	W	T	M	W
1. Königsberg	1538	2616	618	1466	2662	485	−4.7	+0.2	−21.5
2. Gumbinnen	1806	3074	695	1604	2801	551	−11.2	−8.9	−20.7
3. Danzig	1531	2584	607	1510	2640	516	−1.4	+2.2	−15.0
4. Marienwerder	1504	2466	624	1407	2372	533	−6.4	−3.8	−14.6
5. Berlin	1316	2194	554	1592	2672	630	+21.0	+21.8	+13.7
6. Potsdam	1011	1695	362	1235	2163	393	+22.2	+27.6	+8.6
7. Frankfurt	922	1570	345	986	1767	282	+6.9	+12.5	−18.3
8. Stettin	1061	1798	384	1352	2340	448	+27.4	+30.1	+16.7
9. Köslin	944	1615	338	889	1583	251	−5.8	−2.0	−25.7
10. Stralsund	666	1171	222	1015	1808	307	+52.4	+54.4	+38.3
11. Posen	1500	2462	688	1334	2345	509	−11.1	−4.8	−26.0
12. Bromberg	1886	3016	872	1607	2665	657	−14.8	−11.6	−24.7
13. Breslau	1264	2174	500	1295	2342	419	+2.5	+7.7	−16.2
14. Liegnitz	804	1395	303	904	1640	269	+12.4	+17.6	−11.2
15. Oppeln	1724	2925	692	1969	3441	665	+14.2	+17.6	−3.9
16. Magdeburg	950	1549	371	1053	1788	372	+10.8	+15.4	+0.3
17. Merseburg	934	1494	401	962	1608	362	+3.0	+7.6	−9.7
18. Erfurt	887	1526	330	891	1600	285	+0.5	+4.8	−13.6
19. Schleswig	680	1164	215	1002	1672	343	+47.4	+43.6	+59.5
20. Hannover	958	1662	302	1289	2199	433	+34.6	+32.3	+43.4
21. Hildesheim	857	1445	291	845	1476	251	−1.4	+1.4	−13.7
22. Lüneburg	732	1251	218	1029	1757	286	+40.6	+40.4	+31.2
23. Stade	780	1356	209	994	1738	227	+27.4	+28.2	+8.6
24. Osnabrück	533	957	118	595	1084	115	+11.6	+13.3	−2.5
25. Aurich	693	1140	287	864	1536	251	+24.7	+34.7	−12.5
26. Münster	497	897	98	1111	1917	262	+123.5	+113.7	+167.3
27. Minden	449	811	110	659	1207	141	+46.8	+48.8	+27.3
28. Arnsberg	854	1437	223	1324	2214	338	+55.0	+54.1	+51.6
29. Kassel	853	1517	273	780	1448	178	−8.6	−4.5	−34.8
30. Wiesbaden	874	1523	280	1097	1972	290	+25.5	+29.5	+3.6
31. Koblenz	624	1095	176	851	1554	182	+36.4	+41.9	+3.4
32. Düsseldorf	793	1374	219	1413	2399	399	+78.2	+74.6	+82.2
33. Köln	778	1351	235	1613	2703	572	+107.3	+100.1	+143.4
34. Trier	606	1018	205	1286	2132	424	+112.2	+109.4	+106.8
35. Aachen	628	1076	192	856	1503	237	+36.3	+39.7	+23.4
36. Sigmaringen	562	1027	151	537	1020	107	−4.4	−0.7	−29.1
Prussia	1052	1769	395	1248	2157	403	+18.6	+21.9	+2.0
37. Oberbayern	1429	2369	525	1430	2446	507	+0.1	+3.3	−3.4
38. Niederbayern	1324	2324	442	1588	2820	432	+19.2	+21.3	−2.3

Table 10-1, continued

District	1882-91			1902-11			Percent Change		
	T	M	W	T	M	W	T	M	W
39. Pfalz	1526	2713	440	1787	3233	431	+17.1	+19.2	−2.0
40. Oberpfalz	1141	1923	437	1399	2508	389	+22.6	+30.4	−11.0
41. Oberfranken	1054	1823	355	1219	2184	335	+15.7	+19.8	−5.6
42. Mittelfranken	1213	2028	471	1381	2420	428	+13.8	+19.3	−9.1
43. Unterfranken	1058	1906	299	1114	2058	253	+5.3	+8.0	−15.4
44. Schwaben	1038	1797	356	1240	2210	335	+19.5	+23.0	−5.9
Bavaria	1243	2141	424	1409	2498	405	+13.4	+16.7	−4.5
45. Dresden	941	1543	420	1020	1772	375	+8.4	+14.8	−10.7
46. Leipzig	1015	1634	438	1084	1837	387	+6.8	+12.4	−11.6
47. Chemnitz	—	—	—	838	1462	272	—	—	—
48. Zwickau	988	1676	353	1029	1810	342	−5.5	−2.4	−13.0
49. Bautzen	696	1202	258	656	1171	197	−5.7	−2.6	−23.6
Saxony	948	1576	381	969	1679	336	+2.2	+6.5	−11.8
50. Württemberg	876	1548	281	1178	2141	301	+34.5	+38.3	+7.1
51. Baden	873	1548	257	1168	2133	254	+33.8	+37.3	−1.2
52. Hessen	775	1371	224	988	1765	251	+27.5	+28.7	+12.1
53. Meckl-Schwerin	680	1168	225	1059	1860	309	+55.7	+59.2	+37.3
54. Großhz.Sachsen	835	1385	340	1052	1852	315	+26.0	+33.7	−7.4
55. Meckl-Strelitz	723	1241	248	1034	1826	281	+43.0	+47.1	+13.3
56. Oldenburg	691	1200	215	1051	1870	265	+52.1	+55.8	+23.3
57. Braunschweig	956	1536	391	1241	2051	489	+29.8	+33.5	+25.1
58. Sachsen-Mein.	1105	1897	381	1180	2098	331	+6.8	+10.6	−13.1
59. Sachsen-Alt.	871	1406	376	877	1499	294	+0.7	+6.6	−21.8
60. Sach-Cob-Gotha	871	1515	303	822	1510	210	−5.6	−0.3	−30.7
61. Anhalt	1050	1683	453	1213	2018	451	+15.5	+20.0	−0.4
62. Schwz-Sondrz.	1287	2004	636	985	1780	274	−23.5	−11.2	−56.9
63. Schwz-Rudofs.	1473	2477	561	1187	2120	340	−19.4	−14.4	−39.4
64. Waldeck	478	890	139	429	815	90	−10.3	−8.4	−35.3
65. Schaum-Lippe	411	706	129	414	772	80	+0.7	+9.3	−38.0
66. Lippe	538	895	207	630	1180	143	+17.3	+31.8	−30.9
67. Lübeck	936	1695	268	1043	1827	323	+11.4	+7.8	+20.5
68. Bremen	1564	2859	436	2131	3793	503	+36.3	+32.7	+15.4
69. Hamburg	1270	2165	438	1501	2585	456	+18.2	+19.4	+4.1
70. Alsace-Lorr.	758	1337	242	966	1702	259	+27.4	+27.3	+7.0
German Reich	1029	1746	375	1220	2128	378	+18.6	+21.9	+0.8

Key: T = Total; M = Men; W = Women

a. The figures represent the total number of convictions per 100,000 legally liable population of the appropriate gender.

Sources: Unless otherwise indicated, all figures in this and the following tables in this chapter come from *Statistik des Deutschen Reichs* and *Preußische Statistik*. Most of the criminal justice data are from the former series, particularly in yearly volumes entitled *Kriminalstatistik*.

Otherwise only parts of Bavaria, such as Oberbayern, Niederbayern, and Pfalz, and the city-state of Bremen had exceedingly high crime rates. The lowest crime rates were to be found along the western border that Germany shared with Denmark, Holland, Luxembourg, France, and Switzerland, from Schleswig in the north all the way to Konstanz in the south, with only a few exceptions, mostly in central Germany. Moderate levels of criminality prevailed everywhere else, primarily in the German hinterland.

These observations are based on the rather dubious classification of annual convictions per 100,000 legally liable population for all serious crimes and misdemeanors (*Verbrechen und Vergehen*), and adult male criminality accounted for the bulk of the figures as the adult male rate was roughly five times that of the adult female rate and three times that of the juvenile rate. Nonetheless, this same tripartite geographical division would seem to apply for women and juveniles, and for individual offenses such as assault and battery and especially for common theft.[3] Thus the same districts with extremely high or extremely low rates of men's criminality also had extremely high or extremely low rates of female and juvenile criminality (notice in table 10-1, for example, the extremely high rates for all three groups in the northeastern Prussian border districts of Gumbinnen, Bromberg, and Oppeln and the extremely low rates in the western districts of Münster and Minden). Furthermore, if a graph of individual offenses such as theft were presented here, the same kinds of geographical patterns would appear in even bolder relief. During the 1880s some individual *Kreise* in the Prussian northeast, such as Labiau in Königsberg, Heydekrug in Gumbinnen, and Obernik in Posen, had theft rates that exceeded 900, and many more neighboring districts exceeded 800, all of which were between ten to fifteen times the theft rates of many individual *Kreise* in western districts, in Schleswig, Osnabrück, Minden, Münster, Düsseldorf, Cologne, Koblenz, Aachen, and Trier.[4]

These general patterns of criminality did not hold throughout the years of Imperial Germany, however, as one learns from the second map and from the figures in table 10-1. Twenty years later, after the turn of the century, the Prussian northeast and much of Bavaria still had high crime rates, but several former low-crime areas along the western frontier, such as the *Regierungsbezirke* of Düsseldorf, Cologne, and Arnsberg, now registered very high rates of crime as well. Some scholars have pointed out that the western frontier was becoming something akin to the American "wild west" as other western districts, such as Schleswig, Oldenburg, Hannover, Münster, and Trier, also recorded marked increases in their crime rates between the 1880s and the early 1900s.[5] True, the recorded crime rate for Germany as a whole had grown by nearly 20 percent from the 1880s to the 1900s. But Germany's increase in recorded crime was due primarily to new laws enacted in the 1890s for certain politically conceived offenses, such as the laws concerning union workers' insurance. These increases were not common among some large components of the general population, such as women, whose overall crime rate held rather steady. These caveats notwithstanding, the westward expansion of crime was anything but illusory.

Numerous cities, towns, and villages of the Rhine, the Ruhr, and other western regions recorded booms in garden-variety offenses such as theft, assault and battery, and murder that had no obvious political roots. And in the same period many northeastern communities actually had declining crime rates. Some figures to support this statement are given in table 10-2, which lists the fifty-seven largest German cities (all with a legally liable population of over 50,000 by 1905). Here one finds information that helps one to compare changes in the cities' population, and various rates of crime from a five-year period in the 1880s to a five-year period in the early 1990s. The Rhineland cities of Cologne and Düsseldorf, for example, which in the 1880s had very low crime rates, recorded such huge increases in their overall crime totals and in individual offenses such as assault and battery and theft that they ranked among the most crime-infested cities of Germany after the turn of the century. In the Prussian northeast, on the other hand, many cities such as Königsberg, Breslau, and Posen actually recorded modest decreases in most types of crime over these years. These urban examples are not extraordinary. Not only did many other western cities experience a criminal explosion while many northeastern cities had rates that either declined or held relatively steady; many smaller, largely rural communities in the vicinity of the western cities also registered dramatic increases while many smaller, largely rural communities in the vicinity of the northeastern cities registered dramatic decreases.[6]

Hence, by the turn of the century, there was no longer a clear geographical pattern in the distribution of crime rates across the map of Germany. This was true for both women and men and most types of criminal offenses, though more so for property offenses and less so for crimes of violence, which, with some exceptions, remained most highly concentrated in northeastern Prussia and in Bavaria. This breakdown of the old regional distribution of criminality should lead one immediately to question the hypothesis that crime is primarily a learned behavior with fixed geocultural roots. This is not meant to dispute that some criminal activities, especially crimes of passion such as assault, rape, and murder, do seem to have cultural compo-

Table 10–2. Crime and Population Figures for Fifty-seven Largest German Cities (Listed Alphabetically)

City	LLPop.85	LLPop.05	TCR 1883-87	A&B 1883-87	Theft 1883-87	TCR 1903-7	A&B 1903-7	Theft 1903-7
1. Aachen	68,097	108,349	901*	96*	232*	1215	165	260
2. Altona	86,468	124,495	1257	87	345	1585	141	294
3. Augsburg	49,286	70,912	1360	172	400	1595	287	405
4. Barmen	69,750	112,897	850	155	182	966	163	204
5. Berlin	977,802	1,609,527	1213	78	329	1522	131	335
6. Bielefeld	23,645	51,802	1157*	228*	253*	1415	192	239
7. Bochum	25,647	72,370	1460*	254*	333*	1603	305	385
8. Bonn	?	57,485	?	?	?	1525	224	288
9. Braunschweig	88,896	132,824	1010	103	309	1489	126	302
10. Bremen	83,521	159,558	1170	123	330	1897	283	395
11. Breslau	220,744	350,079	2138	195	520	1857	197	340
12. Chemnitz	79,997	176,745	1511	79	460	1188	75	294
13. Colmar	57,873	66,997	626	109	164	1131	208	161
14. Danzig	80,291	112,412	2016	202	700	1732	256	370
15. Darmstadt	58,879	91,167	854	153	214	905	124	173
16. Dessau	41,069	62,499	1008	88	318	1324	164	366
17. Dortmund	51,286	121,551	1232*	203*	301*	1628	242	396
18. Dresden	182,339	379,493	1039	36	332	1251	56	208
19. Düsseldorf	78,796	181,579	989	185	255	1838	235	462
20. Duisburg	30,656	106,385	1335*	215*	389*	1543	251	375
21. Elberfeld	72,756	119,097	888	144	235	1639	202	364
22. Erfurt	40,739	71,294	1526*	97*	416*	1447	83	369

Table 10–2, continued

City	LLPop.85	LLPop.05	TCR 1883–87	A&B 1883–87	Theft 1883–87	TCR 1903–7	A&B 1903–7	Theft 1903–7
23. Essen	43,211	149,782	1151*	197*	306*	1884	323	435
24. Frankfurt	?	257,666	?	?	?	1432	143	301
25. Freiburg	52,489	78,631	1366	181	394	1274	286	288
26. Gelsenkirchen	?	89,760	?	?	?	1595	352	326
27. Giesen	50,286	63,887	787	121	171	757	166	119
28. Görlitz	41,007	63,399	1339	96	360	1543	133	326
29. Hagen	?	53,086	?	?	?	1667	303	349
30. Halle	41,339	50,028	1637	170	411	1272	114	300
31. Hamburg	227,414	608,267	1658	133	490	1468	66	326
32. Hannover	99,265	187,853	1270	124	326	1964	174	381
33. Karlsruhe	64,283	108,864	985	148	300	1437	277	257
34. Kassel	45,069	91,632	1204*	100*	362*	1591	183	325
35. Kiel	34,051	102,066	1701*	101*	525*	2079	160	442
36. Köln	113,859	311,332	931	112	244	2446	322	384
37. Königsberg	109,693	156,445	2066	150	529	2017	262	402
38. Krefeld	62,128	85,004	850*	149*	170*	998	102	196
39. Leipzig	128,084	382,529	1373	52	455	1335	83	292
40. Lübeck	39,559	66,546	959*	84*	276*	984	72	266
41. Magdeburg	110,689	176,127	1461	149	359	1400	123	313
42. Mainz	73,167	104,928	1054	183	303	1740	347	321
43. Mannheim	61,772	138,048	1332	215	439	2209	576	402
44. München	200,493	410,012	1430	210	397	1300	189	302

Kreis	LLPop.85	LLPop.05	TCR	A&B	Theft	TCR	A&B	Theft
45. Münster	30,624	57,882	**1069***	131*	252*	**1163**	132	**261**
46. Mulhausen	103,465	130,880	1152	**255**	**290**	**1180**	**275**	201
47. Nürnberg	84,264	213,752	1445	**191**	**422**	1651	**361**	**344**
48. Posen	47,211	94,788	2252*	**293***	**645***	2241	**370**	**497**
49. Rostock	46,926	66,809	**721**	83	217	1256	154	**275**
50. Schwerin	46,056	54,519	**673**	72	195	**839**	103	191
51. Stettin	71,983	162,958	1501*	**161***	**342***	2258	**278**	**381**
52. Strassburg	75,282	117,444	**1000**	**185**	**296**	1272	187	**254**
53. Stuttgart	92,842	178,163	1005	73	**339**	1307	132	**284**
54. Weimar	61,840	77,789	**949**	68	**323**	**1135**	150	**300**
55. Wiesbaden	41,299	78,373	1506*	122*	**371***	1410	158	**314**
56. Worms	45,693	61,174	**930**	**190**	223	1372	**360**	208
57. Würzburg	40,386	58,761	1191*	**165***	**317***	1231	199	**286**
Averages	93,567	167,734	1219	147	339	1492	215	311
Averages for all Kreise in Reich			1001	153	282	1195	228	239

Note: Figures are in **boldface** if they exceed the national average for all *Kreise* in assault and battery and theft offenses, or if they are less than the average in the total crime category.

Key:
* = figures for 1883–97 substituted for unavailable 1883–87 figures
LLPop.85 = legally liable population (age twelve and over) for 1885
LLPop.05 = legally liable population (age twelve and over) for 1905
TCR = total crime rate (convictions per 100,000 legally liable population)
A&B = assault and battery rate (convictions for serious bodily harm per 100,000 legally liable population)
Theft = theft rate (convictions for simple and grand theft per 100,000 legally liable population)

nents in Germany and in other societies.[7] However, it is meant to suggest that
there must have been other factors at work that would explain the considerable changes in the regional bases of criminality. Developing a theory that
accounts for the changes is no simple task. Several possibilities come quickly to mind, however, most of which hinge on theories stressing the importance of the processes of migration, population growth, and urbanization,
which were popular theories in Germany at the time and which remain popular theories for explaining criminal trends in many countries today.[8]

All students of modern German history know that the last decades of the
nineteenth century were characterized by sharp rises in population and urban growth, dramatically so for many of the industrializing communities in
the Rhine-Ruhr region. And given the significant flight (*Landflucht*) of eastern rural migrants into many of the boom towns of the west during the eight-
ies, nineties, and early 1900s, would not the classic *Gemeinschaft* to *Gesellschaft* and anomie theories of Tönnies and Durkheim explain the perceived
changes in the geographical loci of criminal behavior?[9] Could we not expect
the uprooted immigrants who swelled the western cities and towns to have
experienced alienation and anomie in their strange and new surroundings?

Pregnant as such theories might appear, in reality they are barren. Recent studies of the social impact of nineteenth- and twentieth-century German migration that have been undertaken by American scholars such as
Walter Kamphoefner, James Jackson, Steve Hochstadt, and David Crew and
by German scholars such as Klaus Bade have not found that the migrants'
experiences or the process of migration itself were especially unsettling.[10]
Furthermore, arguments about alienation, anomie, urbanization, and population growth do not apply on their very face when one considers that cities
such as Munich and Leipzig had declining crime rates even though they also
had huge migrant populations and tremendous population growth. Perhaps
part of the explanation for the changing regional bases of criminality, however, still has something to do with migration. But migration per se was of
little or no importance. What was important, however, was who exactly the
migrants were and whether they were received as unwanted *Ausländer* and
whether they met with discrimination and hardship, as was the experience
of many eastern Poles and Lithuanians, or if they were more readily accepted, as was more often the case for Western Europeans such as the Danes,
Dutch, Belgians, and French.[11] But before discussing the significance of hardship and ethnic discrimination in detail, I will consider and put to rest the
tired hypotheses that posit that urbanization, population growth, and urban
living cause crime.

◆ Urban/Rural Differences and Urbanization

The theory that urban growth and big cities engender crime is a long-standing and well-articulated myth. This myth has been widely shared and Germans have done their part to perpetuate it. Based largely on belief, the myth has been very hard to dispel, all the more so because it has often been propagated by the most respected guardians of the people's trust, from pious pastors to prominent politicians. By pointing the finger of blame at the city for generating crime and other social ills, theologians such as Christian Rugge in the *Kaiserreich* and political leaders such as Adolf Hitler some years later hoped to mobilize support for their own ideological aims and mount opposition to their enemies.[12] Housing Jews, workers, socialists, and democrats, the city has been a logical target for conservative ideologues.

The city has also been a convenient and logical target for presumably less-biased trustees of the truth. In Germany perhaps the first "coherent [antiurban] intellectual position," as it was characterized by the American historian Andrew Lees, was worked out by Wilhelm Heinrich Riehl. Riehl was a Bavarian journalist and university professor who wrote a four-volume treatise published between 1854 and 1869 depicting cities as symbols and sources of the worst aspects of the modern world, including ruthlessness, declining national identity, cosmopolitanism, godlessness, social disorder, and crime.[13] Of course, his arguments would be echoed resoundingly by other ultraconservative thinkers and publicists, some of whom, such as Walter Classen in the Kaiserreich or Nazi theorists in Weimar and the Third Reich, even had racist biases against the metropolis.[14] But the antiurban critique became all the more powerful when it was taken up by leading reform-minded thinkers of a less ideological bent, such as the economist Karl Bücher, the intellectual historian Julius Langbehn, and the demographer Adolf Weber. Andrew Lees has studied these antiurban critics in German history perhaps more than has anyone else. Lees wrote: "It is clear . . . that by the early twentieth century criticism of cities was rampant in Germany. . . . Much of this criticism was hostile in the extreme. Conservative clergymen, social theorists, demographers, and publicists painted a dark picture of the urban scene."[15]

But, among the Germans who contributed most significantly to the longstanding myth that cities promote crime and disorder are some of the founders of modern sociology, for example, Georg Simmel, Ferdinand Tönnies, and Max Weber. Their classic works stand alongside those of their French contemporary Emile Durkheim as bulwarks protecting the antiurban mythos. To this day they are trotted out as the standard-bearers of a logic that

seems inescapable. Only very recently has their dogma been seriously challenged, largely by sociologists and historians armed with methodological
weaponry powerful enough to penetrate the fortress of theories that they and
their countless descendants have erected.[16]

Despite the mounting attacks of modern empiricists, the canon still
sounds good. Cities cause crime because they are centers of prostitution and
vice, which eat away at their foundations. People in cities do not know their
neighbors and do not go to church, so the social and moral control supposedly characteristic of small town and village life breaks down. It is easy to steal
from or get into a fight with people one does not know. The population pressure makes one irritable and violent. The grime, dirt, and pollution make one
less respectful of public property. There is more to steal and more people to
assault, and there is less risk of being caught. Cities are centers of pubs, gam-
bling, and nightlife, which attract thieves, rapists, and murderers. They are
purveyors of alcohol and drugs. Crime-prone youths and gangs control the
streets, and otherwise honest adolescents are pressed early into lives of crime.
City dwellers suffer from anomie and alienation and turn to crime to alleviate their anxieties. The mental life of the metropolis is disturbed. Crime is
more acceptable behavior. The possible arguments are endless. But most of
them are simply rubbish.[17]

Cities and for that matter all forms of settlement are what society makes
of them. Of course they can be filthy and stinking, swollen with the homeless and the jobless, the politically emasculated, and the racially discriminated
against, and if so they would logically be breeding grounds for criminality
and other asocial behavior. But they do not have to be, and they have not
always been.

The data to be presented here will show that German cities in the late
nineteenth and early twentieth centuries were not particularly crime ridden
even if, in accord with classical sociological logic and the strength of the
antiurban political and moral forces lodged against them and their inhabitants at the time, they should have been. If the cities of Imperial Germany,
which underwent a growth equal at least to that of any other sizable European or North American land (see table 10-2), can be shown to be relatively
safe and lawful, then no theory accusing urban growth and urban environments as being crime inducing is tenable.[18]

Perhaps German cities were exceptional, as indeed some American visitors such as the publicist Ray Stannard Baker and the police expert Raymond Fosdick thought them to be. We recall how at the turn of the century
Baker found German cities to be uncomfortably overregulated but, possibly

as a result, "safer for strangers, perhaps, than any other in the world." And Fosdick, in 1909, while making a comparative study of crime and police practices in various European countries, was told by a Dresden police commissioner that there was not much crime in his city because "we have no real poverty here." Fosdick compared this with what he was told by the head constable of Liverpool, England, a city of about the same size, who believed that "by far the greater part of the crime of Liverpool is due to poverty."[19] Certainly these observers were not alone in noting the order, cleanliness, and relative lack of poverty that prevailed in German cities. For example, in the 1870s, the British visitor Henry Vizetelly, though complaining about nearly everything under the German sun, from "dully paved roads" to the terrible odor he thought he smelled, was struck by the comparative lack of poverty in Berlin: "Berlin with all its misery has nothing comparing to our London Rookeries."[20]

Though these observations are less than scientific, they can be supported by data showing that measures of relative wealth, such as adult and infant mortality, taxation, school spending, and literacy, correlated positively with the size of urban population in administrative districts in Imperial Germany, while measures of hardship and poverty, such as infant and adult mortality, correlated negatively.[21] This does not mean that German cities were never centers of poverty and criminality, as indeed many were. It does demonstrate, however, that German cities were certainly not generally to be construed as loci of dirt and despair when compared with cities in other countries or with other types of communities in Germany at the time.[22]

Germans might have been particularly adept at handling the huge population and urban growth in the late nineteenth and early twentieth centuries and perhaps largely for this reason there was no great upsurge in criminality in Germany over these years. But in recent studies of lands such as France, Britain, Sweden, and the United States there is much evidence that the second half of the nineteen century, despite the growth of cities everywhere, did not witness a general growth of crime, however it is measured. In fact, the opposite was often the case, for crime rates actually declined in many societies.[23]

But it is dubious to speak of "the crime rate" as declining or growing or staying the same. All crime rates are of questionable validity. At best they measure only a fraction of the actual amount of criminality that takes place. This is true whether the measure of "the crime rate" is based on reported crimes, arrests, trials, or convictions. And worse is that "the crime rate" is in reality cobbled together from a myriad of individual offenses that go in or out of fashion with the whims of citizens and justice officials; ultimately, it is only a kind of broad measure of the statistically reported operations of police and justice official machinery. Prudent scholars now recognize that if one wants to do more than discuss the ebb and flow of reported criminal activity in a particular society at a particular time, and especially if one wants to develop a theory about crime causation that has cross-cultural and cross-temporal validity, one must at the very least separate "the crime rate" into its components and focus only on those crimes—such as theft, murder, and assault and battery—that all societies believe are criminal offenses.

However, even though several scholars in several societies have now done this, no one has successfully woven together the individual threads of scholarship into an acceptable theoretical fabric. Perhaps this is impossible to do. So politicians and ideologues and classroom teachers have been free to fabricate policy out of the old yarn that cities cause crime.

Of the studies with which I am familiar, and from the data that I present here, there is but one slender strand of evidence that could support this conception. It relies primarily on what Charles Tilly, Arthur Stinchcombe, and others have called a "structural theory," whereby certain types of crime are apt to be prominent in certain types of social environments. According to this theory, property crimes such as theft can be expected to have a higher frequency in towns and cities than in rural settings because of the greater abundance of goods to steal and the more materialistic ethos of the city population, which makes more people desire to accumulate goods, by stealing if they must.[24] This theory seems to make some sense, especially when we consider that cities usually have higher concentrations of young adult males (who are often particularly prone to property offenses) than do more rural settings, whose demographic makeup is usually comprised of a larger proportion of older people.

Even admitting all of this, the structural theory is rendered rather limp and questionable when one considers that it is also possible that the more materialistic urban ethos may lead to overcounted property crime statistics. Conceivably, urban inhabitants are more concerned than rural inhabitants with reporting property offenses and more often urge the criminal justice authorities to prosecute property offenders with alacrity. (Dirk Blasius and others have shown how theft offenses skyrocketed in the early 1800s owing to the new practice of vigorously prosecuting people for stealing wood from the forest of the now more materialistic German property owners.) A limited and not thoroughly successful attempt to test this proposition, as conceded openly by its authors, was carried out a few years ago by Charles Tilly,

Allan Levett, A. Q. Lodhi, and Frank Munger, who studied police activity in several societies in Europe and North America in the nineteenth century (though not in Germany). Their findings led them to argue that with the growth of professional police forces, which occurred everywhere, "the intensification of policing undoubtedly tended to raise the proportion of all violations of the law which came to the attention of crime control specialists and thereby become visible," and that "at least part of the widespread increase" in reported crime in the first half of the nineteenth century in many societies "results from a rise in crime's visibility."[25] Since they found that the growth of police forces was generally faster in urban than in rural communities, and they believed that there were greater incentives both to steal and to report stealing in the city than in the village, the crime rates—particularly the property crime rates—could be expected to be overestimated in cities and underestimated in rural areas.

Some final problems with the structural theory are that it says nothing at all about the size of the urban population, the growth rate of the urban population, or the ethnic and economic makeup of the urban population. Nor does it tell us anything about violent acts, which are what politicians and ideologues are most likely to condemn cities for and which most normal citizens probably fear the most (only very property-minded people can be expected to fear the loss of a pocketbook as much as they fear the loss of a life).

The data to be presented here will show that urban and population growth and urban settings themselves had very little to do with explaining crime patterns in Imperial Germany. What was of importance in explaining why some communities had more crime than others at particular times was not whether they were large or small or growing quickly or even depopulating; rather it was what the conditions were of the people who lived in the communities and often who the people were. What too many people have long overlooked is that hardship and discrimination, which along with pure irrationality should be taken to be the real causes of criminality, are not confined by city walls. Just as cities can be dumping grounds for the wretched and the oppressed, they can also be centers of hope and opportunity. The "smiling countryside," as Holmes called it, can easily be the domicile of downtrodden citizens frowning at the violence and criminality that their misery engenders.[26]

There are many ways in which this point can be illustrated. We might take the example of Berlin, by far the largest German city, which had a population growth rate that was one of the highest of all German cities (see table 10–2). In table 10–3 there are statistics showing that in comparison with

Table 10–3. Crime, Population Density, Mortality, and Ethnicity in Twenty-five Largest Prussian Cities (Highest to Lowest Crime Rate)

City	TCR.3–7	TCR.83–87	Pop.06	Population Density	DR.06	%Ethnic Pop.00	Type
1. Köln	2446	931	429,343	3,868	19	1.0	mixed
2. Stettin	2258	1501*	224,423	3,350	22	1.0	Polish
3. Posen	2241	2252*	137,006	4,152	23	56.0	Polish
4. Kiel	2079	1701*	164,009	7,130	16	2.2	mixed
5. Königsberg	2017	2966	223,928	11,196	20	0.6	Lithuanian
6. Hannover	1964	1270	250,201	6,255	16	1.0	mixed
7. Essen	1884	1151	231,991	23,199	17	3.4	Polish
8. Breslau	1857	2138	471,921	13,096	22	1.6	Polish
9. Düsseldorf	1838	989	253,700	5,178	17	1.8	mixed
10. Danzig	1732	2016	159,838	7,992	21	2.6	Polish
11. Elberfeld	1639	888	163,052	5,260	14	0.9	mixed
12. Dortmund	1628	1232*	175,897	6,282	21	3.7	Polish
13. Bochum	1603	1460	118,696	19,783	21	4.0	Polish
14. Gelsenkirchen	1595	?	147,459	12,214	20	8.1	Polish
15. Kassel	1591	1204*	120,583	5,481	14	0.5	mixed
16. Altona	1585	1257	168,445	7,657	16	1.4	mixed
17. Duisburg	1543	1335*	192,754	5,210	19	6.3	Dutch
18. Berlin	1522	1213	2,041,590	32,406	16	1.6	Polish
19. Frankfurt a.M.	1432	?	335,348	3,567	15	1.1	mixed
20. Wiesbaden	1410	1506*	101,038	2,807	16	2.2	mixed
21. Magdeburg	1400	1461	240,845	4,379	17	0.5	mixed
22. Halle	1272	1637	170,167	4,254	21	0.6	mixed
23. Aachen	1215	901*	144,232	3,698	19	2.2	Dutch
24. Krefeld	998	850*	110,463	5,260	14	1.0	Dutch
25. Barmen	966	850	156,289	7,104	13	0.4	mixed

Key:
* = figures for 1883–97 substituted for unavailable 1883–87 figures
TCR.3–7 = total crime rate for 1903–7
TCR.83–87 = total crime rate for 1883–87
Pop.06 = population in 1906
DR.06 = death rate (deaths per 1,000 inhabitants) in 1906
%Ethnic Pop.00 = percent of each district made up of "non-German ethnic" population in 1900
Type = dominant non-German-speaking, ethnic minority; "mixed" means that no dominant ethnic minority prevailed

other German cities, Berlin also had some of the lowest crime rates. Of the twenty-five largest cities of Prussia, all with a population of over 100,000 inhabitants in 1906, Berlin ranked eighteenth in the overall crime rate in the five-year period between 1903 and 1907, even though its population was over ten times that of ten of the cities with a higher overall crime rate and roughly five times that of its nearest rival in size, Cologne, which had the highest overall crime rate of all major Prussian cities in this period.

These omnibus crime figures could, of course, be misleading; they might camouflage some much higher rates of individual offenses that would be more trustworthy than the "overall crime rate." But they are not misleading. In various periods of five years and longer from 1883 until 1912, Berlin had far lower rates of assault and battery than was the average for all communities in Germany, whether they were rural *Landkreise* or urban *Stadtkreise* (see table 10–4). This was also true in homicide offenses, according to both coroners' and court records. In addition, between 1883 and 1897, Berlin had a slightly lower rate of theft than was the average for all German cities and a modestly higher rate of theft than was the average for German *Landkreise*. Only after the turn of the century did Berlin's overall and theft crime rates exceed the average for both other city districts and land districts, and it was at this time that Berlin's crime rate ranked eighteenth of the largest twenty-five Prussian cities.

Many other figures can be brought forward to show that Berlin was not an exceptional case. The figures in table 10–4 show that throughout the years of Imperial Germany, violent criminality such as assault and battery was more characteristic of the village and the countryside than it was of the city, but that property offenses such as theft were somewhat more prevalent in cities than in more rural communities throughout the 1880s and the 1890s and considerably more prevalent in the cities after the turn of the century. However, the growth of the general and the urban population in these years certainly did not bring about more property offenses. The rate of theft declined in both city districts and land districts after the turn of the century, though the decline was much more noticeable in the countryside. Why this was the case is open to speculation, but one suspects that it had to do with relative prosperity and hardship. The decline of the theft rates in the rural communities probably reflected their improved conditions as German agricultural wages certainly improved around the turn of the century with the end of the "Long Depression" and the draining off of the excess rural populations by the great *Landflucht* of the 1880s and 1890s. The theft rates of the urban population may have been retarded in the 1880s and 1890s as their wages steadily improved vis-à-vis the declining agricultural prices.[27]

Table 10–4. Average Yearly Rates of Crime in Selected Periods

Period	Total Crime Rate				Assault and Battery[a]				Theft[b]			
	Entire Reich	Berlin	All Stadtkreise[c]	All Landkreise[d]	ER	B	S	L	ER	B	S	L
1883–87	1001	1216	—	—	153	94	—	—	282	338	—	—
1888–92	1044	1259	—	—	173	106	—	—	274	292	—	—
1893–97	1177	1682	—	—	219	137	—	—	—	—	—	—
1898–1902	—	—	—	—	—	—	—	—	—	—	—	—
1903–7	1195	1522	—	—	228	131	—	—	239	335	—	—
1908–12	1184	1682	—	—	204	122	—	—	249	421	—	—
1883–97	1075	1346	1428	951	183	104	177	190	269	341	345	299
1903–12	1190	1602	1461	1015	216	127	207	240	244	378	323	191

Note: All crime rates are convictions per 100,000 population.

a. *Gefährliche Körperverletzung*
b. *Einfacher und Schwerer Diebstahl*
c. The figures represent the computed means for all *Stadtkreise* in the Reich for which data are available. Only a few cases are missing. In the later period, 1903–12, there were many more *Stadtkreise* than there were in the earlier one, 1883–97 (151 versus 89).
d. The figures are computed means for *Landkreise* in the Reich. Again, only a few cases (18) are missing. $N = 878$.

Whereas these figures would, nevertheless, lend some support to the structural theory, despite its weaknesses noted above, they would strengthen the argument that neither population growth nor urban growth nor city size had any significant impact on crime rates. This statement is supported by the results from several correlation analyses reported in three tables that follow.

In the first of these tables (table 10–5), correlation coefficients between crime rates and several socioeconomic variables for all *Kreise* in the Reich are reported (1,047 communities) for several periods spanning the years of Imperial Germany. The low and sometimes negative (as in the case of assault

Table 10–5. Zero-Order Correlations between Crime Rates and Socioeconomic Variables in All *Kreise* of the Entire Reich, 1883–1912

Dependent Variable	Percent Urban Population[a]	Population Density	Percent Ethnic Population	Death Rate
Total crime rate				
1883–87	−.02	.15	.43	.67
1883–97	.17	.24	.29	.50
1903–7	.31	.25	.27	.42
1908–12	.34	.28	.25	.40
Assault and battery rate				
1883–87	−.13	−.04	.23	.53
1883–97	−.12	−.05	.17	.53
1903–7	−.11	−.03	.20	.50
1908–12	−.15	−.04	.23	.52
Theft rate				
1883–87	−.03	.12	.51	.69
1883–97	.15	.20	.45	.66
1903–7	.37	.28	.39	.45
1908–12	.46	.35	.31	.38
Murder rate[b]				
1904–6	.25	.27	.04	.27

Note: $N = 1,047$ *Kreise*

a. The percentage of people per *Kreis* living in communities of more than 2,000 population.

b. The per capita rate of murders and manslaughters (from coroners' records) in Prussian *Kreise* only.

and battery) coefficients between the crime rates and measures of population and urban concentration demonstrate my point. Only in the case of theft, and only after the turn of the century, did any meaningful correlations emerge. But these are rather spurious correlations. The percentage of variance (R squared) that even the highest of these correlations renders is very low, and all this actually shows is that after the turn of the century theft was more highly concentrated in cities than in the countryside, but that the size of the city did not make any difference.

This finding is demonstrated more clearly in table 10-6, where correlation coefficients are presented for the socioeconomic and crime variables in just the city districts of the Reich after the turn of the century, thus during the time when the city-theft relationship was at its highest. Here we see that, if we consider the individual cities without the clouding caused by adding the land districts into the calculation, the relationship between city size or population density and the crime rates disappears altogether. Furthermore, no significant relationships are found with the introduction of a measure of the growth rate of the urban population. The correlation coefficients for the land districts alone, without the city districts added (table 10-7), show the same trends.

The inclusion of a measure of the murder rate in tables 10-5 through 10-7, especially because that rate is based on the more reliable coroners' records instead of the more dubious court records, as is the case with the other crime variables, helps provide additional confidence to the assertion that urban-rural differences and urban and population growth had very little impact on crime trends. Indicting the city for causing crime is simply unfounded.

Before proceeding to a discussion of the social and economic conditions that one should indict as causes of crime, I believe it only fair to credit those cities that had consistently low rates of crime and to point out those cities that had exceptionally high rates. Referring back to table 10-2, which presents crime rates in two periods, one in the 1880s and one in the early 1900s, for the fifty-seven largest cities in all of Germany (all of which had a legally liable population greater than 50,000 in 1905), one finds that in the 1880s only eighteen cities had an average overall crime rate that was lower than the national average for all land and city districts (i.e., all *Kreise*); and in the period 1903-7 only ten of these cities continued to have lower crime rates than was average for all districts (note the figures in boldface). This trend did not hold for assault-and-battery offenses, however. In the earlier period only a third, or nineteen cities, had higher than average rates and in the later period the total increased by only three cities to twenty-two with higher than average rates for all districts. The overall crime trends in the German cities

Table 10–6. Zero-Order Correlations between Crime Rates and Socio-economic Variables for Prussian *Stadtkreise,* 1903–12

Dependent Variable	City Population	Population Density	Population Growth, 1885–1910	Percent Ethnic[a] Population, 1900	Death Rate, 1904–6
Murder rate					
1904–6	−.07	.31	—	.31	.33
Total crime rate					
1903–7	.07	.12	.20	.61	.48
1908–12	.10	.17	.19	.57	.47
Assault and battery rate					
1903–7	−.09	.14	−.06	.68	.56
1908–12	−.07	.14	−.15	.71	.58
Theft rate					
1903–7	.01	.16	.24	.65	.51
1908–12	.07	.15	.28	.61	.47

Note: $N = 78$

a. The percentage of Germans in each *Stadtkreis* listing their mother tongue as other than German in the 1900 census.

Table 10–7. Zero-Order Correlations between Crime Rates and Socioeconomic Variables for Prussian *Landkreise*, 1903–12

Dependent Variable	Urban Population	Population Density	Percent Ethnic Population, 1900	Death Rate, 1904–6
Murder rate				
1904–6	.10	.15	.05	.29
Total crime rate				
1903–7	.15	.32	.55	.55
1908–12	.20	.37	.51	.53
Assault and battery rate				
1903–7	.11	.34	.54	.50
1908–12	.07	.31	.55	.52
Theft rate				
1903–7	.05	.15	.61	.58
1908–12	.19	.25	.53	.53

Note: $N = 462$

were, on the other hand, directly in step with the patterns of theft offenses. In the earlier period forty had higher than average theft rates and in the later period the total increased to 46 (one needs to keep in mind, however, that figures for three of the cities, Bonn, Frankfurt, and Gelsenkirchen, are missing from the first period so that there was actually very little change that transpired between the two periods).

The information presented here does not allow us to speculate much about the reasons why some of these cities had exceptionally low crime rates. The ten cities that continually had exceptionally low rates (Barmen, Colmar, Darmstadt, Giessen, Krefeld, Lübeck, Münster, Mulhausen, Schwerin, and Weimar) were, however, all relatively small or moderate-sized cities, though all experienced some growth and half of them grew by upward of about 50 percent between the census years of 1885 and 1905. Otherwise there is not much to set these cities apart. They were not concentrated in any geographical region; they could be cities with either a clear Protestant or Catholic majority or they could be religiously mixed; and they could be made up of almost totally German-speaking inhabitants or they could be comprised of large non-German-speaking minorities, as was the case of the French-speaking citizens of Colmar and Mulhausen. Little also can be said about the eight cities that were once in this low-crime group but no longer were after the turn of the century (Aachen, Cologne, Düsseldorf, Dessau, Elberfeld, Karlsruhe, Rostock, and Worms). With the exception of Cologne, all were either small or moderate-sized cities and all had increasing populations, though some, for example, Rostock and Worms, had quite low rates of population growth. Again there was no geographic or religious pattern worthy of note. What might be mildly noteworthy, however, is that only a few cities had exceptionally low rates of one kind of crime and exceptionally high rates of another type. Although there were only three (Hamburg, Leipzig, and Chemnitz) that consistently demonstrated this disparity, and only Berlin could possibly be added from the earlier period, all of them were very large cities by German standards, with only Chemnitz, which was moderate sized, as an exception. It almost goes without saying that all of them had low rates of assault and battery and high rates of theft.

There is a bit more one can say, however, about the cities that had exceptionally high crime rates. To begin with, many of them were located in the Prussian northeast. Table 10–3 shows that five of the ten Prussian cities with the highest crime rates in the 1903–7 period were cities that are today part of either Poland or Russia (Stettin, Posen, Breslau, Danzig, and Königsberg). Since only two cities from the rest of Germany, Bremen and Mannheim, had crime rates that would place them in the top ten, it is clear that most non-

Prussian cities and cities south of the Main River had generally modest crime rates. In addition to this the vast majority of the leading crime cities were port cities, which probably comes as little surprise. Finally, what really set many of the cities and other communities with high crime rates apart from the rest was that they housed a relatively greater amount of human hardship.

◆ Hardship and Ethnicity

If the many Germans who considered the city to be crime inducing were wrong, the many who considered ethnicity and poverty to be determining factors in crime causation were nearer the mark, for these two factors were often of prime importance in distinguishing high-crime communities from low-crime communities in Imperial Germany. Of course ethnicity and poverty have also been found to figure heavily in criminal activity in many other societies,[28] especially because they often march hand in hand. Nonetheless, one must be careful in using these terms. Though poverty, which is usually a relative concept, is often more difficult to measure than ethnicity, which is more concrete, there is probably not as much danger that its impact will be misunderstood or misused. Whereas few people would expect all poor or relatively poor people to be criminals, and would not damn the poor for simply being poor even though many of them may have turned to criminality, many people in many societies are often not so hesitant to stigmatize certain ethnic groups if some of their members can be shown to be guilty of wrongful behavior (in Imperial Germany, for example, Poles were often stigmatized for being habitual and biologically inclined criminals).[29] Accordingly one must be wary of making statements that can be confused with or turned into sociobiological pronouncements.

It must be stressed from the start that even though certain ethnic minorities in Imperial Germany will be shown to have been associated with a high level of criminality, this does not mean that these same ethnic minorities were in any way prone to crime, for their crime rates in other lands, under other social, economic, and political conditions, have often been very low.[30] Indeed it will become clear that a strong association of ethnicity and criminality is mostly a spurious correlation brought about by intervening variables such as social stigmatization, political repression, and economic hardship.[31]

In a previous examination of popular opinion toward criminals and justice, I found that many Germans believed crime to be a foreign phenomenon and that two ethnic groups in particular, Poles and Lithuanians, were frequently singled out as criminals, in both journalistic and literary accounts.[32]

Evidence of the pervasive ethnic bias against these Slavic minorities is easy to find in other places as well, and not just among conservatives, theologians, and others with a political program or an ideological axe to grind. Even leading criminologists such as Gustav Aschaffenburg, who aimed at unbiased and dispassionate analyses of the crime problem and who tried to argue against the notion that the Slavs were congenital criminals by pointing to their poverty as the real cause of their illegal activity, were nonetheless, if unwittingly, often guilty of adding to the racialist stereotyping and stigmatizing of these Slavic peoples. Aschaffenburg stated in his classic text that the persistence of high crime rates in the Prussian northeast was in part due to the fact that these districts were "partly inhabited by a Slavic population" that was "culturally not so highly developed."[33]

To many it appeared that the bias against these groups, the poverty in which many of them lived, and the hostility between them and the government were nearly all pervasive, especially in the case of the Poles. In 1913 the editor of a Polish newspaper in the Westphalian city of Herne wrote that the cause of much recent criminality in his area should be "blamed in the first instance on the anti-Polish system, which the Germans learn. . . . the Poles are (constantly) insulted and ridiculed. . . . Taunts like damned Polacks and other such are heard daily on the street."[34] Indeed the anti-Polish sentiment was so widespread that even foreign visitors seldom failed to take notice and frequently made it a subject of their commentary. In the 1870s the Briton Vizetelly reported on the poor public image of the Slavs in Berlin by writing that "the girls who come from Prussian Poland are credited with being exceedingly untidy and lazy."[35] In 1910 William Dawson put the whole Polish question into perspective for his American readership with the words:

> And today, as for the last hundred years, there still goes on between the Prussian Government and its administrative officials in the Polish districts, on the one hand, and the Polish people on the other, an unceasing feud, an unchanging contest for ascendancy, maintained with equal resolution on both sides, the one seeking to assert German influence, ideas, culture, language, the other tenaciously, unwearyingly, and desperately resisting the onslaught with all the strength and bitterness which pride of race and of history can generate. . . . The present position of the Polish question, then, is this—on the Prussian side repression, on the Polish side embitterment, on both sides suspicion and antagonism.[36]

Surely the large Polish minority population (roughly three million at the turn of the century) and the small but significant Lithuanian population had a bad image and often a bad time in Imperial Germany as both groups were held in low repute, often were compelled because of their poverty to take on the worst kinds of labor, and were confronted with such strong Germanizing policies that they could not school their children in their own language or even represent themselves in court in their native tongue.[37] It is no wonder that these "guestworkers in the German Reich," as they have been referred to in a book by that title, often found themselves on the wrong side of the law.[38]

As the experience of other ethnic minorities in the Reich shows, however, being of non-German ethnic origin was not necessarily to be in bad odor, in particularly trying economic straits, or involved frequently in criminal activity. The German Reich also had sizable Danish, Dutch, Belgian, and French minorities, but these western peoples appeared to fare much better than the downtrodden Slavs. Precisely why this was the case I cannot answer. But the different image, conditions, and treatment of the western European immigrants versus the eastern European immigrants suggests that the dualistic racial policy of the Third Reich had deep roots in German soil.

There is much evidence to support the points made above. One might start by looking back at the correlation coefficients shown in tables 10–5 through 10–7. In table 10–5 we find that, with the exception of the murder rate, there is a positive, consistent, and often quite strong correlation between various crime measures in different periods and the percentage of the population of a community that was of non-German ethnic origin (measured by the percentage of people in a community who listed their mother tongue as other than German in the 1900 census). We see also that there are even higher correlations in the more than 1,000 communities for which figures are available between the crime rates and the death rates, which here are used as a measure of the relative level of poverty or wealth of a community. Even though these measures of ethnicity and poverty correlate more strongly with the crime variables than do measures of population concentration, which makes it clear that they are of more consequence, they are still artificially low.

By using figures for all *Kreise* in the Reich, roughly half of which had nearly no "ethnic" inhabitants, the correlation coefficients are necessarily reduced. Furthermore, by including all ethnic minorities into one lump-sum variable, the relatively low crime rates of some ethnic populations attenuate the effect of the high crime rates of other minorities. And were it possible to use a more exact measure of poverty than the rather crude death rate, it is very likely that the correlation between poverty and criminality would become even more pronounced. In some previous studies, I have in fact used other measures of the relative poverty or wealth of a community, from doctors and taxes per capita to illiteracy rates, and found even higher correlations. But these studies were all based on a much higher level of aggregated data (the Prussian *Regierungsbezirke*) and are thus less reliable.[39] Unfortunately, if, as in this case, one wants to gain more reliability by using much smaller and more numerous units of analysis, one may have to sacrifice some accuracy in the measurement of a concept like poverty, because these other measures are just not available for the smaller districts.

Even if the strength of the correlation coefficients is not as great as I believe it to be, it is still very high and certainly indicates a close relationship between poverty and criminality. There are several reasons why one should accept the death rate as a decent, though far from perfect, measure of poverty. Not only have many other scholars studying Germany and other lands demonstrated, often mathematically, the strong link between poverty and death,[40] but in my other studies I found a very high correlation between the death rate and other measures of hardship at other levels of analysis, and quite similar correlations between crime variables and the death rate and other measures of hardship.[41]

The significance of the poverty and ethnicity variables is even more evident in tables 10–6 and 10–7, which treat Prussian *Stadtkreise* and *Landkreise,* respectively. Whereas the size of the urban population, the total population, and the population growth had very low and sometimes even negative correlations with the crime variables, the correlations between the crime variables and ethnicity and death/poverty are positive and quite strong. Note, for instance, how the correlations between ethnicity and all but the murder rate jump up from the mild coefficients hovering between roughly r = .2 to .5 in table 10–5 to a range of r = .5 to .7 in these two tables. What these figures show is that larger cities and quickly growing cities did not have higher levels of criminality than did smaller cities or medium-sized cities that may have been growing rapidly or not experiencing much growth. But if population pressure accounted for little, hardship and ethnicity counted for a lot. Both in city and land districts taken separately, the crime rates varied directly with a kind of final measure of "un-wellbeing" (death) and with the relative size of the non-German ethnic population.

A way of further illustrating the importance of these two variables is to juxtapose the data presented in tables 10–8 and 10–9, which treat, respectively, the twelve districts with the highest overall level of criminality in the five-year period between 1903 and 1907, and the twelve districts with the lowest overall level of criminality in the same period (out of a total of the more than one

Table 10–8. Twelve *Kreise* with Highest Crime Rates, 1903–7

Kreis	Type	Location	TCR.3–7	Pop.06	Pop. Den.06	DR	% Ethnic.00	Type Ethnic
1. Königshütte	S	Silesia	3391	66,192	11,032	28	44	Polish
2. Kattowitz	S	Silesia	3167	35,167	8,953	19	23	Polish
3. Beuthen	L	Silesia	3094	168,821	1,723	26	73	Polish
4. Zabrze	L	Silesia	3019	139,832	1,165	23	69	Polish
5. Bremen*	L	Bremen	3000	61,585	267	?	0.5	mixed
6. Gleiwitz	S	Silesia	2716	61,441	2,194	21	26	Polish
7. Ludwigshafen*	L	Pfalz	2702	90,474	768	?	0.5	mixed
8. Heydekrug	L	E. Prussia	2647	43,307	54	26	57	Lithuan.
9. Niederung	L	E. Prussia	2386	55,174	62	25	15	Lithuan.
10. Neidenburg	L	E. Prussia	2358	57,426	35	21	25	Polish
11. Oberhausen	S	Westphalia	2447	52,305	4,023	20	?	?
12. Cologne	S	Rhineland	2446	429,343	3,868	19	1	mixed
Averages			2781	105,143	2,845	23	30	mixed

Key:
* = figures for death rates are missing for these two non-Prussian districts
Type = S is *Stadtkreis* (city district), L is *Landkreis* (rural district)
TCR.3–7 = total crime rate for 1903–7
Pop.06 = population in 1906
Pop.Den.06 = population density in 1906
DR = deaths per 1,000 population in 1906
%Ethnic.00 = percent of each district made up of "non-German ethnic" population in 1900
Type Ethnic = Dominant non-German-speaking ethnic minority

Table 10-9. Twelve *Kreise* with Lowest Crime Rates, 1903–7

Kreis	Type	Location	TCR.3–7	Pop.06	Pop. Den.06	DR	% Ethnic.00	Type Ethnic
1. Lübbecke	L	Minden	224	50,879	90	15	.02	PG
2. Wittlage	L	Osnabrück	262	17,998	57	16	.08	PG
3. Gammertingen	L	Sigmaringen	287	12,836	39	23	.12	PG
4. Hümmling	L	Osnabrück	305	17,098	21	16	.25	PG
5. Mühlhausen	L	Erfurt	352	35,906	91	18	.06	PG
6. Warendorf	L	Münster	359	30,986	55	16	.18	PG
7. Tondern	L	Schleswig	369	57,149	32	14	69.00	Danish
8. Montjoie	L	Aachen	369	17,647	49	19	.24	PG
9. Melle	L	Osnabrück	372	26,586	105	15	.09	PG
10. Hufum	L	Schleswig	372	39,741	47	15	13.00	Danish
11. Lingen	L	Osnabrück	375	34,218	43	17	.66	PG
12. Zeven	L	Stade	394	16,388	25	15	.07	PG
Averages			337	29,776	55	16.6	.18*	

Key:
* = the two districts with large Danish populations not included
Type = S is *Stadtkreis* (city district), L is *Landkreis* (rural district)
TCR.3–7 = total crime rate for 1903–7
Pop.06 = population in 1906
Pop.Den.06 = population density in 1906
DR = deaths per 1,000 population in 1906
%Ethnic.00 = percent of each district made up of "non-German ethnic" population in 1900
Type Ethnic = dominant non-German-speaking ethnic minority
PG = almost all native pure German-speaking population.

thousand districts in the entire Reich). Here we see that the districts in table 10–8 had a crime rate that was roughly eight times that of the districts in
table 10–9. The death rate in the high-crime districts was about 50 percent
higher than that in the low-crime districts, and the percentage of ethnic inhabitants was over one hundred times higher in the high-crime districts.
Though half of the high-crime districts were cities and all of the low-crime
districts were composed of mainly rural communities, which accounts for the
higher average population and population density of the high-crime districts,
only one truly large city, Cologne, is to be found in either table.

The most startling differences between these two types of communities
were, then, in their death rates and in the size of minority population. The
type of the ethnic minority population was also of great importance, however, as Poles and Lithuanians were the predominant minority population in
all of the communities with high crime rates and large ethnic minority populations. Most low-crime districts, on the other hand, were made up of purely
German-speaking populations, though two had large Danish-speaking populations (Tondern and Hufum, both in Schleswig). If we return for a moment
to table 10–3, where the twenty-five largest Prussian cities are presented in
rank order from the city with the highest level of crime in this period, Cologne, to the city with the lowest level, Barmen, we find similar trends, though
not quite as pronounced. The death rate and the size of the ethnic population were usually much higher in the cities with higher levels of crime than
in those with lower levels of crime; and Polish and Lithuanian minorities
predominated in the former but were seldom found in the latter, though this
time the communities with lower crime rates could often have significant
Dutch populations.

These figures show clearly that hardship was nearly always a major factor in determining the crime rate of a community, but "ethnicity" only mat-
tered in the case of Poles and Lithuanians, for communities with other types
of ethnic minorities either had unremarkable or low rates of crime. But the
reason the Slavic minorities had such high crime rates was because they were
socially stigmatized, politically repressed, and usually at the bottom of the
economic ladder. Their economic woes and the close relationship between
poverty and criminality is perhaps most sharply demonstrated in the last two
tables to be considered. In table 10–10 we find figures showing that communities with large Polish minorities almost always had greater than average
crime rates (only a quarter of the 173 communities did not) and that all of the
communities with significant Lithuanian minorities had high crime rates
(though there were only nine of them). The vast majority of the communi-

Table 10–10. Crosstabulation of Total Crime Rate and Ethnic Grouping of
All *Kreise* in the Entire Reich, 1908–12

	Crime Rate				
Ethnic Grouping	Lowest	Low-Medium	Medium-High	Highest	*N*
Purely German-speaking (less than 1% foreign)	30%	27%	25%	18%	678
Lithuanian	0	0	22	78	9
Polish	7	20	27	46	173
French	19	50	19	12	16
Dutch	52	9	22	17	23
Danish	63	25	12	0	8
Mixed	9	20	17	54	35
Other	28	33	19	19	36
					978

Note: Each crime rate category represents 25 percent of all *Kreise* in the Reich.

ties with predominantly French-, Dutch-, or Danish-speaking minorities had
lower than average crime rates, and in the case of the Dutch and the Danish,
very low crime rates. The communities without any significant minority
population at all (less than 1 percent foreign speakers) were distributed evenly
in the high, moderate, and low crime categories. The "other" group, which
was made up of a wide variety of ethnic minorities, ranging from tiny groups
such as the Wends to Masurians and Italians, usually had lower than average crime rates and the "mixed" group had higher than average rates (Poles
were usually the largest ethnic minority in these communities but they were
not classified as Polish because the Poles did not make up a clear majority).

Table 10–11 makes plain the strong association between well-being or the
lack of it and the different ethnic minority populations. Whereas communities made up of purely German speakers or communities with sizable western European minority populations had low death rates, and the Danes and
the Dutch had very low death rates, the Polish and Lithuanian minorities
nearly always resided in communities where people lived hard lives and died
young. Crime, poverty, and death haunted the Polish and Lithuanian peoples in Imperial Germany. It did not matter if they lived in the city, the town,
or the countryside, and it did not matter if they stayed in their often hard-
pressed ancestral homelands in the Prussian northeast or if they moved away
to the booming industrial "wild west."

Table 10–11. Crosstabulation of Death Rates and Ethnic Groupings in Prussian *Kreise*, 1904–06

| Ethnic Grouping | Death Rate | | | | N |
	Lowest	Low-Medium	Medium-High	Highest	
Purely German-speaking	35%	29%	24%	12%	309
Lithuanian	0	0	22	78	9
Polish	5	12	32	51	169
French	—	—	—	—	0
Dutch	9	61	26	4	23
Danish	100	0	0	0	8
Mixed	—	—	—	—	24
Other	21	36	7	36	14
					556

Note: Each death rate category represents 25 percent of all Prussian *Kreise*.

Crime, in its many forms and independent of how it was measured, from the reasonably reliable coroners' records of homicide to the more suspect court records of theft and assault and battery,[42] was not caused by the industrial revolution, the growth of cities, the size of cities, population density, anomie, or other intangible and impersonal factors, as the citizens of Germany and many other societies would often like to think. Violent crimes such as murder, manslaughter, and assault and battery may have become more prevalent over the years but had roots that were just as fertile in the countryside as they were in the city. Property offenses such as theft declined in both urban and rural settings, but more so in the countryside after the turn of the century. As the death rate was the only consistent correlate with all crime rates, in all periods, and in all settings, the only sensible conclusion to make is that the best way for society to reduce crime is to reduce human hardship.

Notes

An earlier version of this essay appeared in *Social Science History* 16 (1992):129–76.

1. A growing body of evidence, for example, suggests that the most reliable measure of criminality, homicide, was far more prevalent (perhaps as much as ten times) in premodern and preindustrial society than it is today. Ted Robert Gurr has

summarized the evidence in his "Historical Trends in Violent Crime: A Critical Review of the Evidence," *Crime and Justice: An Annual Review of Research* 3 (1981): 295–343. Most of the work he mentions, however, is based on Britain prior to the eighteenth century. For a good general discussion, an excellent bibliography, and mention of some important British studies that have appeared since Gurr's essay was published, see Lawrence Stone, "Homicide and Violence," in his *The Past and the Present Revisited* (London, 1987), 295–310, 426–32. For a discussion of several important American and European studies on various forms of criminality based on quantitative evidence, see Eric Monkkonen, "The Quantitative Historical Study of Crime and Criminal Justice," in *History and Crime: Implications for Criminal Justice Police,* ed. James A. Inciardi and Charles E. Faupel (Beverly Hills, Calif., 1980), 53–73; Dirk Blasius, "Kriminologie und Geschichtswissenschaft: Bilanz und Perspektiven interdisziplinärer Forschung," *Geschichte und Gesellschaft* 14 (1988): 136–49; and *Quantification and Criminal Justice History in International Perspective,* ed. Eric A. Johnson, special issue of *Historical Social Research/Historische Sozialforschung* 15 (1990). For the history of crime in Germany alone, see Richard J. Evans, "In Pursuit of the *Untertanengeist:* Crime, Law and Social Order in German History," in his *Rethinking German History: Nineteenth-Century Germany and the Origins of the Third Reich* (London, 1987), 156–87; and Richard J. Evans, ed., *The German Underworld: Deviants and Outcasts in German History* (London, 1988).

2. An excellent discussion (and a large though now somewhat dated bibliography) is found in Hermann Mannheim, *Comparative Criminology* (Boston, 1965); see esp. 499–605.

3. Eric A. Johnson and Vincent E. McHale, "Socioeconomic Aspects of the Delinquency Rate in Imperial Germany, 1882–1914," *Journal of Social History* 13 (1980): 384–402; Kelley Reed, "Female Criminality in Imperial Germany" (Central Michigan University Senior Seminar paper, 1981).

4. In the five-year period between 1883 and 1887, Labiau's theft rate (based on convictions per year per 100,000 population of legally liable age) was 994, Heydekrug's was 922, and Obornik's was 941. In the same period, the Schleswig districts of Hufum and Tondern, for example, registered rates of 54 and 68, respectively.

5. See, for example, Evans, *Rethinking German History,* 176.

6. Between the periods of 1883–87 and 1903–7, the average yearly crime rate in Düsseldorf *Stadtkreis* grew from 989 to 1,838, and in Cologne *Stadtkreis* from 931 to 2,446. At the same time it grew in Düsseldorf *Landkreis* from 732 to 1,504, and in Cologne *Landkreis* from 851 to 1,534. In the same period it declined in the almost completely rural districts of Labiau in Königsberg from 2,512 to 2,132, in Oletzko in Gumbinnen from 2,115 to 1,311, and in Obornik in Posen from 2,131 to 1,527.

7. In a previous study, I found a strong correlation between the violent crime rates of Prussian *Regierungsbezirke* in the 1880s and the 1900s (r = greater than .6), but not between property crime rates and other types of crime rates, such as crimes against the state. Other scholars, such as Howard Zehr, have noted this as well,

though I think that Zehr overstated the case by claiming that "the biggest single cause of variance in assault rates" was regional tradition. See Zehr, *Crime and the Development of Modern Society: Patterns of Criminality in Nineteenth-Century Germany and France* (London, 1976), 105ff.

8. For discussions of these theories in German society, see Andrew Lees, "Critics of Urban Society in Germany, 1854–1914," *Journal of the History of Ideas* 40 (1979): 61–83; and idem, "Debates about the Big City in Germany, 1890–1914," *Societas* 5 (1975): 31–47. For a general discussion of these theories as they apply to criminological research, see Mannheim, *Comparative Criminology,* 533–51.

9. For a discussion of the *Landflucht,* especially how it applied to the Poles of northeastern Prussia who moved into the Ruhr, see Christoph Klessmann, *Polnische Bergarbeiter im Ruhrgebiet, 1870–1945: Soziale Integration und nationale Subkultur einer Minderheit in der deutschen Industriegesellschaft* (Göttingen, 1978). For a discussion more centered on economic conditions, see Frank B. Tipton, *Regional Variations in the Economic Development of Germany during the Nineteenth Century* (Middletown, Conn., 1976).

10. See Walter D. Kamphoefner, "The Social Consequences of Rural-Urban Migration in Imperial Germany: The 'Floating Proletariat' Thesis Reconsidered" (Social Science Working Paper, California Institute of Technology, 1982); James H. Jackson, "Migration in Duisburg, 1867–1890: Occupational and Familial Contexts," *Journal of Urban History* 8 (1982): 235–70; Steve L. Hochstadt, "Migration in Germany: An Historical Study" (Ph.D. diss., Brown University, 1983); idem, "Migration and Industrialization in Germany," *Social Science History* 5 (1981): 445–68; David F. Crew, *Town in the Ruhr: A Social History of Bochum, 1860–1914* (New York, 1979); Klaus J. Bade, ed., *Auswanderer-Wanderarbeiter-Gastarbeiter: Bevölkerung, Arbeitsmarkt, und Wanderung in Deutschland seit der Mitte des 19. Jahrhunderts* (Ostfildern, Germany, 1984). For an overview of recent migration research, see James H. Jackson and Leslie Page Moch, "Migration and the Social History of Modern Europe," *Historical Methods* 22 (1989): 27–36.

11. Kamphoefner found that Berlin immigrants from the east did much worse than immigrants from the west in Imperial Germany. Kamphoefner, "Social Consequences of Rural-Urban Migration." Discrimination against the eastern immigrants is discussed at length in Klessmann, *Polnische Bergarbeiter,* esp. 83–93, and in Richard Charles Murphy, *Guestworkers in the German Reich: A Polish Community in Wilhelminian Germany* (Boulder, Colo., 1983).

12. Rugge, a Protestant clergyman, argued that sharply increased rates of crime and vice resulted from the loss of communal controls and the emergence of self-centered personalities in cities: "It [the big city] becomes the dwelling place for masses of criminals. . . . An army of prostitutes and pimps eats away at its foundations." C. Rugge, "Die Bedeutung der Grosstädte für das Volksleben," *Die Reformation: Deutsche evang. Kirchenzeitung für die Gemeinde,* 8 (1909), 389–90, cited in Lees, "Critics of Urban Society," 70.

13. Lees, "Critics of Urban Society," 62; see Wilhelm Heinrich Riehl, *Die Naturgeschichte des Volkes als Grundlage einer deutschen Social-Politik* (Stuttgart, 1854–69, 4 vols.); vol. 1, *Land und Leute,* contains his most extensive criticisms.

14. See Walther Classen, *Das stadtgeborene Geschlecht und seine Zukunft* (Leipzig, 1914).

15. See Karl Bücher, *Die wirtschaftlichen Aufgaben der modernen Stadtgemeinde* (Leipzig, 1898); Julius Langbehn, *Rembrandt als Erzieher* (Leipzig, 1890); Adolf Weber, *Die Großstadt und ihrer sozialen Probleme* (Leipzig, 1908). The remark by Lees is from his "Critics of Urban Society," 82.

16. See, for example, Charles Tilly, *As Sociology Meets History* (New York, 1981), esp. his chapter on "Useless Durkheim."

17. For a further discussion, see Hans H. Burchardt, *Kriminalität in Stadt und Land* (Berlin, 1935); Denis Szabo, *Crimes et villes* (Paris, 1960); Johnson and McHale, "Socioeconomic Aspects of the Delinquency Rate," 384–85; and Mannheim, *Comparative Criminology,* 532–62.

18. In 1871 Germany had eight cities with over 100,000 inhabitants, fourteen in 1880, twenty-six in 1890, thirty-three in 1900, and forty-one in 1905. Gerd Hohorst, Jürgen Kocka, and Gerhard A. Ritter, *Sozialgeschichtliches Arbeitsbuch: Materialien zur Statistik des Kaiserreichs, 1871–1914* (Munich, 1978). See also Adna Weber, *The Growth of Cities in the Nineteenth Century* (Ithaca, N.Y., 1899); Andrew Lees and Lynn Lees, eds., *The Urbanization of European Society in the Nineteenth Century* (Boston, 1976); N. L. Tranter, *Population and Society, 1750–1940* (London, 1985); and H. J. Teuteberg, ed., *Urbanisierung im 19. und 20. Jahrhundert: Historische und Geographische Aspekte* (Cologne, 1983).

19. Ray Stannard Baker, *Seen in Germany* (New York, 1901), 8; Raymond B. Fosdick, *European Police Systems* (New York, 1915), 5. Both Baker and Fosdick begin their accounts with comments on the cleanliness and orderliness of German cities. See also William Harbutt Dawson, *German Life in Town and Country* (New York, 1901), 273ff.

20. Henry Vizetelly, *Berlin: Under the New Empire* (London, 1879; New York, 1968), vol. 1, 25.

21. Regression analysis, path analysis, and factor analysis are used to demonstrate this in Vincent E. McHale and Eric A. Johnson, "Urbanization, Industrialization, and Crime in Imperial Germany: Part 1," *Social Science History* 1 (1976): 45–78. For a good general discussion of recent studies of health, hardship, and social inequality in nineteenth-century Germany, see Hartmut Kaeble, *Industrialization and Social Inequality in Nineteenth-Century Europe* (Leamington Spa, 1986); and Richard J. Evans, *Death in Hamburg: Society and Politics in Hamburg during the Cholera Years, 1830–1910* (Oxford, 1987).

22. For graphic portraits of urban conditions and criminality in Britain and France, often based on literary evidence, see J. J. Tobias, *Urban Crime in Victorian England* (New York, 1972); Louis Chevalier, *Laboring Classes and Dangerous Classes*

in Paris during the First Half of the Nineteenth Century (Princeton, 1981); and Gordon Wright, *Between the Guillotine and Liberty* (New York, 1983).

23. Britain is a classic example. Tobias, using literary sources and fulminating against statistical evidence, nevertheless argued this to be true in his *Urban Crime in Victorian England.* For a defense of the statistical approach, see V. A. C. Gatrell and T. B. Hadden, "Nineteenth-Century Criminal Statistics and Their Interpretation," in *Nineteenth-Century Society,: Essays on the Use of Quantitative Methods for the Study of Social Data,* ed. E. A. Wrigley (London, 1972), 336-96; and Gatrell, "The Decline of Theft and Violence in Victorian and Edwardian England," in *Crime and the Law: The Social History of Crime in Western Europe since 1500,* ed. V. A. C. Gatrell, Bruce Lenman, and Geoffrey Parker (London, 1980), 238-338. Crime rates also appeared to decline in Sweden, Finland and America. For Sweden, see Ted Robert Gurr, Peter N. Grabosky, and Richard C. Hula, *The Politics of Crime and Conflict: A Comparative History of Four Cities* (London, 1977); Jan Sundin, "Theft and Penury in Sweden, 1830-1920: A Comparative Study at the County Level," *Scandinavian Journal of History* 1 (1976): 265-92; Björn Horgby, *Den disciplinerade arbetaren: Brottslighet och social förändring i Norrköping, 1850-1910* (Stockholm, 1986); and Hanns von Hofer, *Brott och straff i Sverige: Historisk kriminalstatistik, 1750-1984* (Örebro, 1985). For Finland, see Heikki Ylikangas, *Knivjunkarna: Valdskriminalitet i Sydösterbotten, 1790-1825* (Borga, 1985), originally published in Finnish as *Puukkojunkkareitten esiinmarssi: Vhakivaltarikollisuus Etelha-Pohjanmaalla, 1790-1825* (Helsinki, 1976). For America, see Roger Lane, *Violent Death in the City: Suicide, Accident and Murder in Nineteenth-Century Philadelphia* (Cambridge, Mass., 1979); and Eric H. Monkkonen, *Hands Up: Police in Urban America, 1860-1920* (New York, 1980). And for a general survey of the recent history of violence in many societies, see J. C. Chesnais, *Histoire de la violence en Occident de 1800 à nos jours* (Paris, 1981).

24. Arthur L. Stinchcombe, "Institutions of Privacy in the Determination of Police Administrative Practices," *American Journal of Sociology* 69 (1963): 150-60; Abdul Qaiyum Lodhi and Charles Tilly, "Urbanization, Crime and Collective Violence in Nineteenth-Century France," *American Journal of Sociology* 79 (1973): 196-218.

25. Charles Tilly, Allan Levett, A. Q. Lodhi, and Frank Munger, "How Policing Affected the Visibility of Crime in Nineteenth-Century Europe and America," CRSO Working Paper 115, Ann Arbor, Michigan. On the growth of German and other European police systems, see Fosdick, *European Police Systems.*

26. In an essay about rural society in Imperial Germany, Cathleen S. Catt argues that in Germany "the study of rural society has been largely neglected." This neglect has, however, been partially rectified by her essay, "Farmers and Factory Workers: Rural Society in Imperial Germany: The Example of Maudach," and by other essays in Richard J. Evans and W. R. Lee, eds., *The German Peasantry: Conflict and Community in Rural Society from the Eighteenth to the Twentieth Centuries* (New

York, 1986). Crime and misery in the German countryside have received some treatment of late, however, especially in the works of Dirk Blasius that deal primarily with the first half of the nineteenth century. See his *Bürgerliche Gesellschaft und Kriminalität: Zur Sozialgeschichte Preußens im Vormärz* (Göttingen, 1975) and *Kriminalität und Alltag: Zur Konfliktgeschichte des Alltagslebens im 19. Jahrhundert* (Göttingen, 1978). See also Carsthen Küther, *Räuber und Gauner in Deutschland: Das organisierte Bandenwesen im 18. und frühen 19. Jahrhundert* (Göttingen, 1976); H. Reif, ed., *Räuber, Volk und Obrigkeit: Studien zur Geschichte der Kriminalität in Deutschland seit dem 18. Jahrhundert* (Frankfurt, 1984); and Evans, *The German Underworld*.

27. On conditions in the northeast leading to the *Landflucht,* see Klessmann, *Polnische Bergarbeiter,* 23–43, and William W. Hagen, *Germans, Poles, and Jews: The Nationality Conflict in the Prussian East, 1772-1914* (Chicago, 1980). For accounts by an American contemporary, see Dawson, *German Life in Town and Country,* esp. 68–92, and idem, *The Evolution of Modern Germany* (New York, n.d.). On the improvement in urban conditions and wages, see W. Masur, *Imperial Berlin* (New York, 1970), 243ff.; Gerhard Bry, *Wages in Germany, 1871-1945* (Princeton, 1960); and Ashok V. Desai, *Real Wages in Germany* (Oxford, 1968). For the interrelationship of wages, prices, and crime, see Edward Renger, *Kriminalität, Preis und Lohn: Eine Kriminalstatistische Untersuchung für Sachsen von 1882 bis 1929* (Leipzig, 1933).

28. Historians of crime in America often point to ethnicity and race (or racism) as being perhaps the key factor in determining crime rates and criminal patterns. Roger Lane, for example, argues that the perceived increase in homicide in post–World War II America is almost totally a function of a huge increase in black homicide rates, which are some twenty times that of white rates, which have not changed at all. The black rates are explained of course in relation to their immiseration. Roger Lane, "Urban Homicide in the Nineteenth Century: Some Lessons for the Twentieth," in Inciardi and Faupel, *History and Crime,* 91–109. For a fuller discussion of ethnicity and homicide in the nineteenth century, see Lane's *Violent Death in the City.* For the importance of ethnicity in colonial America, see Douglas Greenberg, *Crime and Law Enforcement in the Colony of New York, 1691-1776* (Ithaca, N.Y., 1976), 25ff. For a discussion of the impact of race and racism throughout American history, see Samuel Walker, *Popular Justice: A History of American Criminal Justice* (New York, 1980). On the impact of ethnicity and poverty in nineteenth-century French criminality, see David Cohen and Eric A. Johnson, "French Criminality: Urban-Rural Differences in the Nineteenth Century," *Journal of Interdisciplinary History* 12 (1982): 477–501. The classic statement of the importance of poverty is Willem Bonger, *Crime and Economic Conditions* (1905; Bloomington, Ind., 1969).

29. Klessmann, *Polnische Bergarbeiter,* 79.

30. Roger Lane, for example, found that the homicide rates of Poles in nineteenth-century America were very low. See his "Urban Homicide in the Nineteenth Century," 99.

31. On the stigmatization and miserable economic conditions of Poles, see Klessmann, *Polnische Bergarbeiter.*

32. Eric A. Johnson, *Urbanization and Crime: Germany, 1871-1914* (New York, 1995), esp. chaps. 2 and 3.

33. Gustav Aschaffenburg, *Crime and Its Repression* (1913; Montclair, N.J., 1968), 58. It should be noted, however, that Aschaffenburg was also quick to point to the economic hardships of these people as the major cause of their high crime rates. See also, P. Frauenstädt, "Die preußischen Ostprovinzen in kriminal-geographischer Beleuchtung," *Zeitschrift für Sozialwissenschaft* 9 (1906): 570-83.

34. Cited in Klessman, *Polnische Bergarbeiter,* 81.

35. Vizetelly, *Berlin Under the New Republic,* 31.

36. Dawson, *Evolution of Modern Germany,* 490, 496.

37. See Klessmann, *Polnische Bergarbeiter*; Murphy, *Guestworkers in the German Reich.* For other discussion of the conditions, image, and treatment of Poles in Germany, see Barrington Moore Jr., *Injustice: The Social Bases of Obedience and Revolt* (White Plains, N.Y., 1978), 119-274; Elizabeth Wiskemann, *Germany's Eastern Neighbors* (New York, 1956), chaps. 1 and 2; and Piotr S. Wandycz, *The Lands of Partitioned Poland, 1795-1918* (Seattle, 1974).

38. See Murphy, *Guestworkers in the German Reich.*

39. Using data from the thirty-six Prussian *Regierungsbezirke,* McHale and I found, for example, that the correlation between a crude rate of literacy and the overall level of crime was −.86 in the 1880s. McHale and Johnson, "Urbanization, Industrialization, and Crime," 236.

40. For a mathematical treatment in German history, see R. Spree, *Wealth and Social Class in Imperial Germany* (Leamington Spa, 1987); for a nonquantitative treatment in British history, see E. P. Thompson, *The Making of the English Working Class* (New York, 1966), 314-50. For an intriguing and prescient analysis of the former Soviet Union during the post–World War II period, see Nick Eberstadt, "The Health Crisis in the U.S.S.R.," *New York Review of Books,* 19 Feb. 1981, 23-31. For a further discussion on the usefulness of mortality rates as a measure of poverty, see my "The Roots of Crime in Imperial Germany," *Central European History* 15 (1982): 370.

41. See Johnson and McHale, "Socioeconomic Aspects of the Delinquency Rate," and McHale and Johnson, "Urbanization, Industrialization, and Crime."

42. In his overview of the history of violent criminality, Lawrence Stone argues that homicide is the "one crime about which the evidence is most reliable" as "homicide is the most difficult crime to conceal." Stone, "Homicide and Violence," 295-96.

Bibliography

Ågren, Maria. "Att lösa ekonomiska tvister domstolarnas främsta sysselsättning på 1700-talet?" *Historisk Tidskrift* 4 (1988): 481–511.

Allmand, Christopher. *The Hundred Years' War.* Cambridge, 1988.

Amabile, Luigi. *Fra Tommaso Campanella, i suoi processi e la sua pazzia.* 3 vols. Naples, 1882.

———. *Il Santo Officio della Inquisizione in Napoli.* 2 vols. Città di Castello, 1892.

Andreae, S. J. Fockema. *De Nederlandse Staat onder de Republiek.* Amsterdam, 1969.

Ankarloo, Bengt. *Trolldomsprocesserna i Sverige.* Lund, 1971.

Ankarloo, Bengt, and Gustav Henningsen, eds. *Häxornas Europa, 1400–1700.* Lund, 1987.

Aronsson, Peter. *Bönder för politik: Det lokala sjålostyret som social arena i tre Smålandssocknar, 1680–1850.* Lund, 1992.

Aschaffenburg, G. *Crime and Its Repression.* 1913. Montclair, N.J., 1968.

Asplund, Johan. *Det sociala livets elementära former.* Göteborg, 1987.

Bade, K. J., ed. *Auswanderer-Wanderarbeiter-Gastarbeiter: Bevölkerung, Arbeitsmarkt und Wanderung in Deutschland seit der Mitte des 19. Jahrhunderts.* Ostfildern, 1984.

Bain, Joseph, ed. *The Border Papers: Calendar of Letters and Papers Relating to the Affairs of the Borders of England and Scotland Preserved in Her Majesty's Public Record Office.* Vol. 2. Edinburgh, 1896.

Bairoch, Paul, et al. *La population des villes Européennes: Banque de données et analyse sommaire des résultats, 800–1850.* Geneva, 1988.

Baker, R. S. *Seen in Germany.* New York, 1901.

Basin, Thomas. *Histoire des règnes de Charles VII et de Louis XI.* 4 vols. Edited by Jules Quicherat. Paris, 1855–59.

Bayard, Françoise. "Les crimes de sang en Lyonnais et Beaujolais aux 17e et 18e siècles." In *Histoire et criminalité, de l'Antiquité au 20e siècle: Nouvelles approches,* edited by Benoît Garnot, 273–81. Actes du colloque de Dijon-Chenove, 3–5 October 1991.

Bayley, D. H. "Knowledge of the Police." In *Control in the Police Organization,* edited by M. Punch. Cambridge, Mass., 1983.

Beattie, J. B. *Crime and the Courts in England, 1660–1800.* Oxford, 1986.

Becker, Marvin B. "Changing Patterns of Violence and Justice in Fourteenth- and Fifteenth-century Florence." *Comparative Studies in Society and History* 18, no. 3 (1976): 281–96.

Beier, A. L. *Masterless Men: The Vagrancy Problem in England, 1560–1640.* London, 1985.

Berents, Dirk Arend. *Misdaad in de middeleeuwen: Een onderzoek naar de criminaliteit in het laat-middeleeuwse Utrecht.* N.p., 1976.

———. *Het werk van de vos: Samenleving en criminaliteit in de late middeleeuwen.* Zutphen, Netherlands, 1985.

Blasius, D. *Bürgerliche Gesellschaft und Kriminalität: Zur Sozialgeschichte Preußens im Vormärz.* Göttingen, 1975.

———. *Kriminalität und Alltag: Zur Konfliktgeschichte des Alltagslebens im 19. Jahrhundert.* Göttingen, 1978.

———. "Kriminologie und Geschichtswissenschaft: Bilanz und Perspektiven interdisziplinärer Forschung." *Geschichte und Gesellschaft* 14 (1988): 136–49.

Blok, Anton. *De Bokkerijders: Roversbenden en Geheime Genootschappen in de Landen van Overmaas (1730–1774).* Amsterdam, 1991.

———. "The Peasant and the Brigand: Social Banditry Reconsidered." *Comparative Studies in Society and History* 14 (1972): 494–503.

———. "The Symbolic Vocabulary of Public Executions." In *History and Power in the Study of Law: New Directions in Legal Anthropology,* edited by J. F. Collier and J. Starr, 31–55. Ithaca, N.Y., 1989.

———. "Zinloos en zinvol geweld." *Amsterdams Sociologisch Tijdschrift* 18, no. 3 (1991): 189–207.

Bonger, W. *Crime and Economic Conditions.* 1905. Bloomington, Ind., 1969.

Boomgaard, Jan. "Het Amsterdamse criminaliteitspatroon in de late middeleeuwen." In *Misdaad, zoen en straf: Aspekten van de middeleeuwse strafrechtsgeschiedenis in de Nederlanden,* edited by Herman A. Diederiks and H. W. Roodenburg, 101–19. Hilversum, 1991.

———. *Misdaad en straf in Amsterdam: Een onderzoek naar de strafrechtspleging van de Amsterdamse schepenbank, 1490–1552.* Zwolle, Netherlands, 1992.

Boutruche, Robert. "The Devastation of Rural Areas during the Hundred Years' War and the Agricultural Recovery of France." In *The Recovery of France in the Fifteenth Century,* edited by P. S. Lewis, 23–59. London, 1971.

Brackett, John K. *Criminal Justice and Crime in Late Renaissance Florence, 1537–1609.* Cambridge, 1992.

Braithwaite, John. *Crime, Shame and Reintegration.* Cambridge, 1989.

Brewer, John, and John Styles, eds. *An Ungovernable People: The English and Their Law in the Seventeenth and Eighteenth Centuries.* London, 1980.

Brown, Keith. *Bloodfeud in Scotland, 1573–1625: Justice and Politics in an Early Modern Society.* Edinburgh, 1986.

Bry, G. *Wages in Germany, 1871–1945.* Princeton, 1960.

Bücher, Karl. *Die wirtschaftlichen Aufgaben der modernen Stadtgemeinde.* Leipzig, 1898.

Burchardt, Hans H. *Kriminalität in Stadt und Land.* Berlin, 1936.

Byock, Jesse L. *Medieval Iceland: Society, Sagas, and Power.* Berkeley, 1988.

Cameron, Iain A. *Crime and Repression in the Auvergne and the Guyenne, 1720–1790.* Cambridge, 1981.

Castan, Nicole. *Les criminels de Languedoc: Les exigences d'ordre et les voies du ressentiment dans une société pré-révolutionnaire, 1750–1790.* Toulouse, 1980.

Champion, P. "Notes pour servir à l'histoire des classes dangereuses en France des origines à la fin du XVe siècle." Appendix to Lazar Sainéan, *Les sources de l'argot ancien,* 2 vols. Paris, 1912.

Chatterton, M. "Police Work and Assault Charges." In *Control in the Police Organization,* edited by M. Punch, 194–221. Cambridge, Mass., 1983.

Chesnais, Jean-Claude. *Histoire de la violence en Occident de 1800 à nos jours.* Paris, 1981.

Chesney, K. *The Victorian Underworld.* 1970. Harmondsworth, 1972.

Chevalier, Louis. *Laboring Classes and Dangerous Classes in Paris during the First Half of the Nineteenth Century.* Translated by Frank Jellinek. Princeton, 1981.

Clark, J. C. D. *English Society, 1688–1832.* Cambridge, 1985.

Classen, W. *Das stadtgeborene Geschlecht und seine Zukunft.* Leipzig, 1914.

Cobb, R. "La Bande d'Orgères." In R. Cobb, *Reactions to the French Revolution,* 181–215. London, 1972.

———. *The Police and the People: French Popular Protest, 1789–1820.* Oxford, 1970.

———. "La Route du Nord: The Bande à Salembier." In R. Cobb, *Paris and Its Provinces, 1792–1802,* 194–210. London, 1975.

———. "La Route du Nord: The Band Juive." In R. Cobb, *Paris and Its Provinces, 1792–1802,* 141–93. London, 1975.

———. *A Sense of Place.* London, 1975.

———. "La Vie en Marge: Living on the Fringe of the French Revolution." In R. Cobb, *Reactions to the French Revolution,* 128–79. London, 1972.

Cockburn, J. S. "The Nature and Incidence of Crime in England, 1559–1625: A Preliminary Survey." In *Crime in England, 1550–1800,* edited by J. S. Cockburn, 49–71. London, 1977.

———. "Patterns of Violence in English Society: Homicide in Kent, 1560–1985." *Past and Present* 130 (1991): 70–106.

Cohen, D., and Eric A. Johnson. "French Criminality: Urban-Rural Differences in the Nineteenth Century." *Journal of Interdisciplinary History* 12 (1982): 477–501.

Contamine, Philippe. *La guerre de cent ans.* Paris, 1968.

Danker, U. *Räuberbanden im Alten Reich um 1700: Ein Beitrag zur Geschichte von Herrschaft und Kriminalität in der frühen Neuzeit.* 2 vols. Frankfurt, 1988.

Davis, Jennifer. "Prosecutions and Their Context." In *Policing and Prosecution in Britain 1750–1850,* edited by Douglas Hay and Francis Snyder, 397–426. Oxford, 1989.

Davis, Natalie Zemon. *Fiction in the Archives: Pardon Tales and Their Tellers in Sixteenth-Century France.* Stanford, 1987.

Dawson, W. H. *The Evolution of Modern Germany*. New York, n.d.

———. *German Life in Town and Country*. New York, 1901.

Dekker, Rudolf M. "Ontwikkelingsperspectief of gezichtsbedrog?" *Amsterdams Sociologisch Tijdschrift* 10, no. 3 (Dec. 1983): 593–96.

———. " 'Politiek geweld' en het proces van staatsvorming in de geschiedenis van de Nederlanden." *Amsterdams Sociologisch Tijdschrift* 10, no. 2 (Oct. 1983): 335–52.

Desai, A. V. *Real Wages in Germany*. Oxford, 1968.

Diederiks, Herman. "Criminality and Its Repression in the Past: Quantitative Approaches: A Survey." *Economic and Social History in the Netherlands* 1 (1989): 67–86.

———. "Gevangenen en gevangenis te Hoorn in de negentiende eeuw." *Criminaliteit in de negentiende eeuw, Hollandse Studien* 22 (1989): 83–94.

———. "Patterns of Criminality and Law Enforcement during the Ancien Régime: The Dutch case." *Criminal Justice History* 1 (1980): 157–74.

———. *Een stad in verval: Amsterdam omstreeks 1800: demografisch, economisch, ruimtelijk*. Amsterdam, 1982.

———. "Stadt und Umland im Lichte der Herkunftorte der Kriminellen in Leiden im 17. und 18. Jahrhundert." In *Städtisches Um- und Hinterland in vorindustrieller Zeit*, edited by H. K. Schulze, 191–92. Cologne, 1985.

Diederiks, Herman A., and Pieter Spierenburg. "Delitti e pene in Olanda (1550–1810)." In *Cheiron, materiali e strumenti di aggiornamento storiografico: Il piotere di guidicare, giustizia, pena e controllo sociale negli stati d'antico regime* 1 (1983): 85–108.

Diederiks, Herman A., S. Faber, and A. H. Huussen Jr. *Strafrecht en criminaliteit: Cahiers voor lokale en regionale geschiedenis*. Zutphen, Netherlands, 1988.

Ditton, Jason. *Controlology: Beyond the New Criminology*. London, 1979.

Dollinger, P. "Le chiffre de la population de Paris au XIVe siècle." *Revue historique* 216 (1956): 35–44.

Duplès-Agier, M., ed. *Registre criminel du Châtelet de Paris du 6 septembre 1389 au 18 mai 1392*. 2 vols. Paris, 1861–64.

Eberstadt, Nick. "The Health Crisis in the U.S.S.R." *New York Review of Books,* 19 Feb. 1981, 23–31.

Egmond, Florike. *Banditisme in de Franse Tijd: Profiel van de Grote Nederlandse Bende, 1790–1799*. Amsterdam, 1986.

———. "Crime in Context: Jewish Involvement in Organized Crime in the Dutch Republic." *Jewish History* 4 (1990): 75–100.

———. "Hoge Jurisdicties van het 18e-eeuwse Holland, een aanzet tot de bepaling van hun aantal, ligging en begrenzingen." *Holland: Regionaal-historisch tijdschrift* 19 (1987): 129–61.

———. *Underworlds: Organized Crime in the Netherlands, 1650–1800*. Cambridge, 1993.

Elias, Norbert. *The Civilising Process*. 2 vols. Oxford, 1982.

Emsley, Clive. *Crime and Society in England 1750–1800*. London, 1987.

Eshof, P. van den, and E. J. C. Weimar. "Moord en doodslag in Nederland: Nederlandse gegevens in internationaal perspectief." *Justitiële Verkenningen* 17, no. 1 (1991): 8–34.

Evans, R. J. *Death in Hamburg: Society and Politics in Hamburg during the Cholera Years, 1830–1910.* Oxford, 1987.

———. *Rethinking German History: Nineteenth-Century Germany and the Origins of the Third Reich.* London, 1987.

———, ed. *The German Underworld: Deviants and Outcasts in German History.* London, 1988.

Evans, R. J., and W. R. Lee, eds. *The German Peasantry: Conflict and Community in Rural Society from the Eighteenth to the Twentieth Centuries.* New York, 1986.

Faber, Sjoerd. "Kindermoord, in het bijzonder in de 18e eeuw te Amsterdam." *Bijdragen en Mededelingen betreffende de Geschiedenis der Nederlanden* 93 (1978): 224–40.

———. *Strafrechtspleging en criminaliteit te Amsterdam, 1680–1811: De nieuwe menslievendheid.* Arnhem, 1983.

Fällström, Anne-Marie. *Konjunkturer och kriminalitet: Studier i Göteborgs sociala historia 1800–1840.* Göteborg, 1974.

Farge, Arlette, and André Zysberg. "Les théâtres de la violence à Paris au 18ième siècle." *Annales* 34 (1979): 984–1015.

Farinacci, Prospero. *Praxis et theoricae criminalis.* Lugduni, 1631.

Favier, Jean. *La guerre de cent ans.* Paris, 1980.

———. *Paris au XVe siècle, 1380–1500.* Paris, 1974.

Flaherty, David. "Law and the Enforcement of Morals in Early America." *Perspectives in American History* 5 (1971): 203–53.

Fosdick, R. B. *European Police Systems.* New York, 1915.

Foucault, Michel. *Discipline and Punish: The Birth of the Prison.* Trans. Alan Sheridan. Harmondsworth, 1986.

Foucher, I. "Deux bandes de voleurs au XVIIIe siècle." M.A. thesis, University of Paris, 1990.

Fourquin, Guy. "La population de la région parisienne aux environs de 1328." *Le moyen âge* 62 (1956): 63–91.

Franke, Herman. "Geweldscriminaliteit in Nederland: Een historisch-sociologische analyse." *Amsterdams Sociologisch Tijdschrift* 18, no. 3 (1991): 13–45.

———. *Twee Eeuwen gevangen: Misdaad en straf in Nederland.* Aula, Holland, 1990.

Frauenstädt, P. "Die preußischen Ostprovinzen in kriminal-geographischer Beleuchtung." *Zeitschrift für Sozialwissenschaft* 9 (1906): 570–83.

Garland, David. *Punishment and Modern Society: A Study in Social Theory.* Oxford, 1990.

———. *Punishment and Welfare: A History of Penal Strategies.* Aldershot, 1985.

Garnot, Benoît. *Un crime conjugal au 18e siècle.* Paris, 1993.

Gatrell, V. A. C. "The Decline of Theft and Violence in Victorian and Edwardian England." In *Crime and the Law: The Social History of Crime in Western Europe since 1500,* edited by V. A. C. Gatrell, Bruce Lenman, and Geoffrey Parker, 238–338. London, 1980.

Gatrell, V. A. C., and T. B. Hadden. "Nineteenth-Century Criminal Statistics and Their Interpretation." In *Nineteenth-Century Society: Essays in the Use of Quantitative Methods for the Study of Social Data,* edited by E. A. Wrigley, 336–96. London, 1972.

Gauvard, Claude. *De Grâce Especial: Crime, état et société en France à la fin du moyen âge*. 2 vols. Paris, 1991.

George, M. D. *London Life in the Eighteenth Century*. 1925. Harmondsworth, 1985.

Geremek, Bronislaw. "La lutte contre le vagabondage à Paris aux XIVe et XVe siècles." In *Ricerche storiche ed economiche in memoria di Corrado Barbagallo*, 2 vols., edited by Luigi de Rosa, 2:211-36. Naples, 1970.

———. *Les marginaux parisiens aux XIVe et XVe siècles*. Paris, 1976.

———. "Paris, la plus grande ville de l'occident médiéval?" *Acta Poloniae historica* 18 (1968): 18-37.

Gijswijt-Hofstra, Marijke. *Wijkplaats voor vervolgden: Asielverlening in Culemborg, Vianen, Buren, Leerdam en IJsselstein van de 16de tot eind 18de eeuw*. Dieren, Netherlands, 1984.

Graafhuis, A., et al. "Misdaad en straf in de stad Utrecht in de tweede helft van de 16e eeuw." In *Recht en Slecht: Een registratie van misdaad en straf in de stad Utrecht, 1550-1575*, edited by the Gemeentelijke Archiefdienst Utrecht, 17-89. Utrecht, 1976.

Greenberg, D. *Crime and Law Enforcement in the Colony of New York*. Ithaca, N.Y., 1976.

Grendi, Edouardo. "Falsa monetazione e strutture monetarie degli scambi nella Repubblica di Genova fra Cinque e Seicento." *Quaderni storici* 66 (1987): 803-37.

Guenée, Bernard. *Tribunaux et gens de justice dans le bailliage de Senlis à la fin du moyen âge*. Paris, 1963.

Gurevich, Aron. *Categories of Medieval Culture*. London, 1985.

Gurr, Ted Robert. "Historical Trends in Violent Crime: A Critical Review of the Evidence." *Crime and Justice: An Annual Review of Research* 3 (1981): 295-353.

Gurr, Ted Robert, T. N. Grabowsky, and R. C. Hula. *The Politics of Crime and Conflict: A Comparative History of Four Cities*. London, 1977.

Gustafsson, Harald. "Bland grevar och avskedade soldater: Sockensjälvstyrelsen på 1840-talet." *Historisk Tidskrift* 4 (1986): 484-501.

Haas, J. A. K. *De verdeling van de landen van Overmaas 1644-1662: Territoriale desintegratie van een betwist grensgebied*. Assen, Netherlands, 1978.

Habermas, Jürgen. *Strukturwandel der Öffentlichkeit: Untersuchungen zu einer Kategorie der bürgerlichen Gesellschaft*. 2d ed. Berlin, 1965.

Hagen, W. W. *Germans, Poles, and Jews: The Nationality Conflict in the Prussian East, 1772-1914*. Chicago, 1980.

Hanawalt, Barbara A. *Crime and Conflict in English Communities, 1300-1348*. Cambridge, Mass., 1979.

———. "Fur-Collar Crime: The Pattern of Crime among the Fourteenth-Century English Nobility." *Journal of Social History* 8 (1975): 1-17.

Harrison, Brian. *Drink and the Victorians*. London, 1971.

Hastrup, Kirsten. *Culture and History in Medieval Iceland: An Anthropological Analysis of Structure and Change*. Oxford, 1985.

Hay, Douglas. "Poaching and the Game Laws on Cannock Chase." In *Albion's Fatal Tree:*

Crime and Society in Eighteenth-Century England, edited by Douglas Hay et al., 189–254. London, 1975.

———. "War, Dearth and Theft in the Eighteenth Century: The Record of the English Courts." *Past and Present* 95 (1982): 117–60.

Hay, Douglas, and Francis Snyder, eds. *Policing and Prosecution in Britain, 1750–1850.* Oxford, 1989.

Herrup, C. B. *The Common Peace: Participation and the Criminal Law in Seventeenth-Century England.* Cambridge, 1987.

Hill, Christopher. "The Many-Headed Monster in Late Tudor and Early Stuart Thinking." In *From the Renaissance to the Counter Reformation: Essays in Honour of Garrett Mattingley,* edited by C. H. Carter, 296–324. London, 1966.

Hobsbawm, Eric J. *Bandits.* New York, 1981.

Hochstadt, S. L. "Migration and Industrialization in Germany." *Social Science History* 5 (1981): 445–68.

Hoeven, Anton van den. "Ten exempel en afschrik: Strafrechtspleging en criminaliteit in Haarlem, 1740–1795." M.A. thesis, University of Amsterdam, 1982.

Hofer, Hanns von. *Brott och straff i Sverige: Historisk kriminalstatistik, 1750–1825.* Stockholm, 1985.

Hoffer, Peter C., and N. E. H. Hull. *Murdering Mothers: Infanticide in England and New England, 1558–1803.* New York, 1981.

Hohorst, Gerd, Jürgen Kocka, and Gerhard A. Ritter. *Sozialgeschichtliches Arbeitsbuch: Materialien zur Statistik des Kaiserreichs, 1871–1914.* Munich, 1978.

Horgby, Björn. *Den disciplinerade arbetaren: Brottslighet och social förändring i Norrköping 1850–1910.* Stockholm, 1986.

Howson, Gerald. *Thief-Taker General: Jonathan Wild and the Emergence of Crime and Corruption as a Way of Life in Eighteenth-Century England.* New Brunswick, N.J., 1985.

Hufton, Olwen. *The Poor of Eighteenth-Century France, 1750–1789.* Oxford, 1974.

———. "Women and Violence in Early Modern Europe." In *Writing Women into History,* edited by Fia Dieteren and Els Kloek, 75–95. Amsterdam, 1990.

Inciardi, James A., and Charles E. Faupel, eds. *History and Crime: Implications for Criminal Justice Policy.* Beverly Hills, Calif., 1980.

Jackson, James H. "Migration in Duisburg, 1867–1890: Occupational and Familial Contexts." *Journal of Urban History* 8 (1982): 235–70.

Jackson, James H., and L. P. Moch. "Migration and the Social History of Modern Europe." *Historical Methods* 22 (1989): 27–36.

Jacobs, B. C. M. *Justitie en Politie in 's-Hertogenbosch voor 1629: De bestuursorganisatie van een Brabantse stad.* Assen, Netherlands, 1986.

Jean de Roye. *Chronique scandaleuse.* 2 vols. Edited by Bernard de Mandrot. Paris, 1894–95.

Jelgersma, H. G. *Galgebergen en Galgevelden in West- en Midden Nederland.* Zutphen, Netherlands, 1978.

Johansson, Kenneth. "Brott, straff och rättens funktioner i Albo härad i Småland ca. 1600–1850." Forthcoming.

Johnson, Eric A. "The Crime Rate: Longitudinal and Periodic Trends in Nineteenth- and Twentieth-Century German Criminality: From Vormärz to Late Weimar." In *The German Underworld: Deviants and Outcasts in German History*, edited by R. J. Evans, 159–88. London, 1988.

———. "The Roots of Crime in Imperial Germany." *Central European History* 15 (1982): 351–76.

———. *Urbanization and Crime: Germany, 1871–1914*. New York, 1995.

———, ed. *Quantification and Criminal Justice History in International Perspective*, special issue of *Historical Social Research/Historische Sozialforschung* 15 (1990).

Johnson, Eric A., and Vincent E. McHale. "Socioeconomic Aspects of the Delinquency Rate in Imperial Germany." *Journal of Social History* 13 (1980): 384–402.

Jones, David J. V. *Crime, Protest, Community and Police in Nineteenth-Century Britain*. London, 1982.

———. "The Poacher: A Study in Victorian Crime and Protest." *Historical Journal* 22 (1979): 325–60.

Jones, Gareth Stedman. *Languages of Class: Studies in English Working-Class History, 1832–1982*. Cambridge, 1983.

Jüngen, Jean A. G. "Doodslagers en hun pakkans in het 16e eeuwse Amsterdam." In *Scherp Toezicht: Van "Boeventucht" tot "Samenleving en Criminaliteit,"* edited by Cyrille Fijnaut and Pieter Spierenburg, 79–97. Arnhem, Netherlands, 1990.

———. "God betert: De Amsterdamse lijkschouwingsrapporten in de jaren 1560, 1570, 1580 en 1590." M.A. thesis, Free University Amsterdam, 1982.

———. "Een stad van justitie? Een verkenning van misdaad en maatschappij in Amsterdam in de 2e helft van de 16e eeuw." M.A. thesis, Free University Amsterdam, 1979.

Kaeble, H. *Industrialisation and Social Inequality in Nineteenth-Century Europe*. Leamington Spa, 1986.

Kamphoefner, W. D. "The Social Consequences of Rural-Urban Migration in Imperial Germany: The 'Floating Proletariat' Thesis Reconsidered." Social Science Working Paper, California Institute of Technology, Pasadena, 1982.

Kekkonen, Jukka. "Explaining Historical Change in Social Control." In *Theatres of Power: Social Control and Criminality in Historical Perspective*, edited by Heikki Pihlajamäki, 143–57. Jyväskylä, Finland, 1991.

Klessmann, C. *Polnische Bergarbeiter im Ruhrgebiet, 1870–1945: Soziale Integration und nationale Subkultur einer Minderheit in der deutschen Industriegesellschaft*. Göttingen, 1978.

Küther, C. *Menschen auf der Straße: Vagierende Unterschichten in Bayern, Franken und Schwaben in der zweiten hälfte des 18. Jahrhunderts*. Göttingen, 1983.

———. *Räuber und Gauner in Deutschland: Das organisierte Bandenwesen im 18. und frühen 19. Jahrhundert*. Göttingen, 1976.

———. "Räuber, Volk und Obrigkeit: Zur Wirkungsweise und Funktion staatlicher

Strafverfolgung im 18. Jahrhundert." In *Räuber, Volk und Obrigkeit: Studien zur Geschichte der Kriminalität in Deutschland seit dem 18. Jahrhundert,* edited by H. Reif, 17–42. Frankfurt, 1984.

Lane, Roger. "Urban Homicide in the Nineteenth Century: Some Lessons for the Twentieth." In *History and Crime: Implications for Criminal Justice Policy,* edited by James A. Inciardi and Charles E. Faupel, 91–109. Beverly Hills, Calif., 1980.

———. *Violent Death in the City: Suicide, Accident, and Murder in Nineteenth-Century Philadelphia.* Cambridge, Mass., 1979.

Langbehn, Julius. *Rembrandt als Erzieher.* London, 1890.

Langbein, John. *Torture and the Law of Proof: Europe and England in the Ancien Régime.* Chicago, 1977.

Langlois, Monique, and Yvonne Lanhers, eds. *Confessions et jugements de criminels au Parlement de Paris (1319–1350).* Paris, 1971.

Larsson, Lars-Olof. *Småländsk historia: Stormaktstiden.* Växjö, Sweden, 1982.

Laxdaela Saga. Translated by Magnus Magnusson and Hermann Pálsson. Harmondsworth, 1969.

Lees, A. "Critics of Urban Society in Germany, 1854–1918." *Journal of the History of Ideas* 40 (1979): 61–83.

———. "Debates about the Big City in Germany, 1890–1914." *Societas* 5 (1975): 31–47.

Lees, A., and L. Lees, eds. *The Urbanization of European Society in the Nineteenth Century.* Boston, 1976.

Lenman, Bruce, and Geoffrey Parker. "The State, the Community and the Criminal Law in Early Modern Europe." In *Crime and the Law: The Social History of Crime in Western Europe since 1500,* edited by V. A. C. Gatrell, Bruce Lenman, and Geoffrey Parker, 11–48. London, 1980.

Lindegren, Jan. "Kriget och arbetskraften."

———. *Utskrivning och utsugning: Produktion och reproduktion i Bygdeå, 1620–1640.* Uppsala, 1980.

Lodhi, A. Q., and C. Tilly. "Urbanization, Crime, and Collective Violence in Nineteenth-Century France." *American Journal of Sociology* 79 (1973): 196–218.

Longnon, Auguste. *Paris pendant la domination anglaise (1420–1436).* Paris, 1878.

Macfarlane, Alan. *The Culture of Capitalism.* Oxford, 1987.

———. *The Justice and the Mare's Ale: Law and Disorder in Seventeenth-Century England.* Oxford, 1981.

———. *The Origins of English Individualism.* Oxford, 1978.

Magnusson, Lars. *Den bråkiga kulturen: Förläggare och smideshantverkare i Eskilstuna, 1800–1850.* Vänersborg, Sweden, 1988.

Mannheim, H. *Comparative Criminology.* Boston, 1965.

Marsilje, J. W., et al. *Bloedwraak, partijstrijd en pacificatie in laat-middeleeuws Holland.* Hilversum, 1990.

Maso, Benjo. "Riddereer en riddermoed: Ontwikkelingen van de aanvalslust in de late middeleeuwen." *Sociologische Gids* 29, no. 3/4 (1982): 296–325.

Masur, G. *Imperial Berlin.* New York, 1970.

McHale, Vincent E., and Eric A. Johnson. "Urbanization, Industrialization, and Crime in Imperial Germany, Part 1." *Social Science History* 1 (1976): 45–78.

———. "Urbanization, Industrialization, and Crime in Imperial Germany, Part 2." *Social Science History* 2 (1977): 210–47.

McIntosh, Marjorie K. *Autonomy and Community: The Royal Manor of Havering, 1200–1500.* Cambridge, 1986.

McIntosh, Mary. "Changes in the Organisation of Thieving." In *Images of Deviance,* edited by S. Cohen, 98–133. Harmondsworth, 1971.

———. *The Organisation of Crime.* London, 1975.

McMullan, J. "Criminal Organization in Sixteenth- and Seventeenth-Century London." *Social Problems* 29 (1982): 311–23.

Metz, Guillebert de. "Description de Paris sous Charles VI." In A. Leroux de Lincy and L. M. Tisserand, *Paris et ses historiens aux XIVe et XVe siècles.* Paris, 1867.

Misraki, Jacqueline. "Criminalité et pauvreté en France à l'époque de la Guerre de Cent Ans." In *Etudes sur l'histoire de la pauvreté,* 2 vols., edited by Michel Mollat, 1:535–46. Paris, 1974.

Mitterauer, Michael, and Reinhard Sieder. *Vom Patriarchat zur Partnerschaft: Zum Strukturwandel der Familie.* Munich, 1977.

Monicat, Jacques. *Les grandes compagnies du Velay, 1358–1392.* 2d ed. Paris, 1928.

———, ed. *Comptes du domaine de la ville de Paris.* 2 vols. Paris, 1958.

Monkkonen, Eric H. *Police in Urban America, 1860–1920.* New York, 1981.

———. "The Quantitative Historical Study of Crime and Criminal Justice." In *History and Crime: Implications for Criminal Justice Policy,* edited by James A. Inciardi and Charles E. Faupel, 53–73. Beverly Hills, Calif., 1980.

Moore, B. *Injustice: The Social Bases of Obedience and Revolt.* White Plains, N.Y., 1978.

Moranvillé, Henri, ed. "Le songe véritable, pamphlet politique d'un parisien du XVe siècle." *Mémoires de la Société de l'histoire de Paris et de l'Ile-de-France* 17 (1891): 236.

Muchembled, Robert. *L'Invention de l'homme moderne: Sensibilités, moeurs et comportements collectifs sous l'ancien régime.* Paris, 1988.

———. *La violence au village: Sociabilité et comportements populaires en Artois du 15e au 17e siècle.* Turnhout, 1989.

Munsche, P. B. *Gentlemen and Poachers: The English Game Laws, 1671–1831.* Cambridge, 1981.

Murphy, R. C. *Guestworkers in the German Reich: A Polish Community in Wilhelminian Germany.* Boulder, Colo., 1983.

Naess, Hans Eyvind. *Trolldomsprosessene i Norge pa 1500–1600-tallet: En retts- og sosialhistorisk undersøkelse.* Oslo, 1982.

Njal's Saga. Translated by Magnus Magnusson and Hermann Pálsson. Harmondsworth, 1960.

Österberg, Eva. "Bönder och statsmakt i det tidigmoderna Sverige: Konflikt-kompromiss-politisk kultur." *Scandia* 55, no. 1 (1989): 73–95.

———. "Brott och straff i svenska smastäder under medeltid och vasatid: Svensk kriminalitet i europeiskt perspektiv." In *Över gränser: Festskrift till Birgitta Odén,* edited by J. Norlid et al., 473–504. Lund, 1987.

———. "Civilisationsprocesser och 1600-talets svenska bondesamhälle-en historia med förhinder." *Saga och sed* (1985): 13–23.

———. "Criminality, Social Control, and the Early Modern State: Evidence and Interpretations in Scandinavian Historiography." *Social Science History* 16, no. 1 (1992): 67–98.

———. "Den gamla goda tiden: Bilder och motbilder i ett modernt forskningsläge om det äldre agrarsamhället." *Scandia* 48, no. 1 (1982): 31–60.

———. "Social Arena or Theatre of Power? The Courts, Crime and the Early Modern State in Sweden." In *Theatres of Power: Social Control and Criminality in Historical Perspective,* edited by Heikki Pihlajamäki, 8–24. Jyväskylä, Finland, 1991.

———. "Violence among Peasants: Comparative Perspectives on Sixteenth- and Seventeenth-Century Sweden." In *Europe and Scandinavia: Aspects of the Process of Integration in the Seventeenth Century,* edited by Göran Rystad, 257–89. Lund, 1983.

Österberg, Eva, and Dag Lindström. *Crime and Social Control in Medieval and Early Modern Swedish Towns.* Uppsala, 1988.

Parrella, Anne. "Industrialization and Murder: Northern France, 1815–1904." *Journal of Interdisciplinary History* 22, no. 4 (1992): 627–54.

Perroy, Edouard. *The Hundred Years' War.* London, 1965.

Petersen, M. A. *Gedetineerden onder dak: Geschiedenis van het gevangeniswezen in Nederland van 1795 af, bezien van zijn behuizing.* Leiden, 1978.

Petersson, Birgit. *Den farliga underklassen: Studier i brottslighetoch fattigdom i 1800-talets Sverige.* Umeå, Sweden, 1983.

Peveri, P. "Les Pickpockets à Paris au XVIII siècle." *Revue d'histoire moderne et contemporaine* 29 (1982): 3–35.

Philips, David. *Crime and Authority in Victorian England.* London, 1977.

Phillips, Roderick. *Putting Asunder: A History of Divorce in Western Society.* Cambridge, 1988.

Pike, Ruth. "Capital Punishment in Eighteenth-Century Spain." *Histoire Sociale/Social History* 18 (1985): 375–86.

Reed, Kelly. "Female Criminality in Imperial Germany." Seminar Paper, Department of History, Central Michigan University, 1981.

Reif, H., ed. *Räuber, Volk und Obrigkeit: Studien zur Geschichte der Kriminalität in Deutschland seit dem 18. Jahrhundert.* Frankfurt, 1984.

Reinhardt, Steven G. "Crime and Royal Justice in Ancien Régime France: Modes of Analysis." *Journal of Interdisciplinary History* 13 (1983): 437–60.

Reinke, H., ed. *Historical Social Research/Historische Sozialforschung.* Vol. 37, *Crime and Criminal Justice History.* Cologne, 1986.

Renger, E. *Kriminalität, Preis und Lohn: Eine kriminalstatistische Untersuchung für Sachsen von 1882–1929.* Leipzig, 1933.

Riehl, W. H. *Die Naturgeschichte des Volkes als Grundlage einer deutschen Sozial-Politik.* 4 vols. Stuttgart, 1854–69.

Roebroeck, E. *Het land van Montfort: Een agrarische samenleving in een grensgebied, 1647–1820.* Assen, Netherlands, 1967.

Romeo, Giovanni. *Aspettando il bòia: Condannati a morte, confortatori e inquisitori nella Napollie della Coantroriforma.* Florence, 1993.

———. *Inquisitori, esorcisti e streghe nell' Italia della Controriforma.* Florence, 1990.

———. "Per la storia del sant' Ufficio a Napoli tra '500 e '600: Documenti e problemi." *Campania sacra* 7 (1976): 5–109.

———. "Una città, due inquisizioni: l'anomalia del Sant' Ufficio a Napoli nel tardo '500." *Rivista di storia e letteratura religiosa* 24 (1988): 42–67.

Rossiaud, Jacques. "Prostitution, jeunesse et société dans les villes du Sud-Est au XVe siècle." *Annales* (1976): 289–325.

Rugge, C. "Die Bedeutung der Großstädten für das Volksleben." *Die Reformation: Deutsche evang. Kirchenzeitung für die Gemeinde* 8 (1909): 389–90.

Ruller, Sibo van. *Genade voor recht: Gratieverlening aan ter dood veroordeelden in Nederland, 1806–1870.* Amsterdam, 1987.

Saga of Gisli. Translated by George Johnston. London, 1963.

Samaha, Joel. *Law and Order in Historical Perspective: The Case of Elizabethan Essex.* New York, 1974.

Sandnes, Jörn. *Kniven, ölet og aeren: Kriminalitet og samfunn i Norge pa 1500- og 1600-tallet.* Oslo, 1990.

Sauval, Henri. *Histoire et recherches des antiquités de la ville de Paris.* Vol. 2. Paris, 1724.

Schwerhoff, Gerd. *Köln im Kreuzverhör: Kriminalität, Herrschaft und Gesellschaft in einer frühneuzeitlichen Stadt.* Bonn, 1991.

Sharpe, James A. "Crime and Delinquency in an Essex Parish, 1600–1640." In *Crime in England, 1550–1800,* edited by J. S. Cockburn. London, 1977.

———. *Crime in Early Modern England, 1550–1750.* London, 1984.

———. *Crime in Seventeenth-Century England: A County Study.* Cambridge, 1983.

———. *Early Modern England: A Social History, 1550–1760.* London, 1987.

———. "The History of Crime in England c. 1300–1914." *British Journal of Criminology* 28 (1988): 254–67.

———. "The History of Crime in Late Medieval and Early Modern England: A Review of the Field." *Social History* 7 (1982): 188–203.

———. "The History of Violence in England: Some Observations." *Past and Present* 108 (1985): 206–15.

Shelley, L. I. *Crime and Modernization: The Impact of Urbanization and Industrialization on Crime.* Carbondale, Ill., 1981.

Sindall, Rob. *Street Violence in the Nineteenth Century.* Leicester, 1991.

Slenders, J. A. M. "Het Theatrum Anatomicum in de Noordelijke Nederlanden, 1555–1800." *Scripta Tironum* 17/18 (1989): 30.

Söderberg, Johan. "En fråga om civilisering: Brottmål och tvister i svenska häradsrätter 1540–1660." *Historisk Tidskrift* 2 (1990): 229–58.

Spierenburg, Pieter. "Evaluation of the Conditions and Main Problems Relating to the Contribution of Historical Research to the Understanding of Crime and Criminal Justice—Report." In *Historical Research on Crime and Criminal Justice: Reports Presented to the Sixth Criminological Colloquium, 1983,* Council of Europe Publications, 49–95. Strasbourg, 1985.

———. "Judicial Violence in the Dutch Republic: Corporal Punishment, Executions and Torture in Amsterdam, 1650–1750." Ph.D. diss., University of Amsterdam, 1978.

———. "Justice and the Mental World: Twelve Years of Research and Interpretation of Criminal Justice Data, from the Perspective of the History of Mentalities." *IAHCCJ Newsletter* 14 (Oct. 1991): 38–79.

———. *The Prison Experience: Disciplinary Institutions and Their Inmates in Early Modern Europe.* New Brunswick, N.J., 1991.

———. *The Spectacle of Suffering: Executions and the Evolution of Repression: From a Preindustrial Metropolis to the European Experience.* Cambridge, 1984.

Spree, R. *Wealth and Social Class in Imperial Germany.* Leamington Spa, 1987.

Stinchcombe, A. L. "Institutions of Privacy in the Determination of Police Administrative Practices." *American Journal of Sociology* 69 (1963): 150–60.

Stone, Lawrence. "Interpersonal Violence in England: A Rejoinder." *Past and Present* 108 (1985): 216–24.

———. "Interpersonal Violence in English Society, 1300–1983." *Past and Present* 102 (1983): 22–33.

———. *The Past and the Present Revisited.* London, 1987.

Stones, E. L. G. "The Folvilles of Ashby-Folville, Leicestershire, and Their Associates in Crime, 1326–1341." *Transactions of the Royal Historical Society,* 5th Series, vol. 7 (1957): 117–36.

Sundin, Jan. "Bandits and Guerilla Soldiers: Armed Bands on the Border between Sweden and Denmark in Early Modern Times." In *Bande armate banditi: Banditismo e repressione di giustizia negli stati europei di antico regime,* edited by Gherardo Ortalli, 141–66. Venice, 1986.

———. "Control, Punishment and Reconciliation: A Case Study of Parish Justice in Sweden before 1850." In *Tradition and Transition: The Demographic Data Base,* edited by Anders Brändström and Jan Sundin, 9–65. Umeå, Sweden, 1981.

———. *För Gud, Staten och Folket: Brott och rättskipning i Sverige, 1600–1840.* Lund, 1992.

———. "Keeping Sex within Marriage: Legal Prosecution of Extra-Marital Sex in Pre-Industrial Sweden." *Social Science History* 16, no. 1 (1992): 99–128.

———. "Kontroll-straff och försoning: Kyrklig rättvisa pa sockennivå före 1850." In *Kontroll och kontrollerade: Formell och informell kontroll i ett historiskt perspektiv,* edited by Sundin, 39–85. Umeå, Sweden, 1982.

———. "Prisons préventives et reformatrices: Ambitions et réalités dans la Suède du XIX siècle." In *La Prison, le bagne et l'histoire: Deviance et societé,* edited by Jacques G. Petit, 201–11. Geneva, 1984.

———. "The Sinful Sex: Criminalization of Sexual Relations in Sweden 1600–1839." Unpublished manuscript, 1988.

———. "Theft and Penury in Sweden, 1830–1920: A Comparative Study at the County Level." *Scandinavian Journal of History* 1 (1976): 265–92.

———, ed. *Kontroll och kontrollerade: Formell och informell kontroll i ett historiskt perspektiv.* Umeå, Sweden, 1982.

Sveri, Knut. "Brottslighetens volym och struktur." In *Samhällsförändringar och brottslighet,* edited by Ake Daun et al. Stockholm, 1974.

Szabo, D. *Crimes et villes.* Paris, 1960.

Tanon, Louis. *Histoire des justices des anciennes églises et communautés de Paris.* Paris, 1883.

———, ed. *Registre criminel de la justice de Saint-Martin-des-Champs.* Paris, 1887.

Taussi Sjöberg, Marja. *Brott och straff i Västernorrland 1861–1890.* Umeå, Sweden, 1981.

———. "Staten och tinget und 1600–talet." *Historisk Tidskrift* 2 (1990): 161–90.

———. "Tinget som social arena." In *Historia nu-18 Umeaforskare om det förflutna,* edited by Taussi Sjöberg. Umeå, Sweden, 1988.

Teuteberg, H. J., ed. *Urbanisierung im 19. und 20. Jahrhundert: Historische und geographische Aspekte.* Cologne, 1983.

Thompson, E. P. "Happy Families." *New Society* 41 (1977): 499.

———. *The Making of the English Working Class.* New York, 1966.

———. *Whigs and Hunters: The Origin of the Black Act.* Harmondsworth, 1977.

Thompson, E. P., and Eileen Yeo, eds. *The Unknown Mayhew: Selections from the Morning Chronicle, 1849–1850.* Harmondsworth, 1971.

Thompson, Flora. "Larkrise to Candleford." In David Jones, *Crime, Protest, Community and Police in Nineteeth-Century Britain.* London, 1982.

Thunander, Rudolf. "Lagbrytare i bondesamhället." Unpublished manuscript, Växjö, Sweden, 1988.

———. "Tusen brott i Småland." Unpublished manuscript, Växjö, Sweden, 1988.

Tilly, Charles. *As Sociology Meets History.* New York, 1981.

Tilly, Charles, Allan Levett, A. Q. Lodhi, and Frank Munger. "How Policing Affected the Visibility of Crime in Nineteenth-Century Europe and America." CRSO Working Paper 115, Ann Arbor, Michigan, 1982.

Tipton, Frank B. *Regional Variations in the Economic Development of Germany during the Nineteenth Century.* Middletown, Conn., 1976.

Tobias, J. J. *Crime and Industrial Society in the Nineteenth Century.* Harmondsworth, 1967.

———. *Urban Crime in Victorian England.* New York, 1972.

Tranter, N. L. *Population and Society, 1750–1940.* London, 1985.

Tuetey, A., ed. *Journal d'un bourgeois de Paris.* Paris, 1881.

Vejbrink, Martin. "En kontrollerad brottsling som historiskt fenomen." In *Kontroll och kontrollerade,* edited by Jan Sundin, 159–95. Umeå, Sweden, 1982.

Vizetelly, H. *Berlin under the New Empire.* Vol. 1. 1879. New York, 1968.

Vries, Jan de. *Barges and Capitalism: Passenger Transportation in the Dutch Economy, 1632–1839.* 1978. Utrecht, 1981.

———. *European Urbanization, 1500–1800.* London, 1984.

Walker, S. *Popular Justice: A History of American Criminal Justice.* New York, 1980.

Wandycz, P. S. *The Lands of Partitioned Poland, 1795–1918.* Seattle, 1974.

Weber, A. *Die Großstadt und ihre sozialen Probleme.* Leipzig, 1908.

Weber, A. F. *The Growth of Cities in the Nineteenth Century.* Ithaca, N.Y., 1899.

Weel, Toon van. "De interjurisdictionele betrekkingen in criminele zaken van het Amsterdamse gerecht (1700–1811)." In *Nieuwe licht op oude justitie, misdaad en straf ten tijde van de republiek,* edited by Sjoerd Faber, 23–48. Muiderberg, 1989.

Wehler, Hans-Ulrich. *Modernisierungstheorie und Geschichte.* Göttingen, 1975.

Weinberger, Barbara. "Law Breakers and Law Enforcers in the Late Victorian City." Ph.D. diss., University of Warwick, 1981.

Weisser, Michael R. *Crime and Punishment in Early Modern Europe.* Hassocks, 1979.

Wettmann-Jungblut, Peter. "Penal Law and Criminality in Southwestern Germany: Forms, Patterns and Developments." Paper presented at the conference *Justice pénale et construction de l'état, 12e-18e siècle,* Brussels, 19 Feb. 1993.

Weustink, J. M. *De rechtsgeschiedenis van de stad Oldenzaal en van de Mark Berghuizen tot 1795.* Assen, Netherlands, 1962.

Wilterdink, Nico. "Inleiding [introduction to special issue on violence in Dutch society]." *Amsterdams Sociologisch Tijdschrift* 18, no. 3 (1991): 7–12.

Winslow, Cal. "Sussex Smugglers." In *Albion's Fatal Tree: Crime and Society in Eighteenth-Century England,* edited by Douglas Hay et al., 119–66. London, 1975.

Wiskemann, E. *Germany's Eastern Neighbors.* New York, 1956.

Wright, G. *Between the Guillotine and Liberty.* New York, 1983.

Wrightson, Keith. "Two Concepts of Order: Justices, Constables and Jurymen in Seventeenth-Century England." In *An Ungovernable People: The English and Their Law in the Seventeenth and Eighteenth Centuries,* edited by John Brewer and John Styles. London, 1980.

Wrightson, Keith, and David Levine. *Poverty and Piety in an English Village: Terling, 1525–1700.* New York, 1979.

Ylikangas, Heikki. "Die Gewaltkriminalität in der Finnischen Geschichte." In *Theatres of Power: Social Control and Criminality in Historical Perspective,* edited by Heikki Pihlajamäki, 41–54. Jyväskylä, Finland, 1991.

———. *Knivjunkarna: Våldskriminalitet i Sydösterbotten, 1790–1825.* Borgå, Finland, 1985.

———. "Major Fluctuations in Crimes of Violence in Finland: A Historical Analysis." *Scandinavian Journal of History* 1 (1976): 81–103.

———. *Puukkojunkkareitten esiinmarssi: Vhakivaltarikollisuus Etelha-Pohjanmaalla, 1790–1825.* Helsinki, 1976.

Young, Malcolm. *An Inside Job: Policing the Police Culture in Britain.* Oxford, 1991.

Zehr, Howard. *Crime and the Development of Modern Society: Patterns of Criminality in Nineteenth-Century Germany and France.* London, 1976.

Zwaan, Ton. "Nogmaals politiek geweld in ontwikkelingsperspectief." *Amsterdams Sociologisch Tijdschrift* 10, no. 3 (1983): 597–601.

———. "Politiek geweld, maatschappelijke structuur en burgerlijke civilisatie: Een verkenning van de binnenstatelijke geweldpleging in de ontwikkeling van de Nederlandse samenleving, 1648–1960." *Amsterdams Sociologisch Tijdschrift* 9, no. 3 (1982): 433–75.

———. "Politiek geweld in ontwikkelingsperspectief." *Amsterdams Sociologisch Tijdschrift* 10, no. 3 (1983): 353–68.

Contributors

♦ ESTHER COHEN is an associate professor of medieval history at the Hebrew University, Jerusalem. She has worked on popular religion in the Middle Ages and the history of crime and law in late medieval northern France, and is currently researching attitudes toward physical pain in the later Middle Ages. She is the author of several articles and of the book *The Crossroads of Justice: Law and Society in Late Medieval France* (1986).

♦ HERMAN DIEDERIKS was a Hoofddocent in the Department of History at the University of Leiden, the Netherlands, and president of the International Association for the History of Crime and Criminal Justice. He is the author of *Een stad in verval: Amsterdam omstreeks 1800: Demografisch, economisch, ruimtelijk* (1982) and the coauthor, with S. Faber and A. H. Huussen Jr., of *Strafrecht en criminaliteit: Cahiers voor lokale en regionale geschiedenis* (1988).

♦ FLORIKE EGMOND is affiliated with the law faculty of Leiden University and the Huizinga Graduate Institute for Cultural History in the Netherlands. Her publications include *Underworlds: Organized Crime in the Netherlands, 1650–1800* (1993) and a forthcoming book cowritten with Peter Mason concerning their joint excursions into microhistory and morphology. She is currently working on the history of punishment and on Renaissance botany and zoology.

♦ ERIC A. JOHNSON is a professor of history at Central Michigan University and was a member of the Institute for Advanced Study, Princeton, New Jer-

sey, during 1995–96. He has held visiting professorships at the University of
Strathclyde (1988–89) and the Zentralarchiv für empirische Sozialforschung
of the University of Cologne (1989–90 and 1992–95). He is the author of several studies of crime and violence in European history, including *Urbanization and Crime: Germany 1871–1914* (1995), and is completing a book on
social control and political dissent in the Third Reich.

◆ MICHELE MANCINO is on the faculty in the Department of History at the
University of Naples. He has researched French Calvinism in the sixteenth
century and is investigating topics relating to Italian religious life between
1500 and 1700, particularly the regulations and controls of the Catholic
Church exerted through ecclesiastical and criminal courts. He has published
a number of articles and reviews.

◆ ERIC H. MONKKONEN is the author of *The Dangerous Class: Crime and Poverty in Columbus, Ohio, 1860–1885* (1975), *Police in Urban America, 1860 to
1920* (1981), *America Becomes Urban: The Development of U.S. Cities and
Towns* (1988), and numerous articles. He is professor of history at the University of California at Los Angeles.

◆ EVA ÖSTERBERG is Distinguished Professor of History at Lund University. She is a specialist in medieval and early modern history, with emphasis
on social and cultural aspects of Scandinavian history. Her publications in
English include *Crime and Social Control in Medieval and Early Modern
Swedish Towns* (with Dag Lindström, 1988) and *Mentalities and Other Realities* (1991). Her most recent book in Swedish is *Folk förr: Historiska essäer* (1995).

◆ JAMES A. SHARPE, a member of the Department of History at the University of York, has published extensively about the history of crime and violence in England. His articles have appeared in journals such as the *British
Journal of Criminology, Past and Present,* and *Social History.* His books
include *Crime in Seventeenth-Century England: A County Study* (1983),
Crime in Early Modern England, 1550–1750 (1984), and *Early Modern England: A Social History, 1550–1760* (1987).

◆ PIETER SPIERENBURG has investigated the historical sociology of prisons,
punishment, and violence in preindustrial Europe. He is the secretary of the
International Association for the History of Crime and Criminal Justice and

the author of *The Spectacle of Suffering: Executions and the Evolution of Repression: From a Preindustrial Metropolis to the European Experience* (1984), *The Prison Experience: Disciplinary Institutions and Their Images in Early Modern Europe* (1991), and several other studies. He is a Hoofddocent in the Department of History at Erasmus University, Rotterdam.

◆ JAN SUNDIN conducts research on the history of crime and legal institutions and the social history of medicine and health. He has published numerous studies about crime and its control in preindustrial Sweden, including *För Gud, Staten och Folket: Brott och rättskipning i Sverige, 1600–1840* (1992). He is a professor in the Department of Health and Society at the University of Linköping, Sweden, and chairs the International Network for the History of Medicine and Health.

◆ BARBARA WEINBERGER is senior research fellow at the Centre for Social History, University of Warwick, England. Her work has focused on aspects of the history of policing. Her publications include *Keeping the Peace? Policing Strikes in Britain, 1906–1926* (1991) and *The Best Police in the World: An Oral History* (1995).

Index